XAVIER VEILHAN
1999–2009

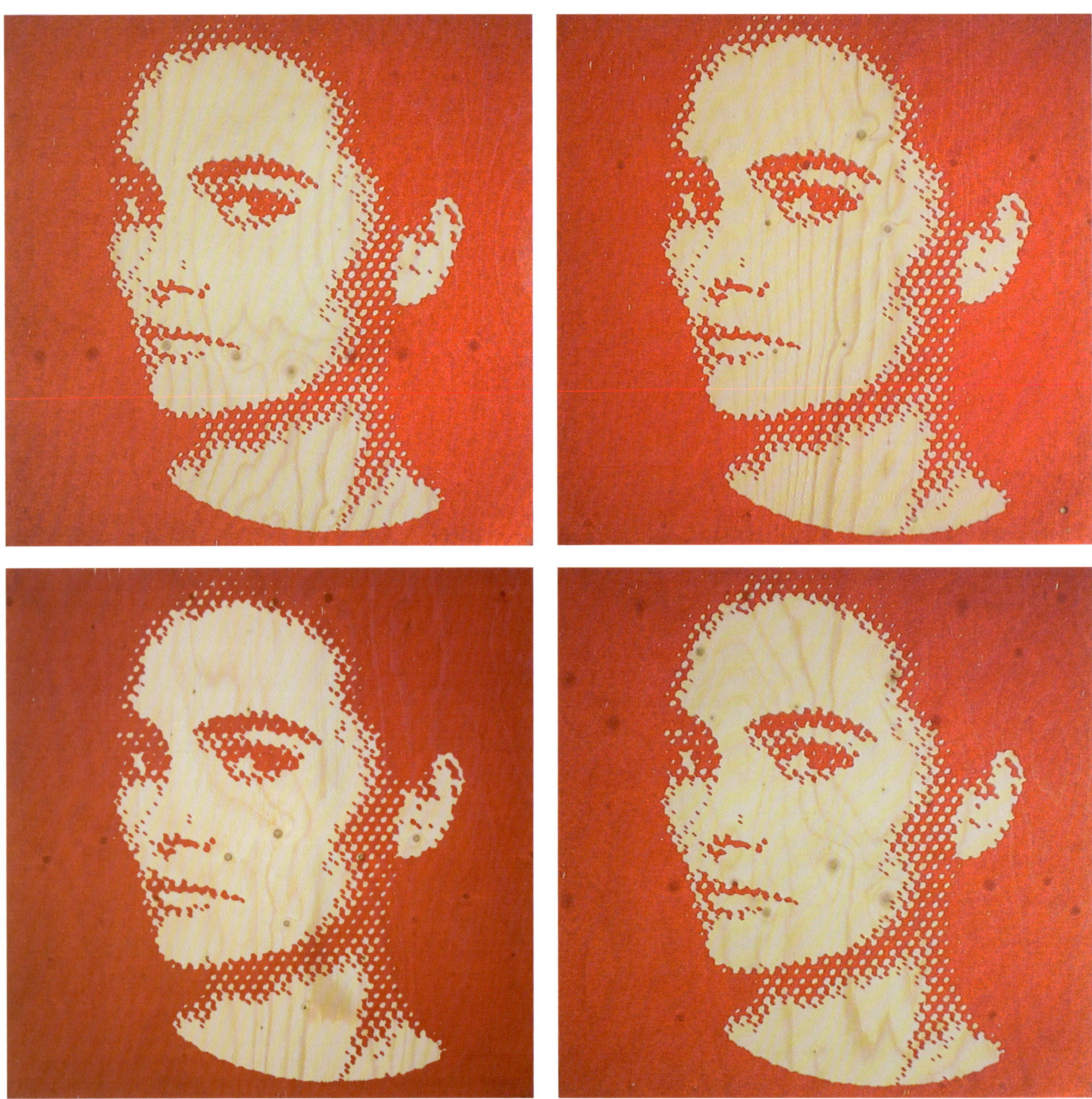

RED CATHERINE N° 1, N° 2, N° 5, AND N° 6, 2002

3

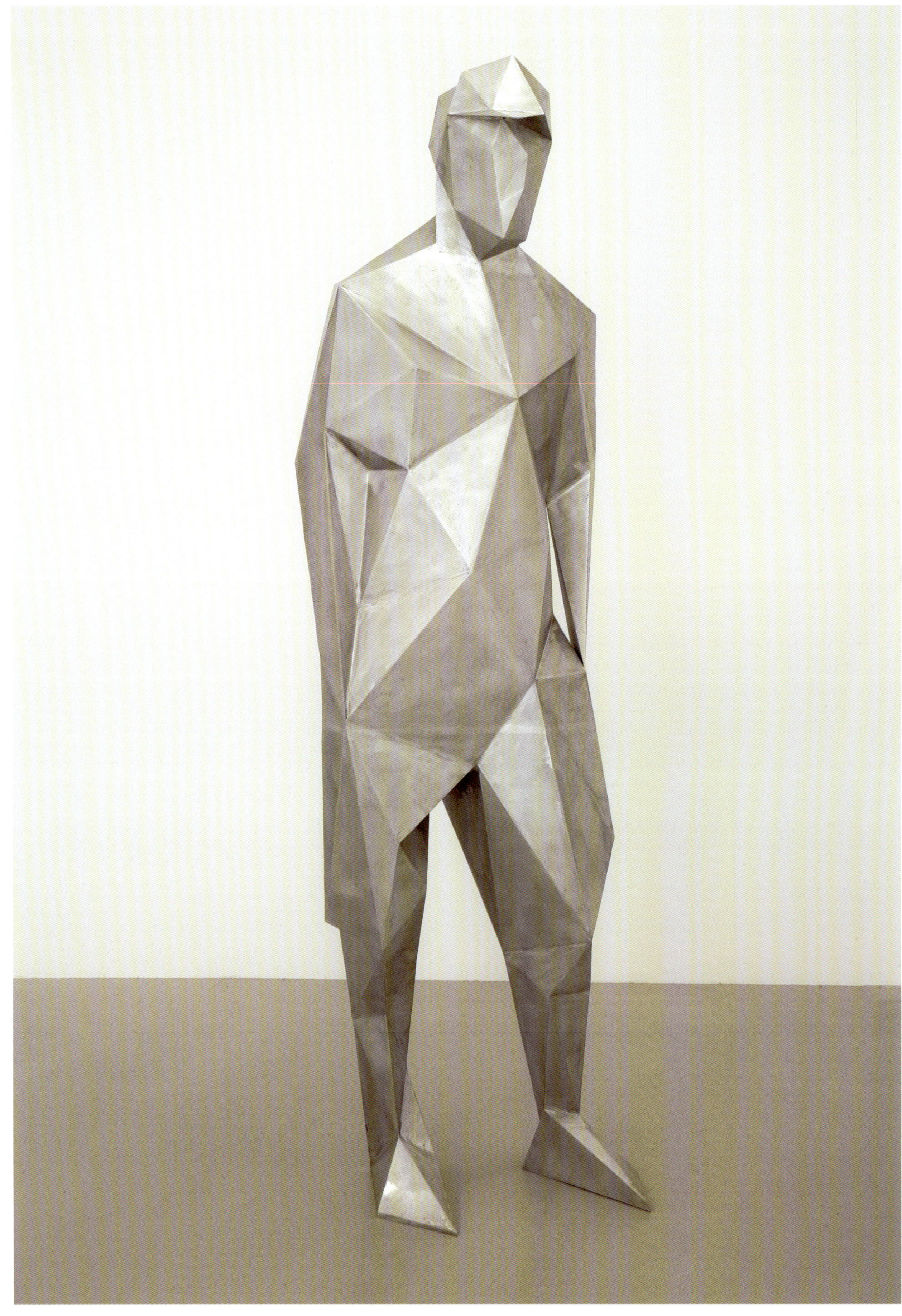

JEANROCH, 2007

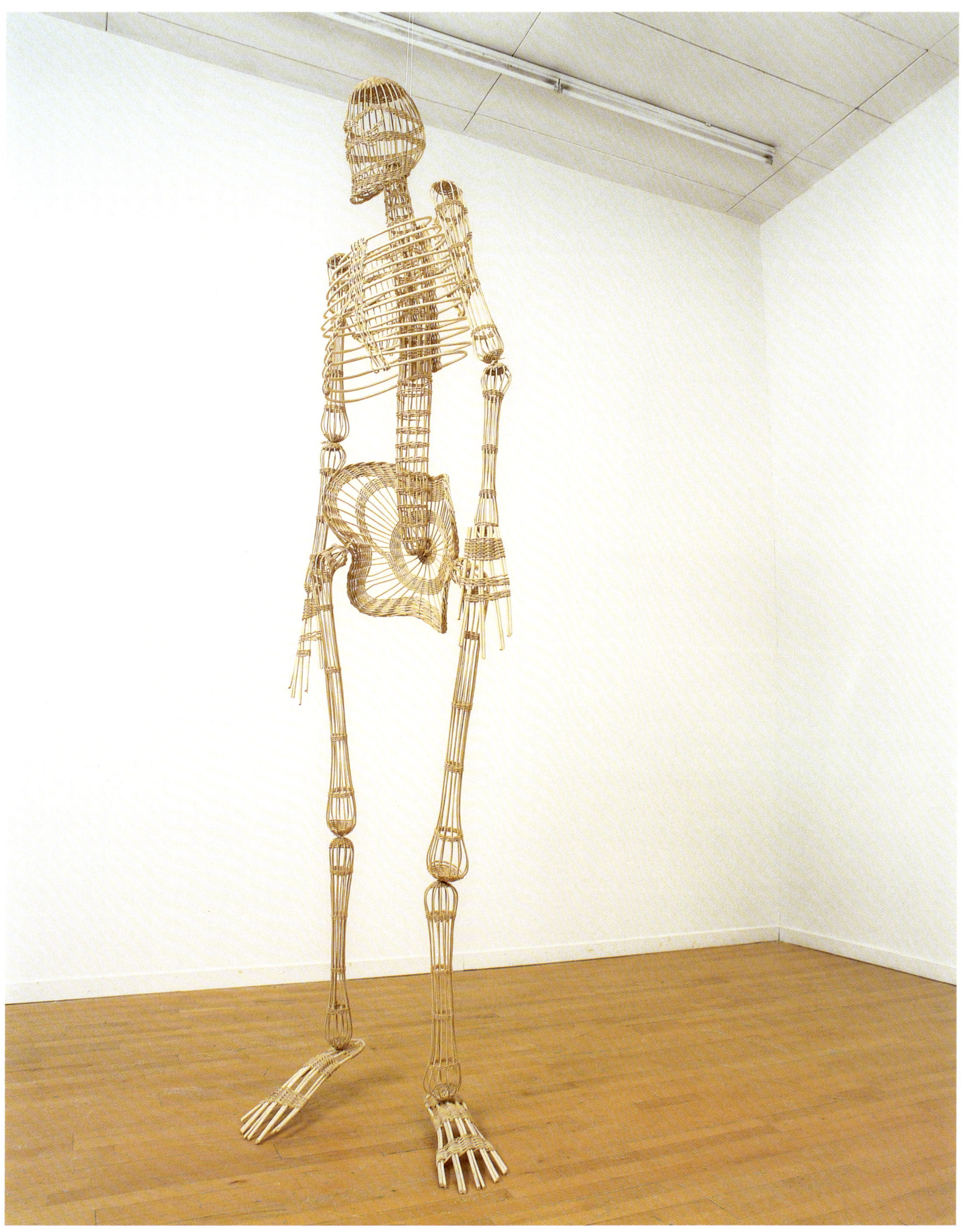

LE SQUELETTE (THE SKELETON), 1999

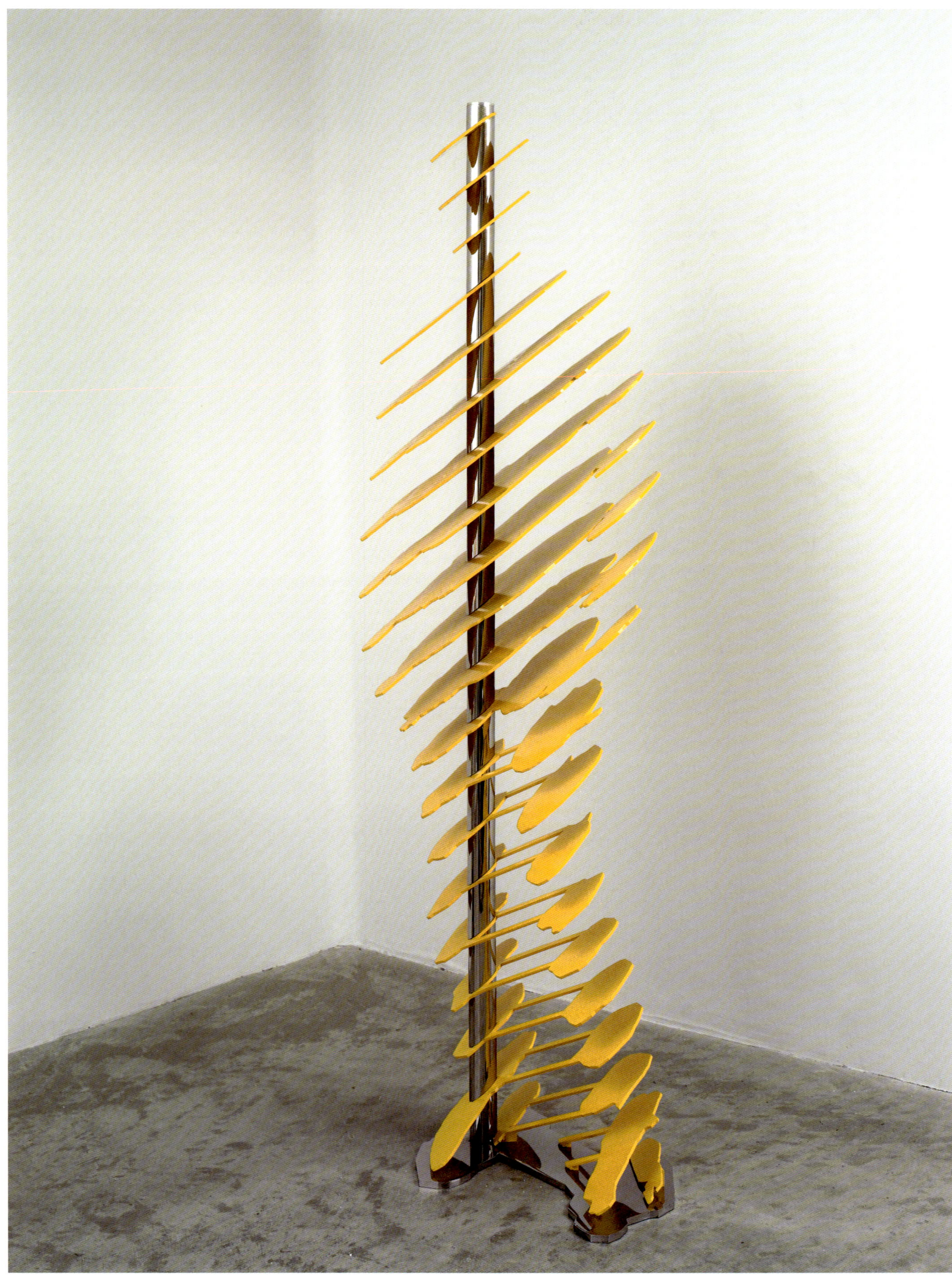

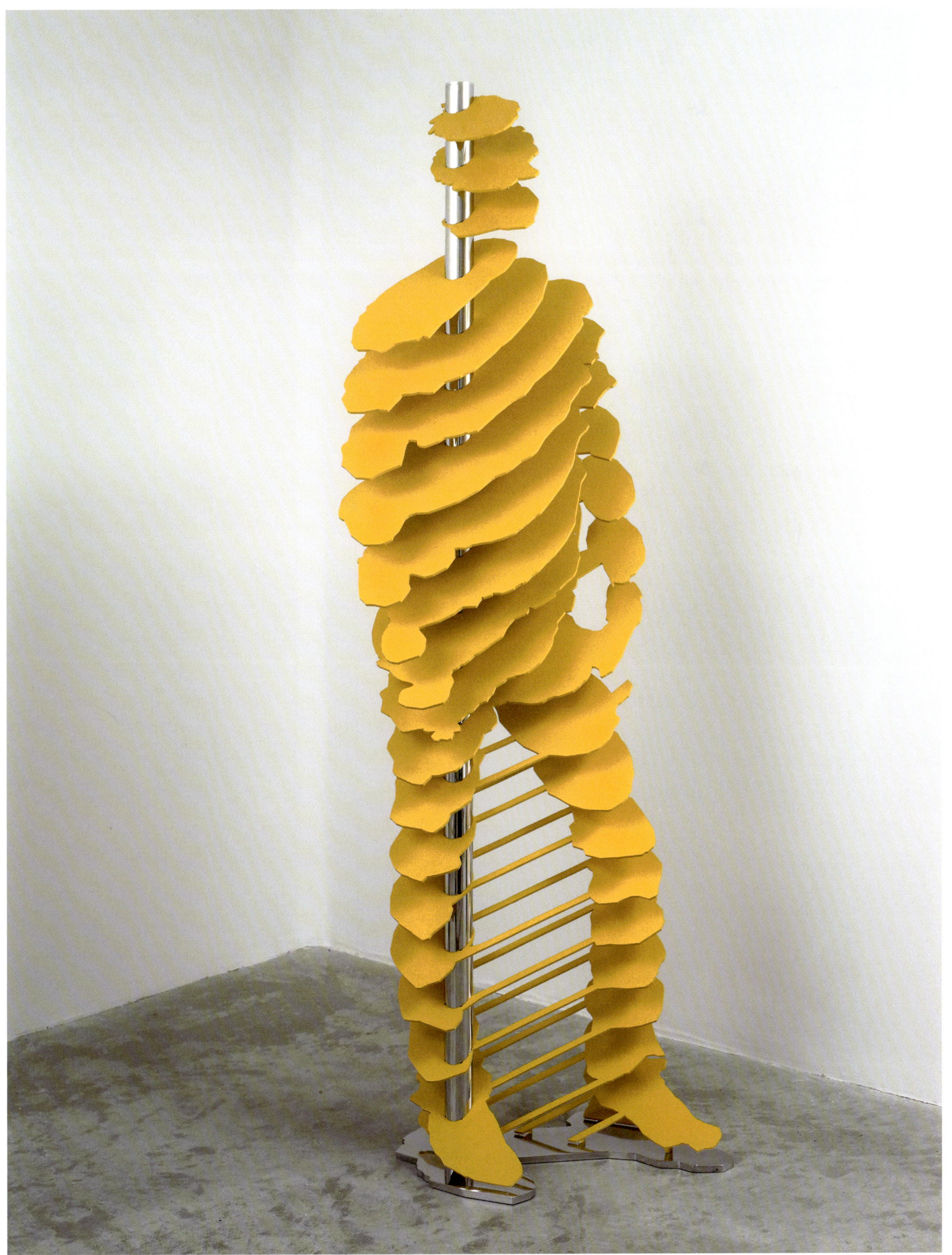

BLIND SCULPTURE JORDAN, 2006

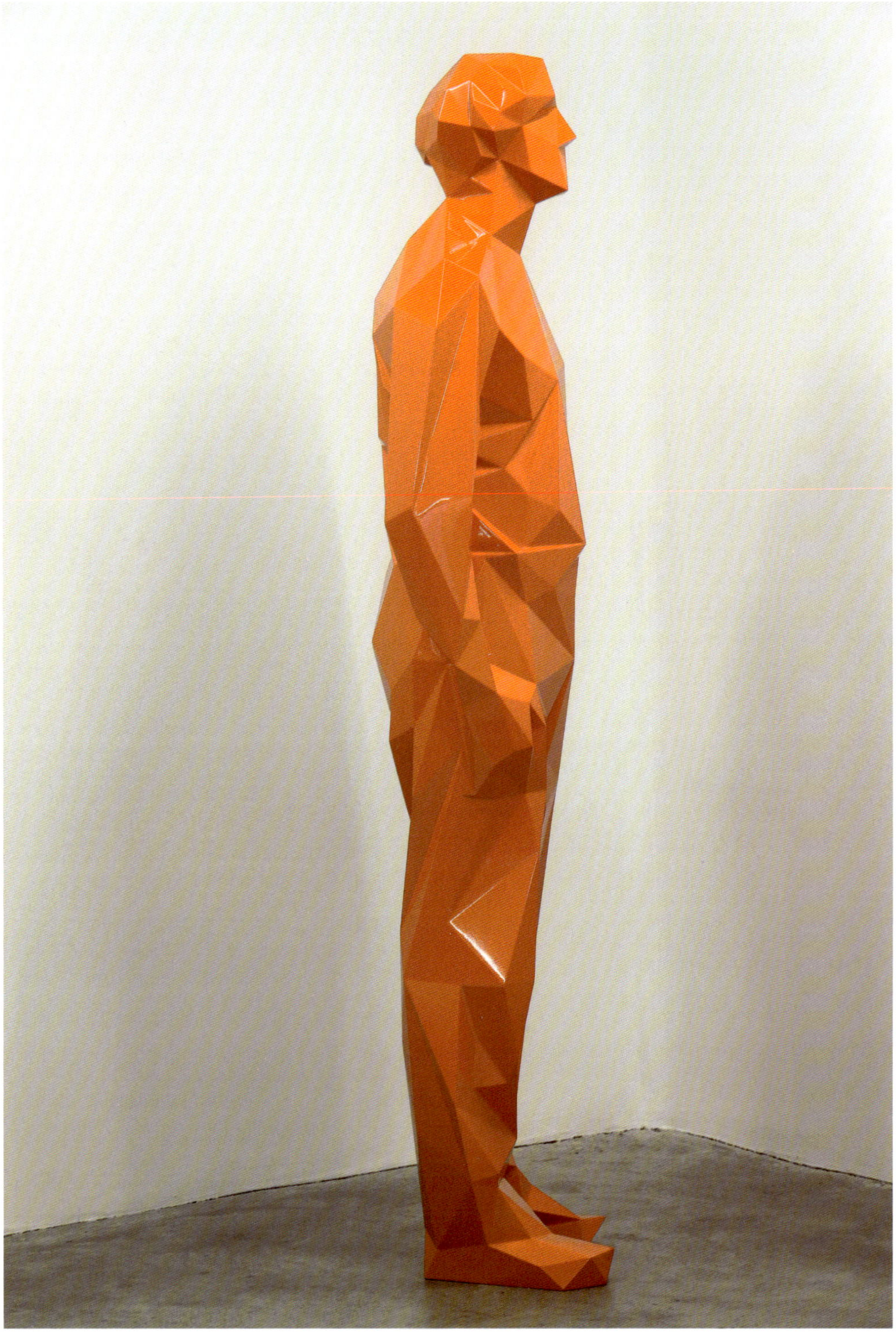

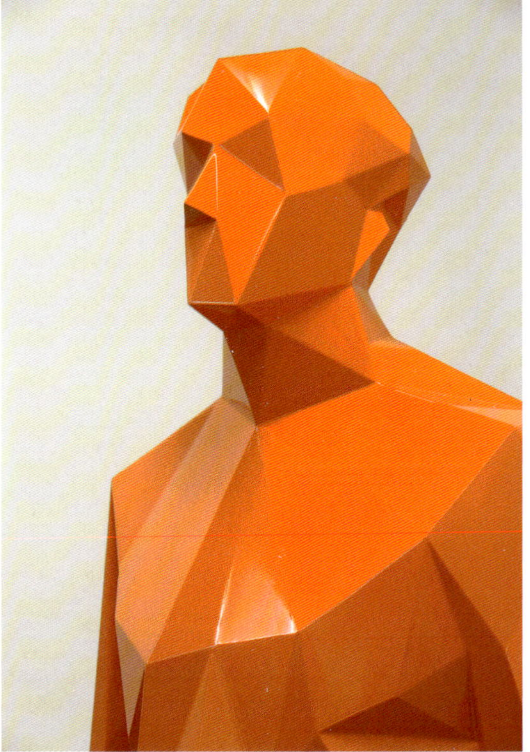

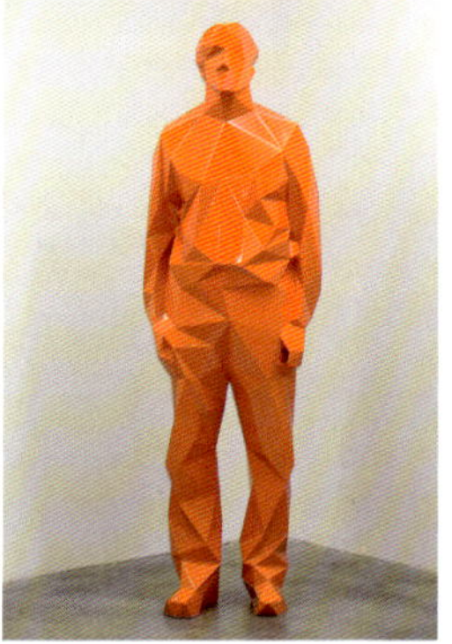

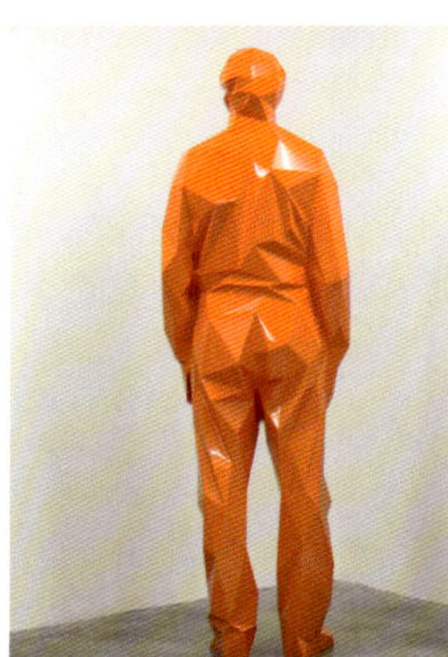

RENAUD, 2007

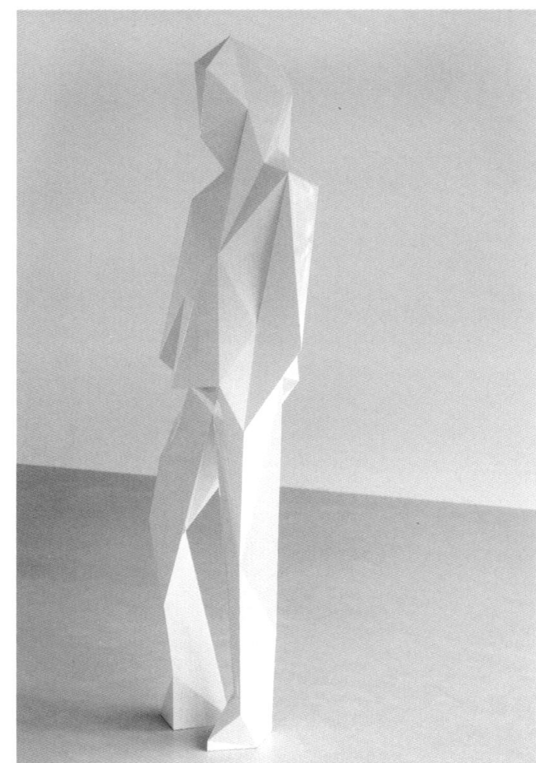

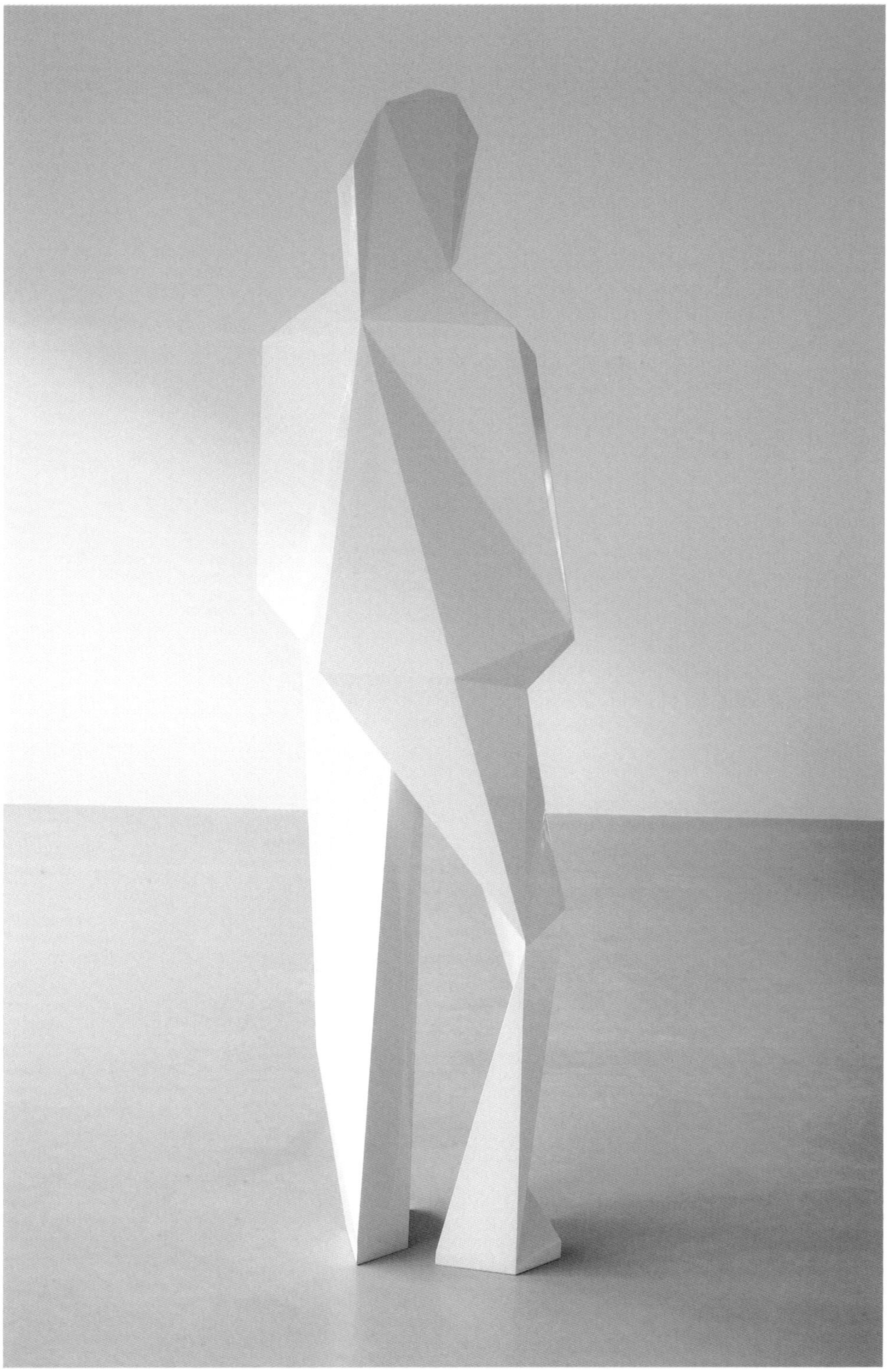

EMMANUELLE, 2007

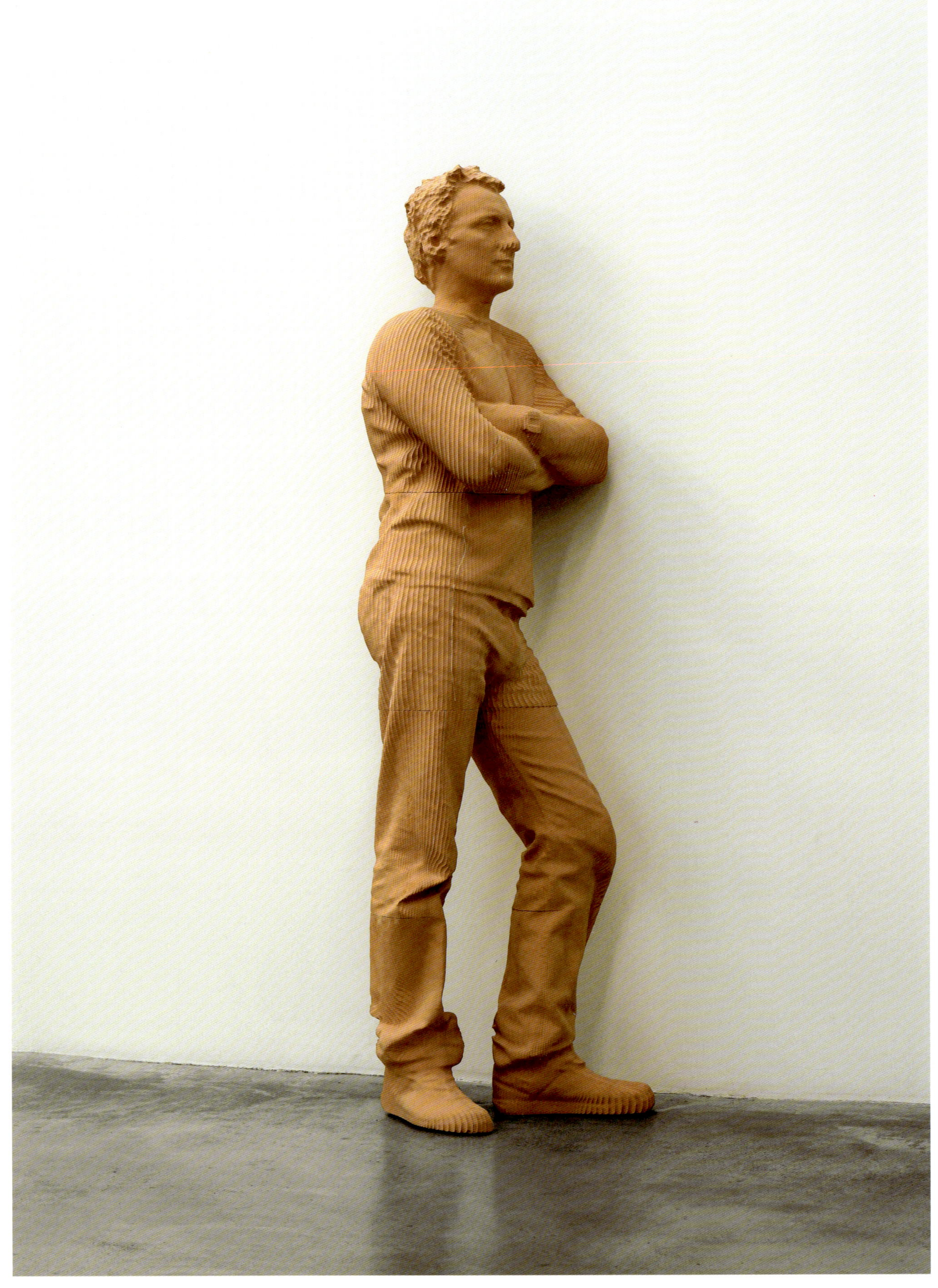

XAVIER, 2006

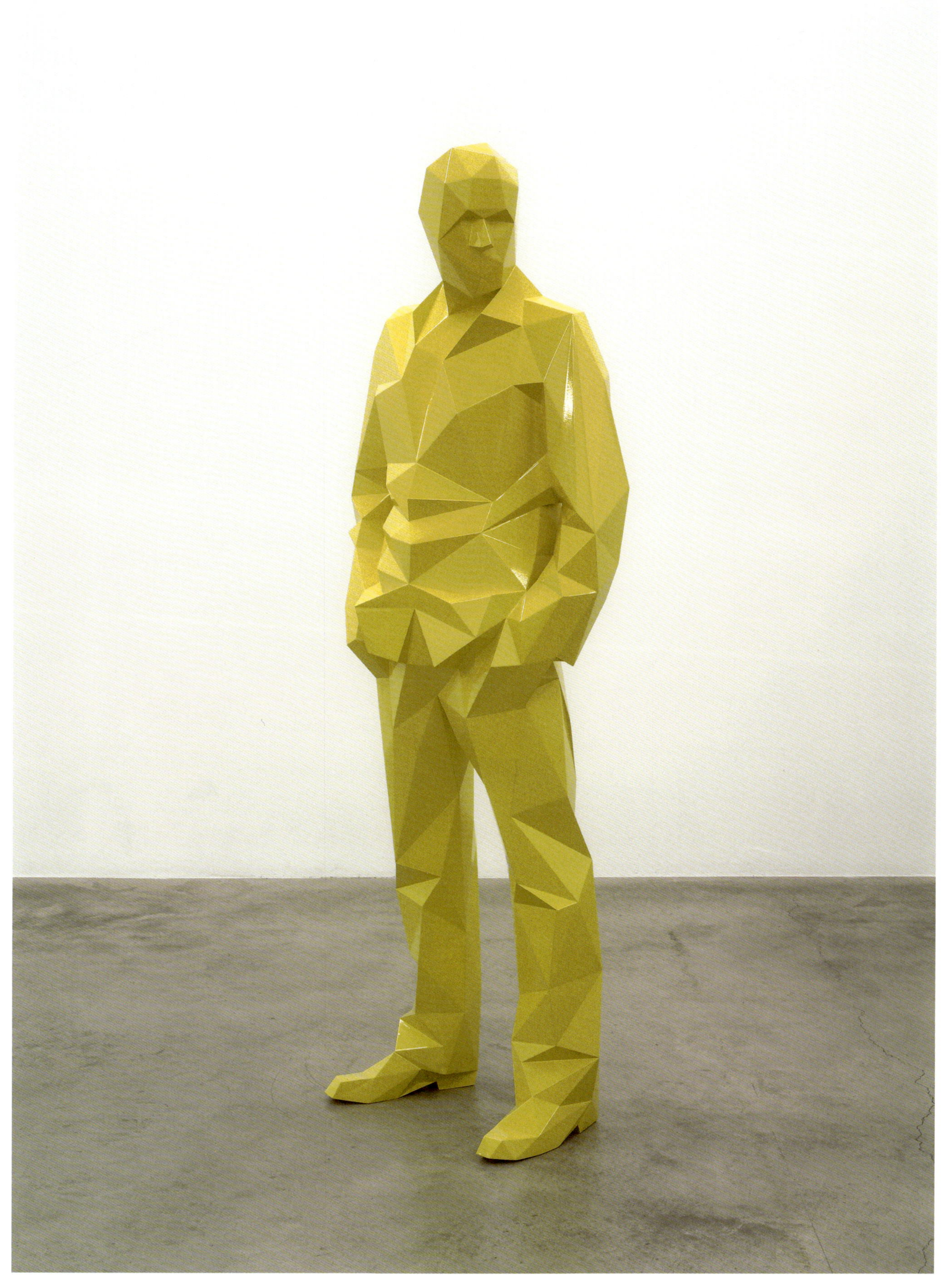

LAURENT (DEUTSCHE GRAMMOPHON), 2006

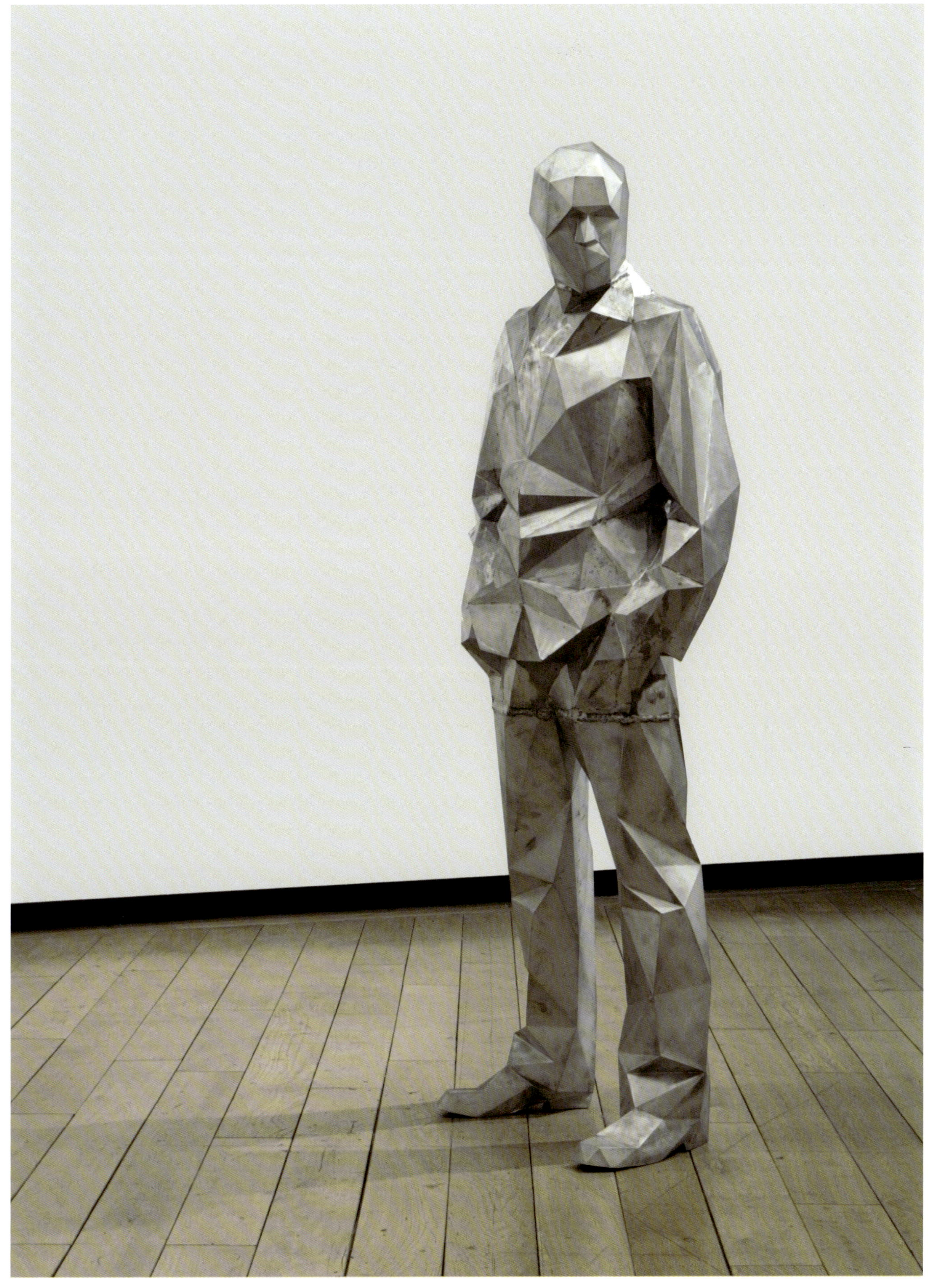

LAURENT, 2005

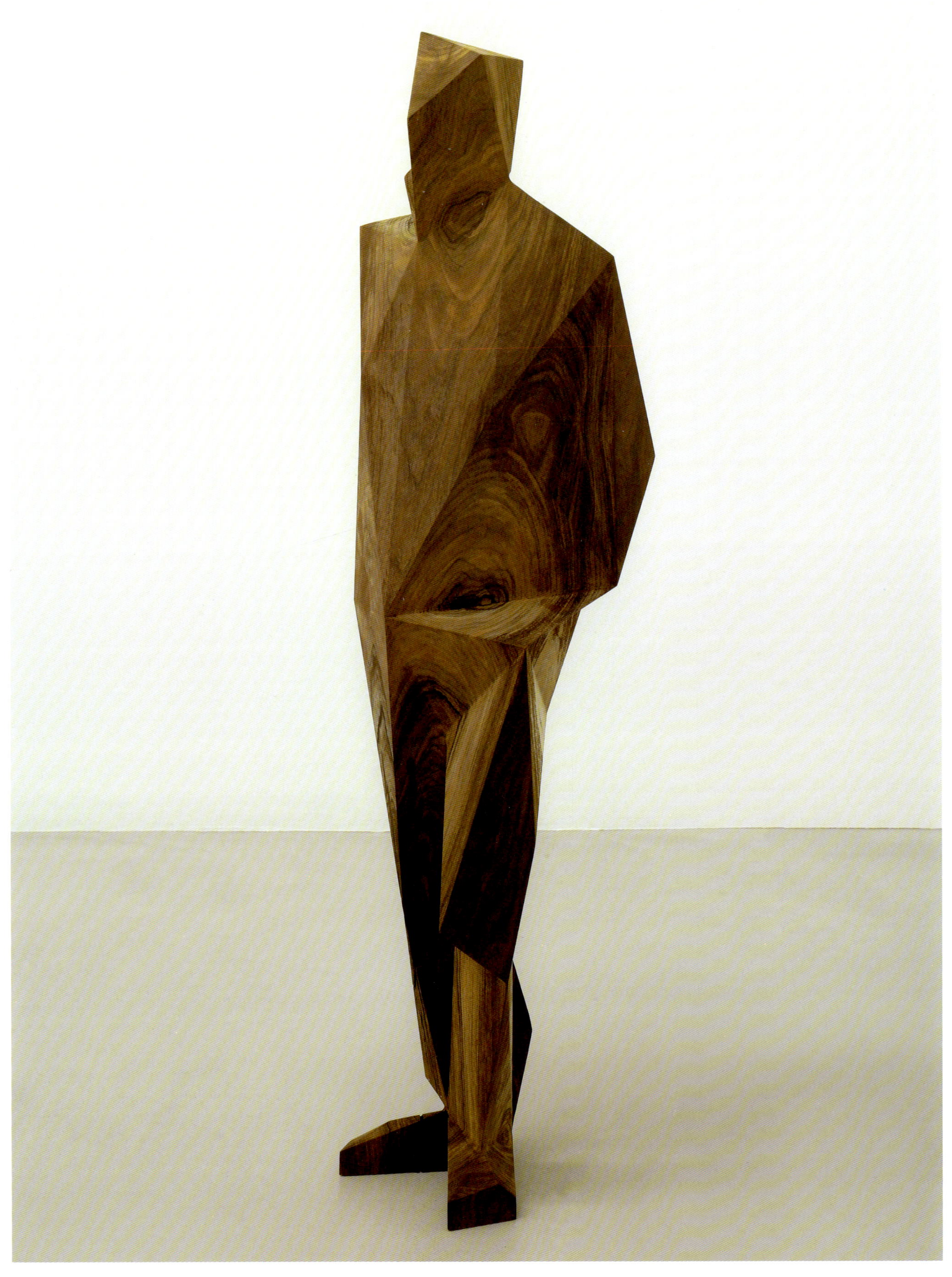

PIERRE N° 4, 2008

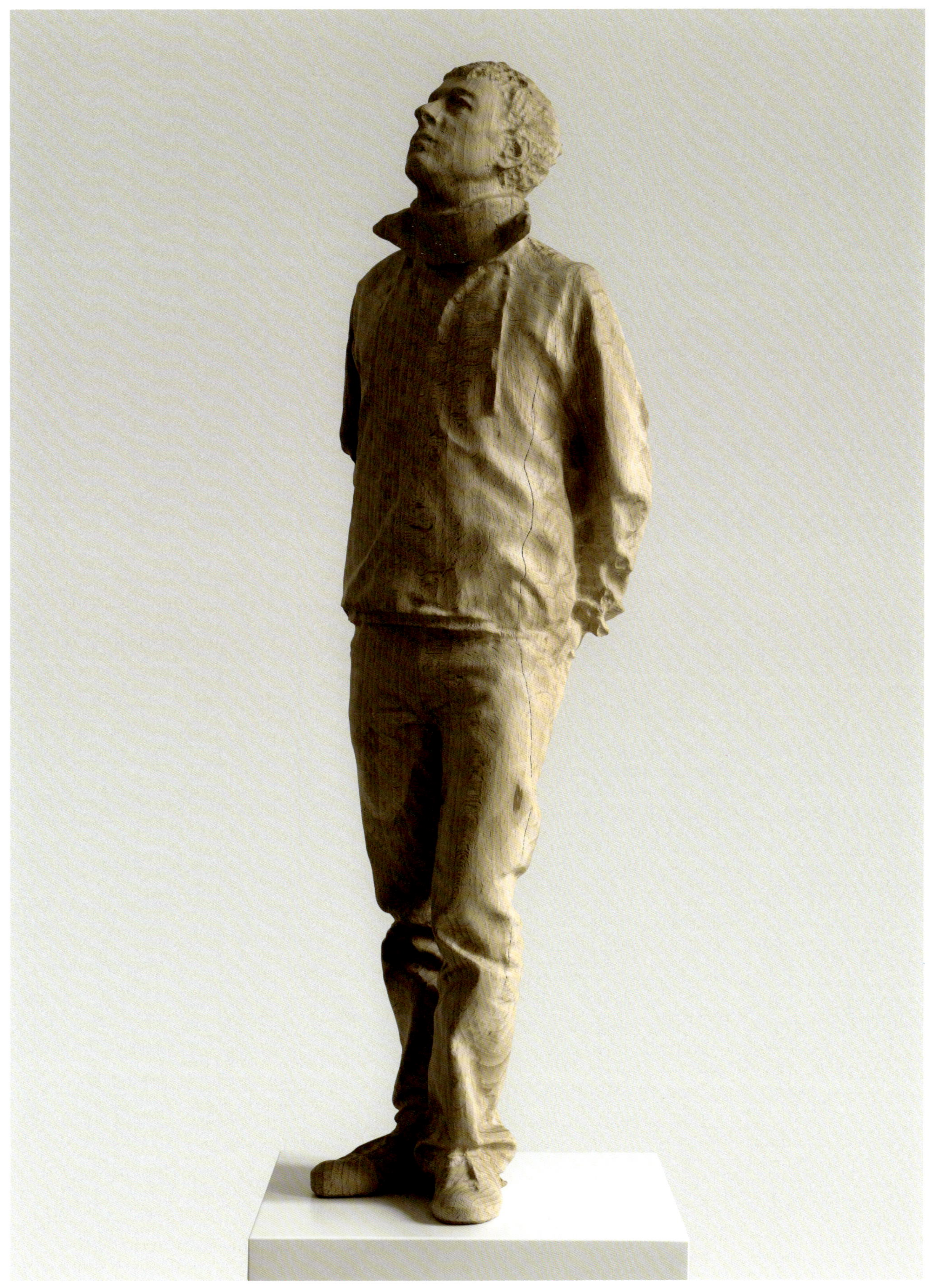

PIERRE N°1, 2008

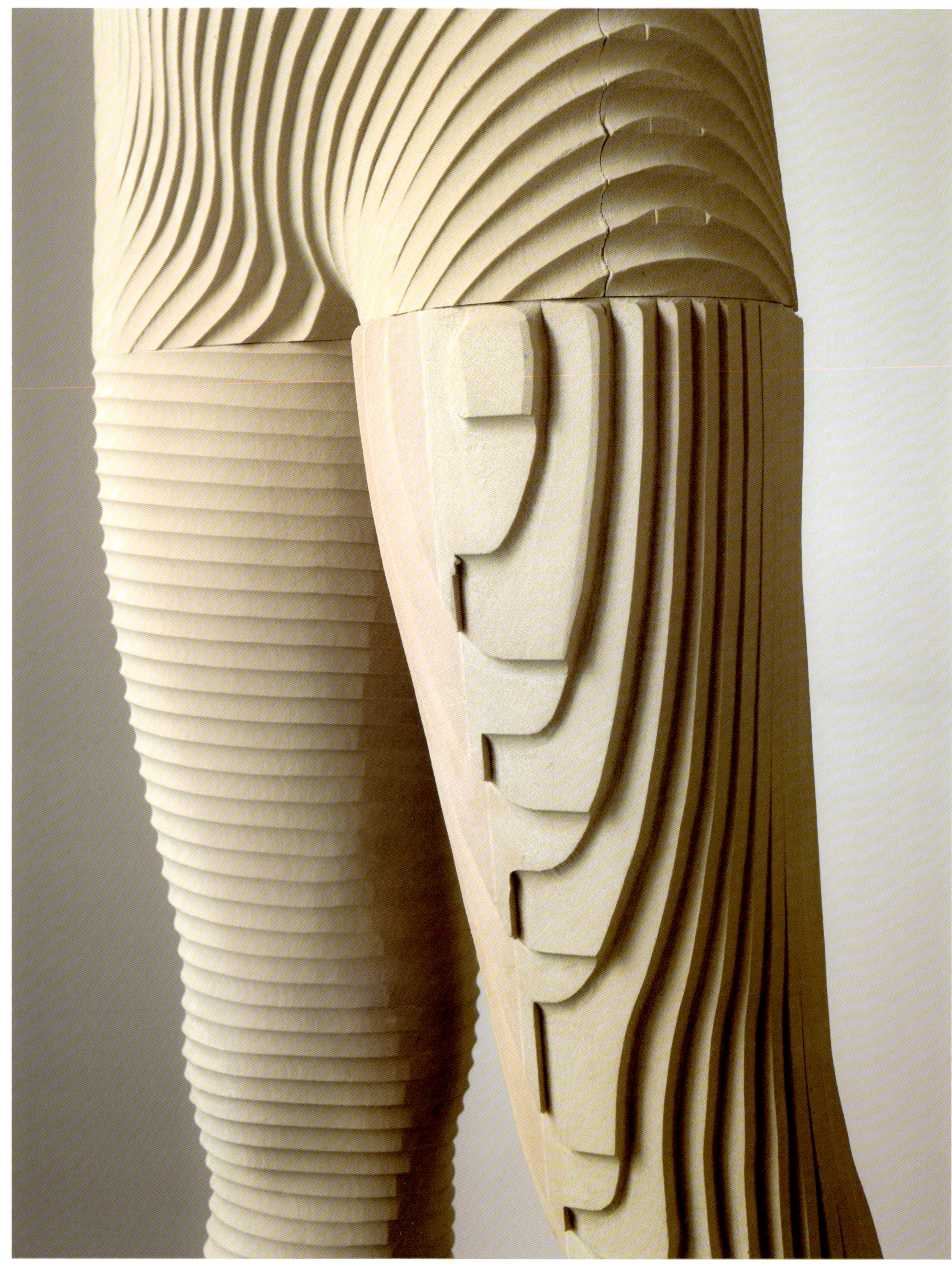

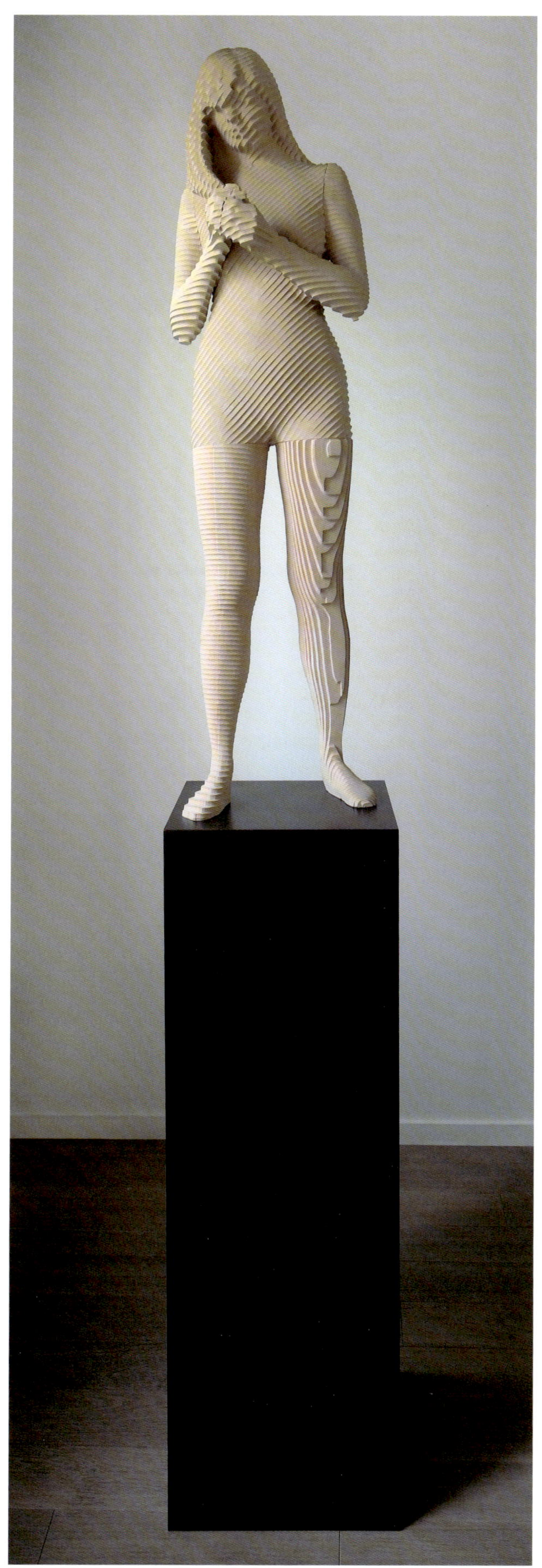

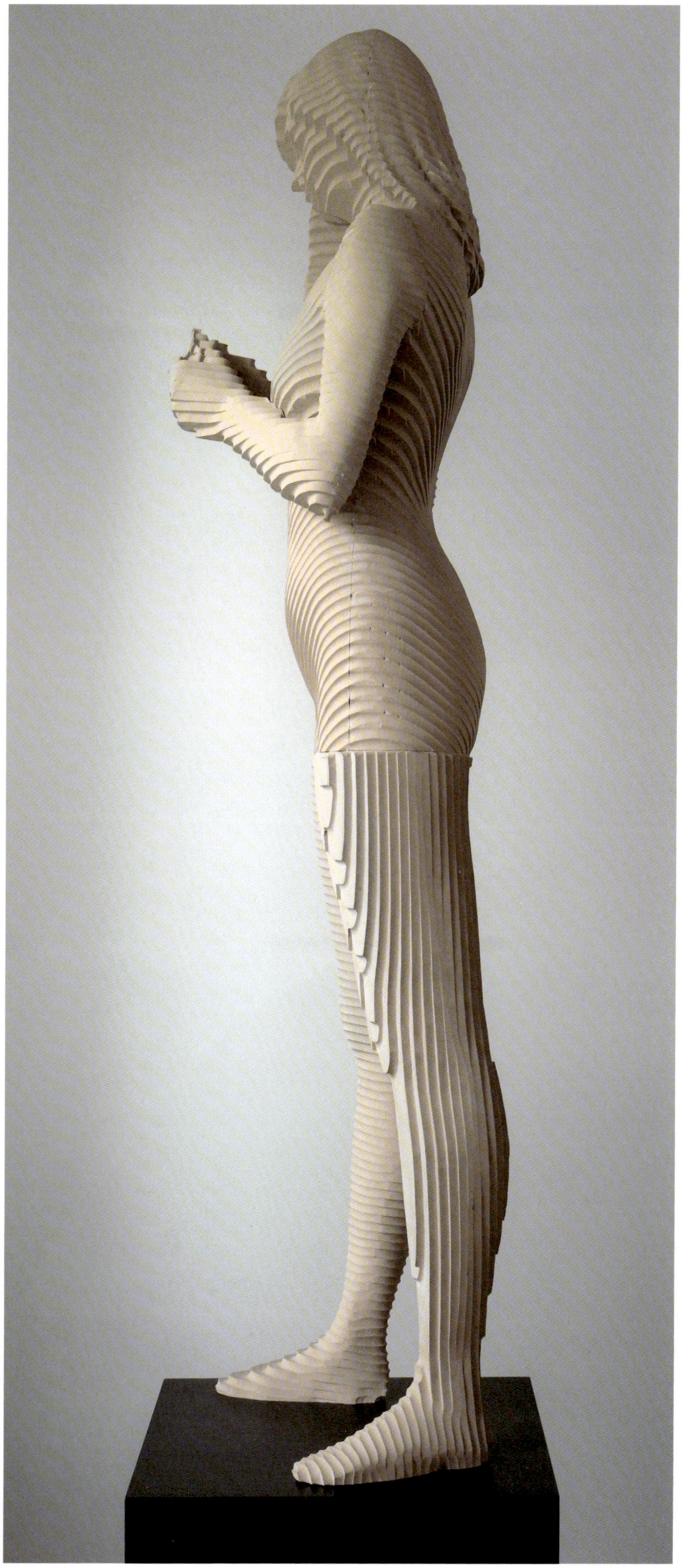

DEBORA, 2006

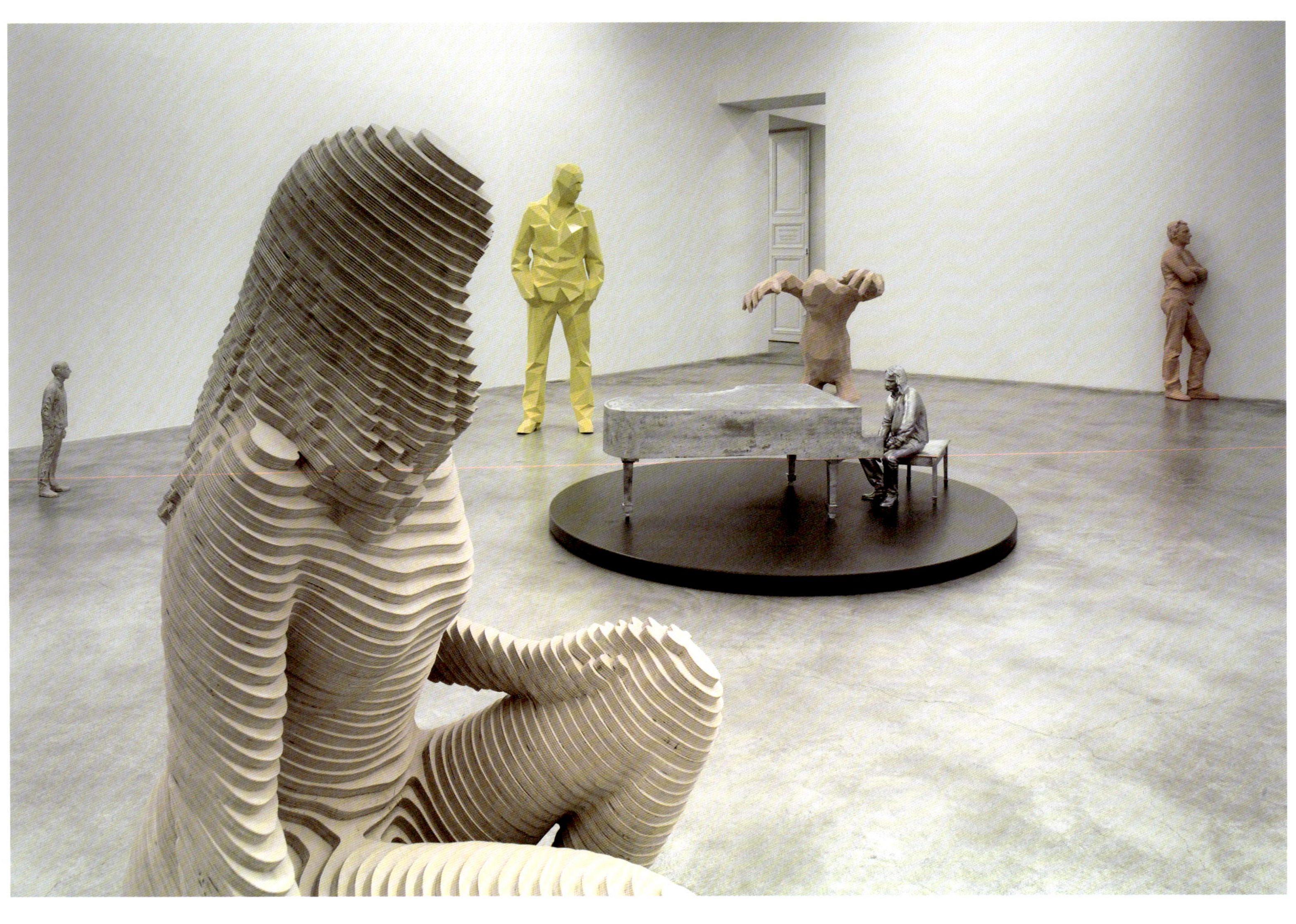

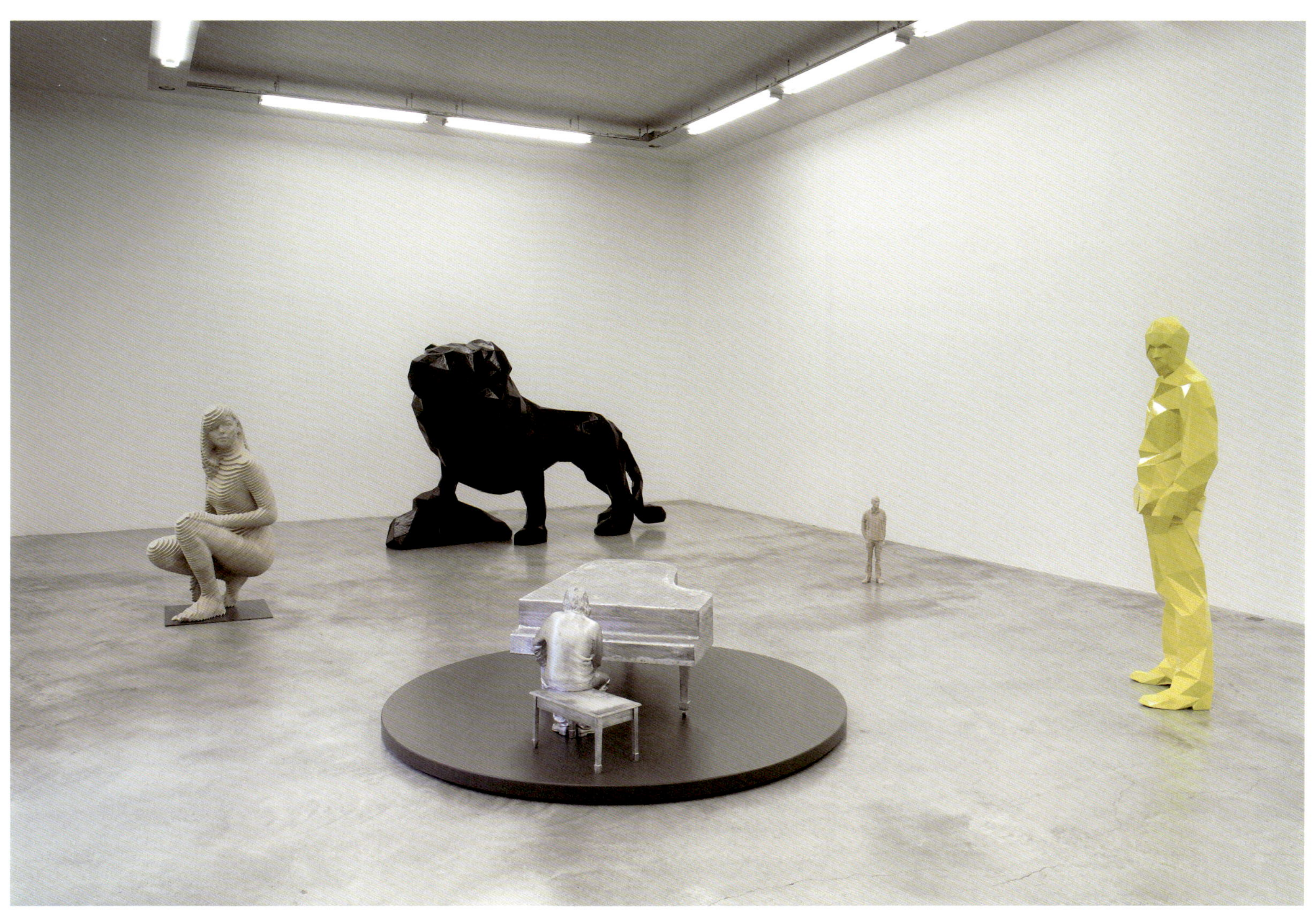

VIEWS OF THE EXHIBITION *SCULPTURES AUTOMATIQUES*, GALERIE EMMANUEL PERROTIN, PARIS, 2006

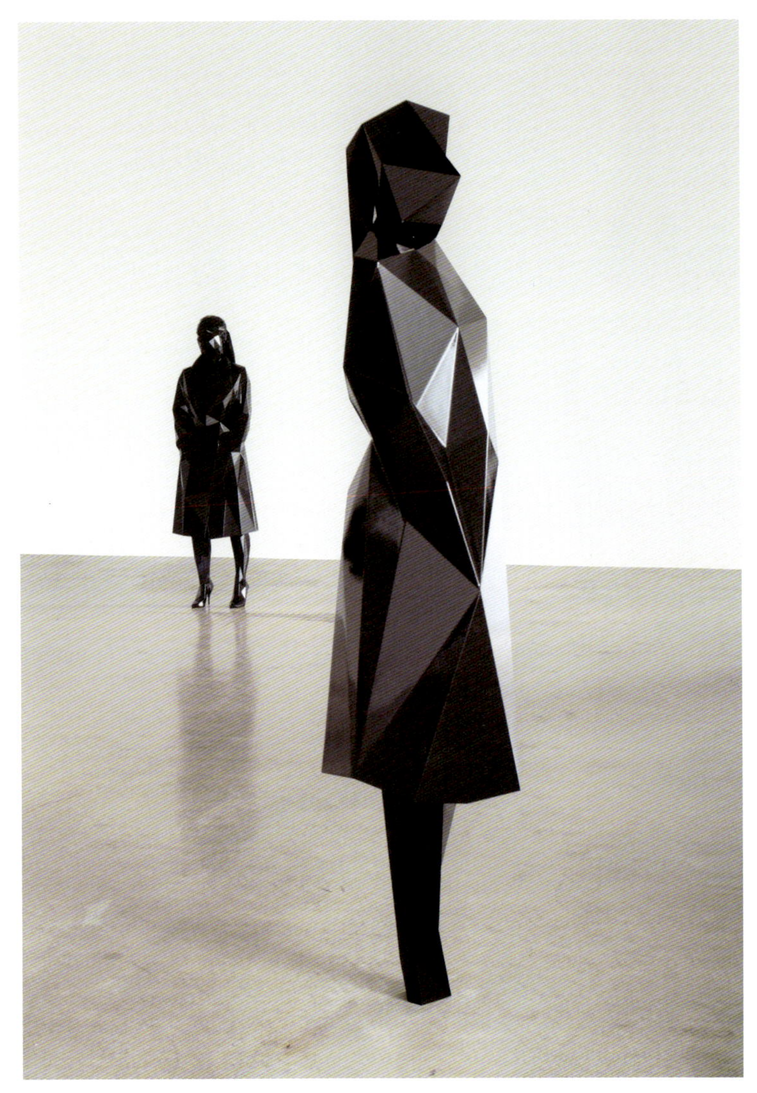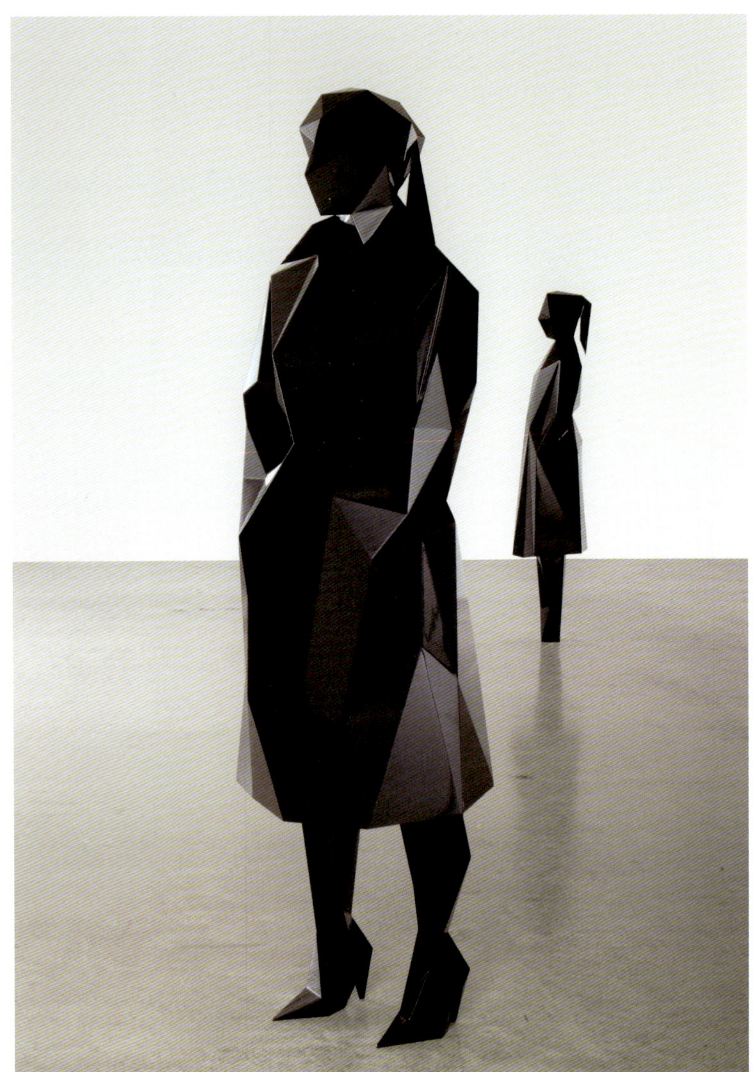

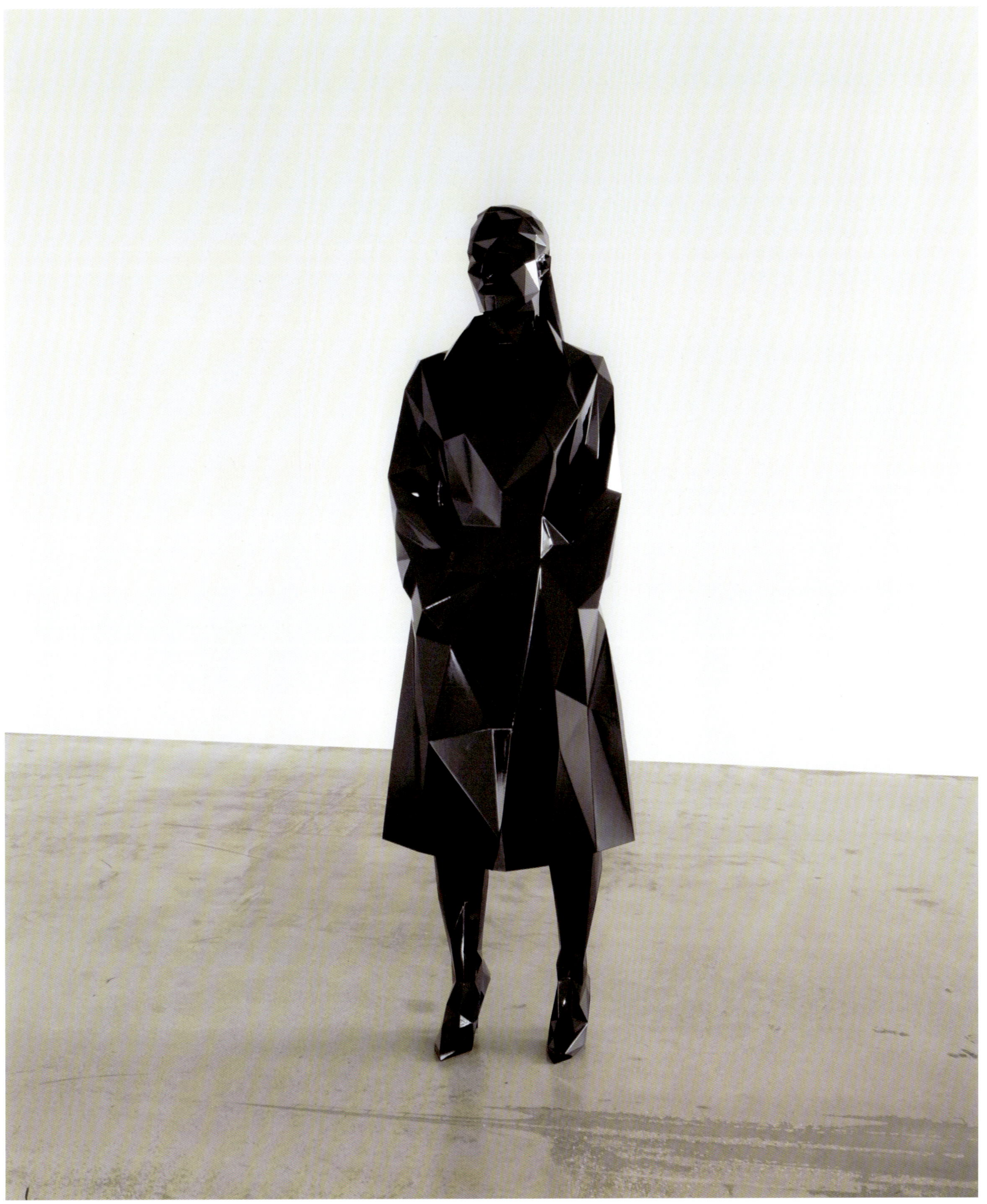

THE THREE SOPHIES, 2006

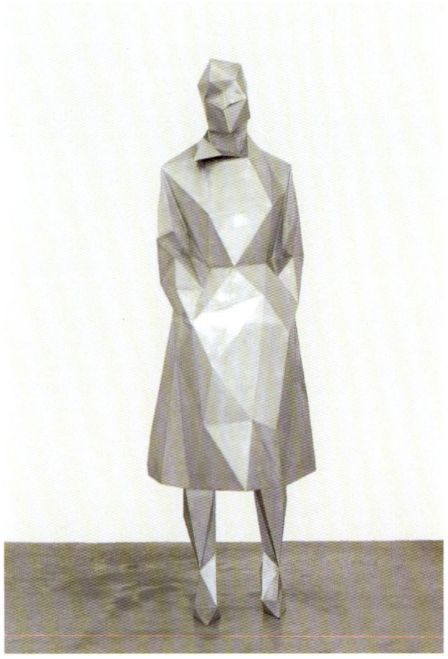

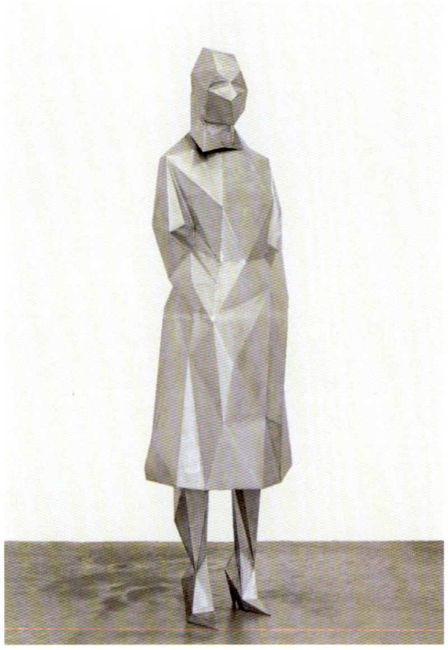

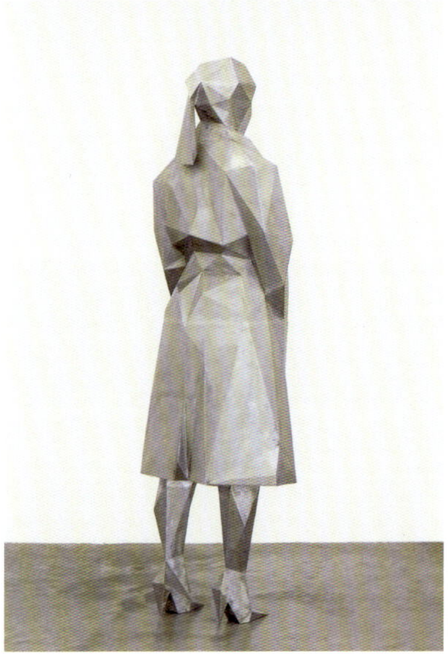

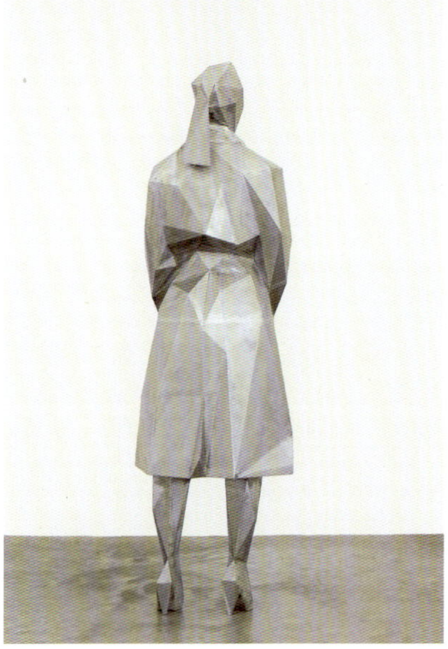

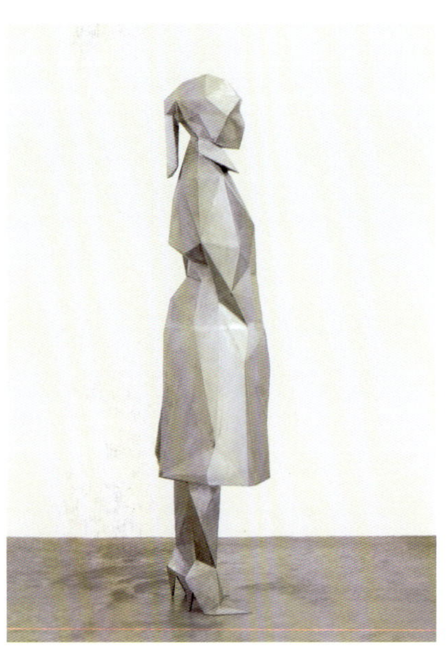
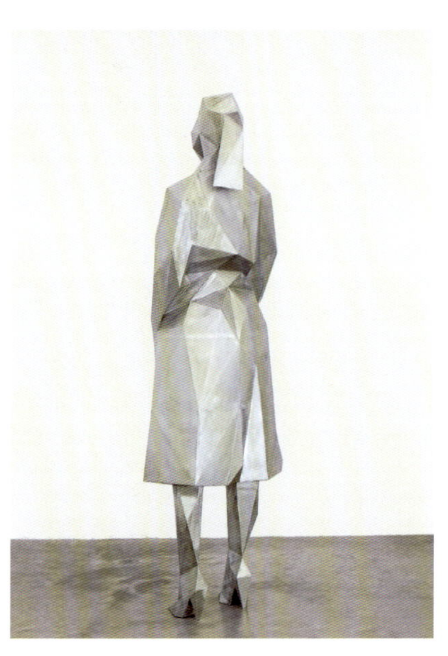

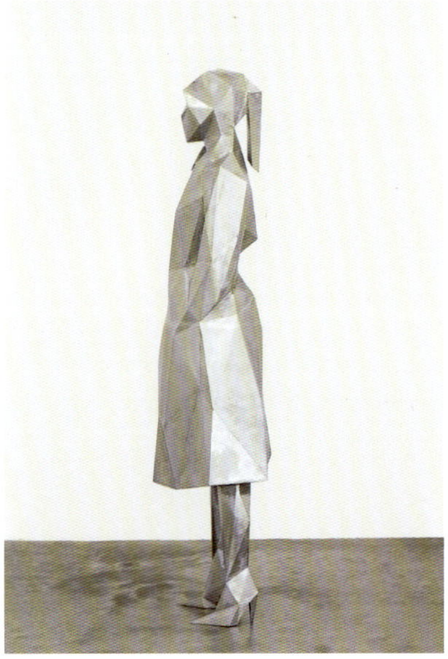

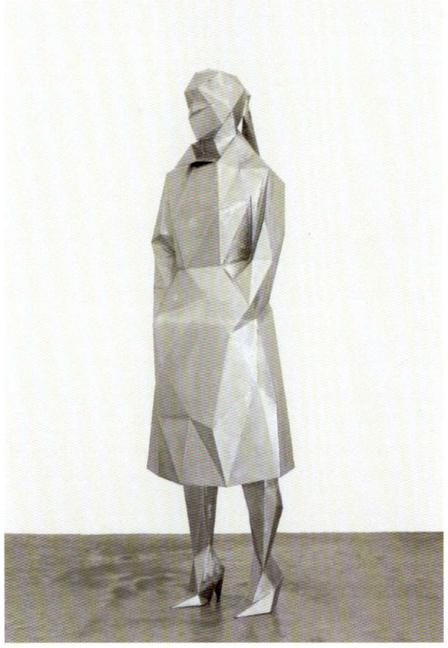

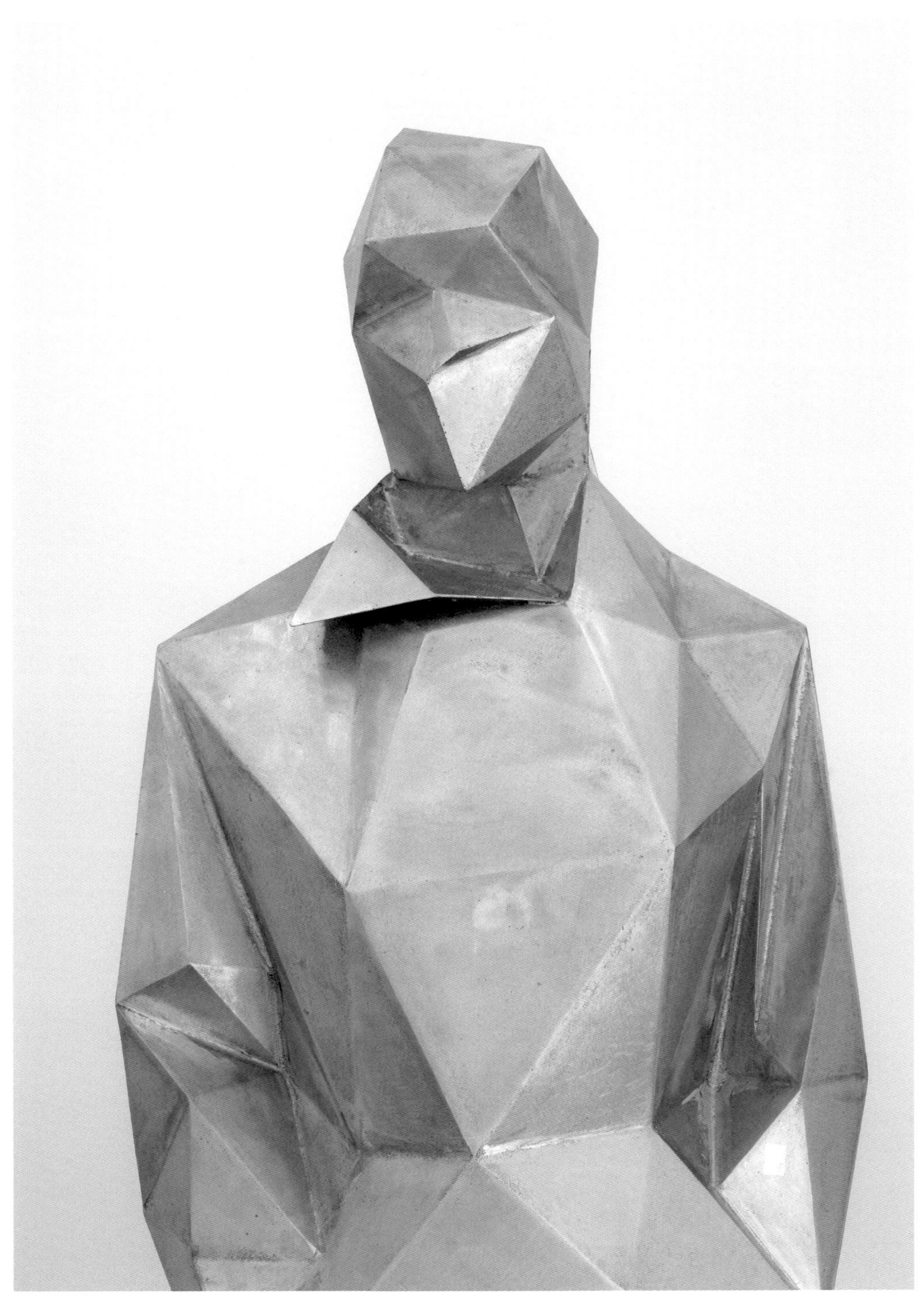

SOPHIE N° 2, 2006

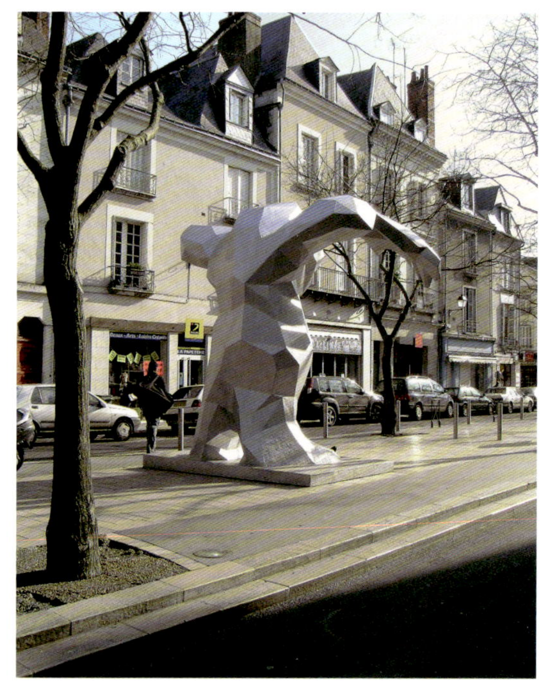

LE MONSTRE (THE MONSTER), 2004. PERMANENT INSTALLATION, PLACE DU GRAND MARCHÉ, TOURS
[→ P. 26–29] LE REQUIN (THE SHARK), 2008

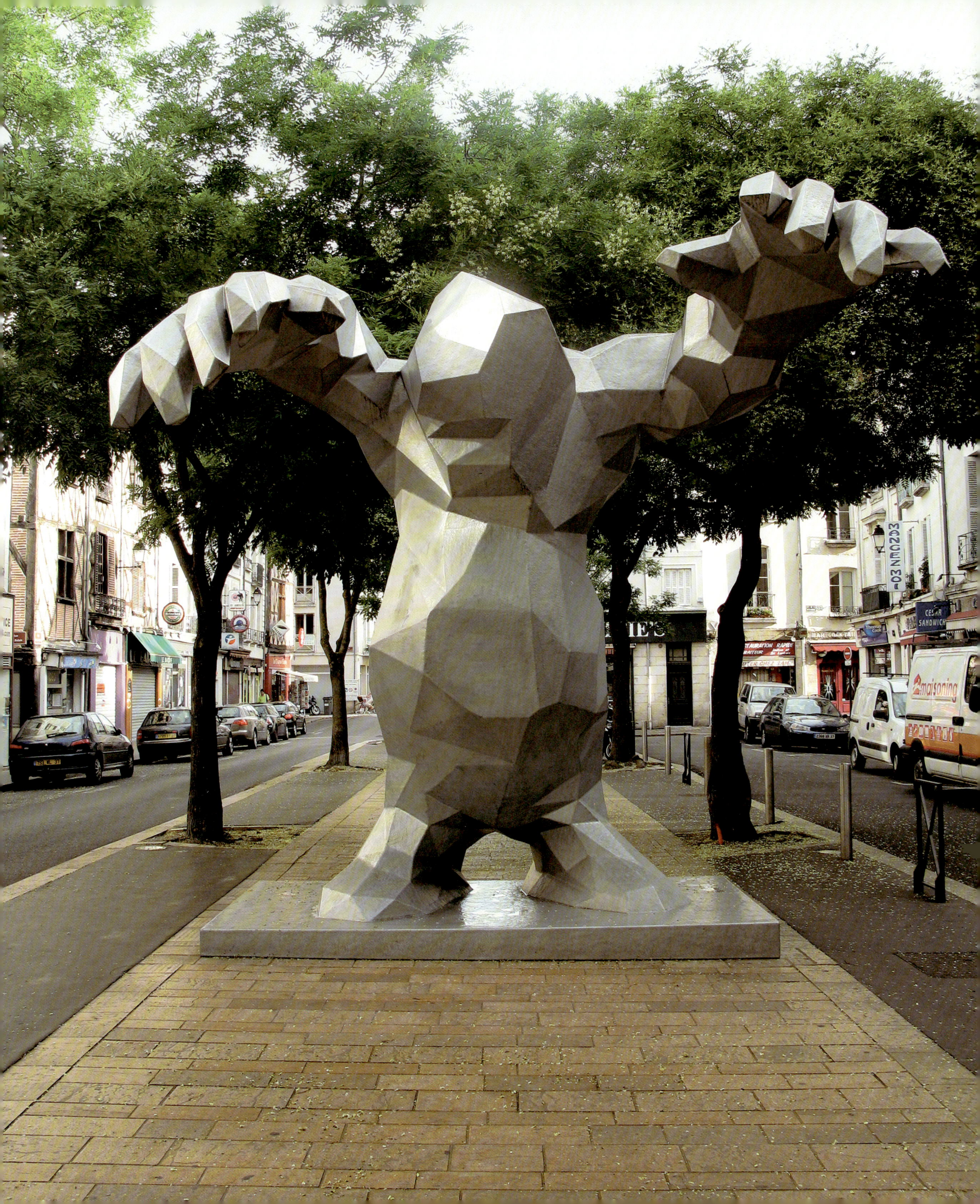

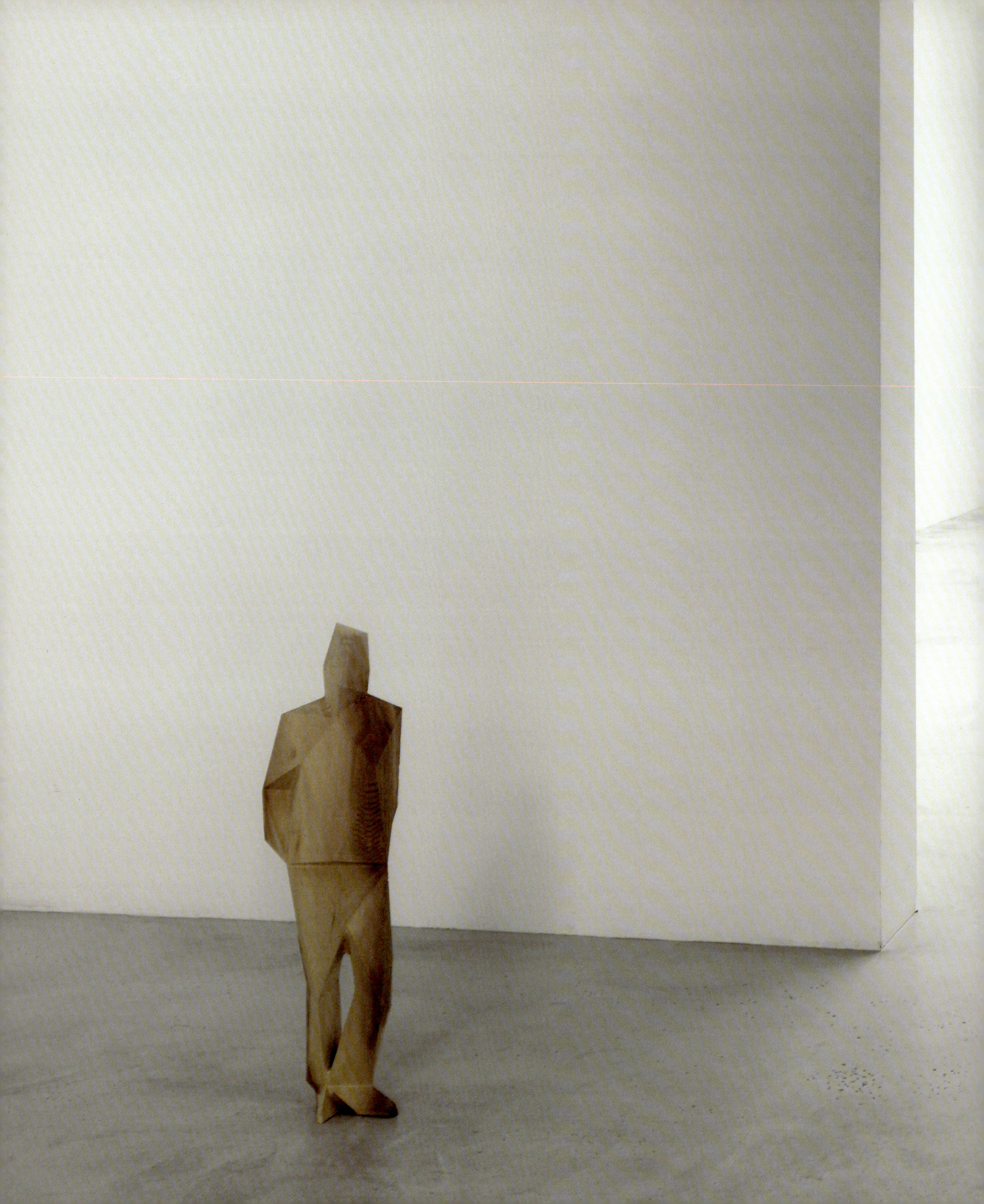

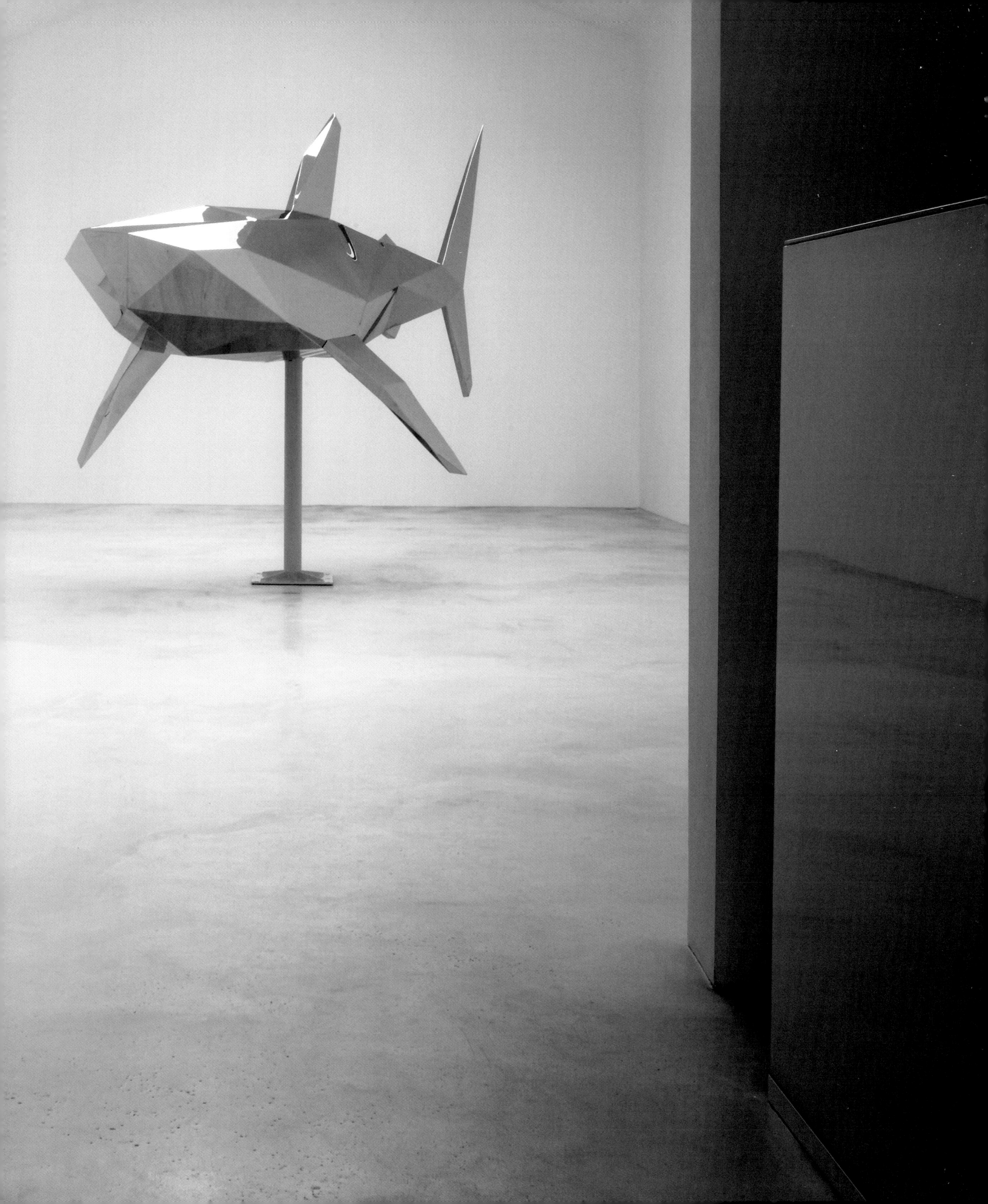

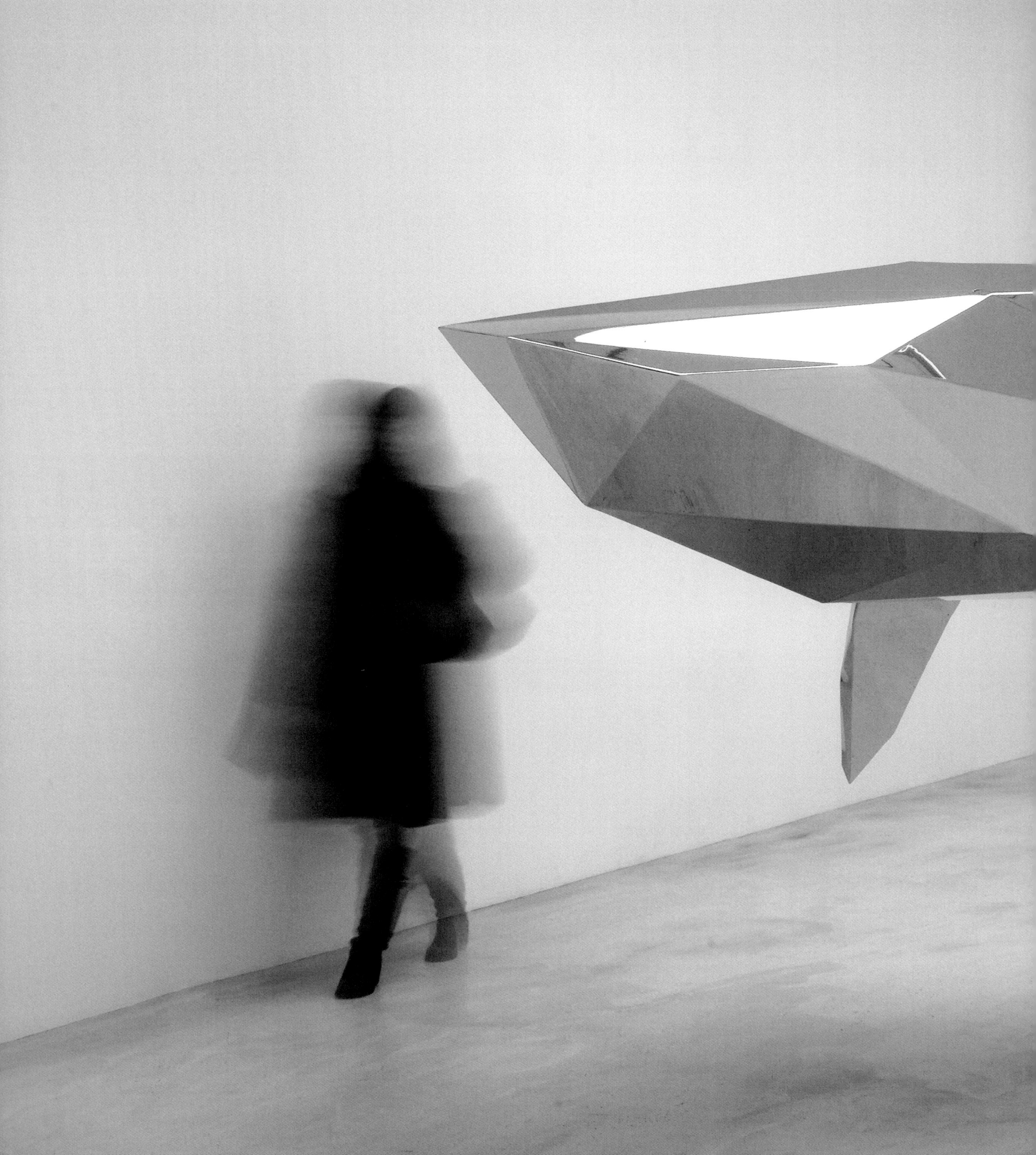

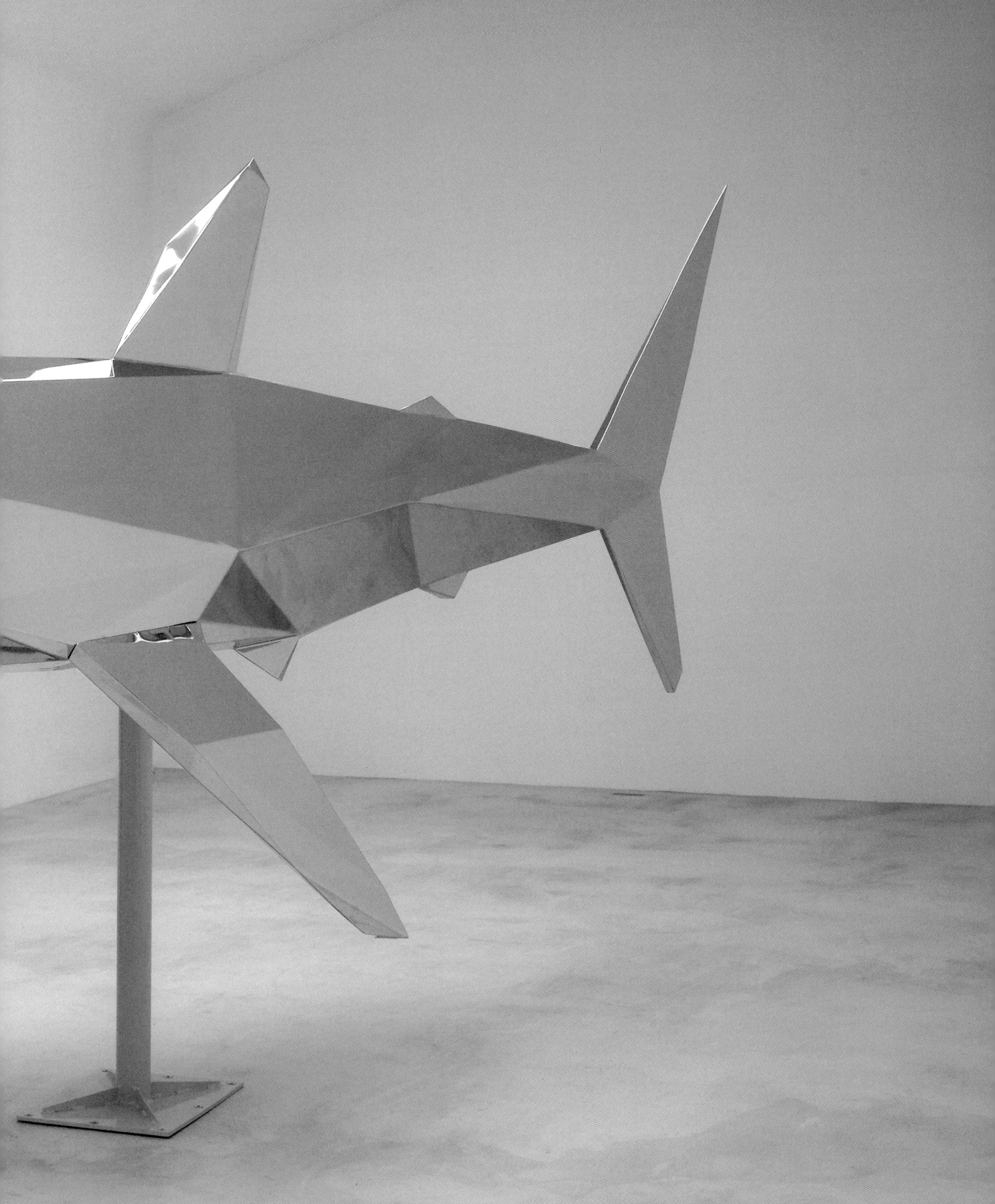

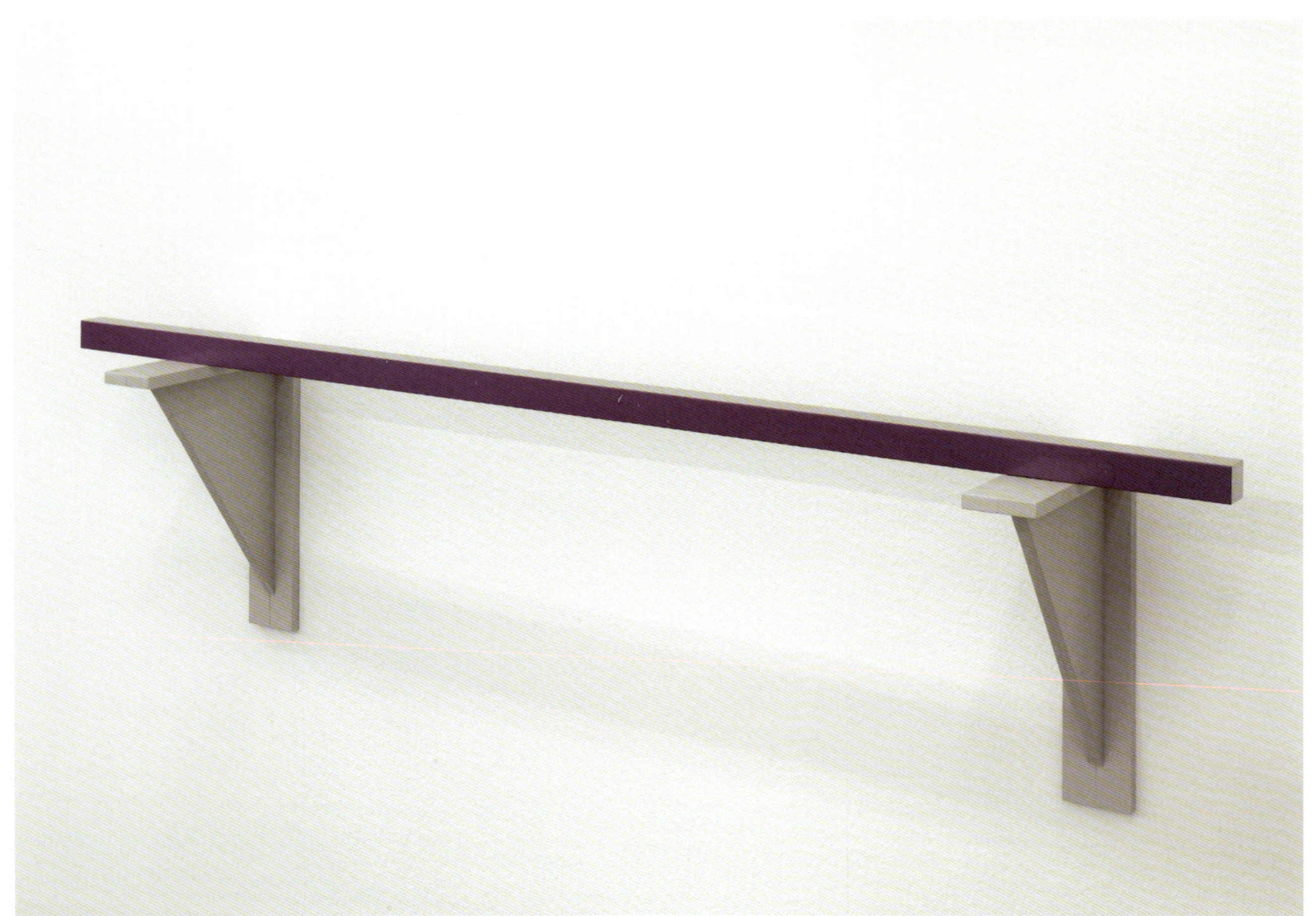

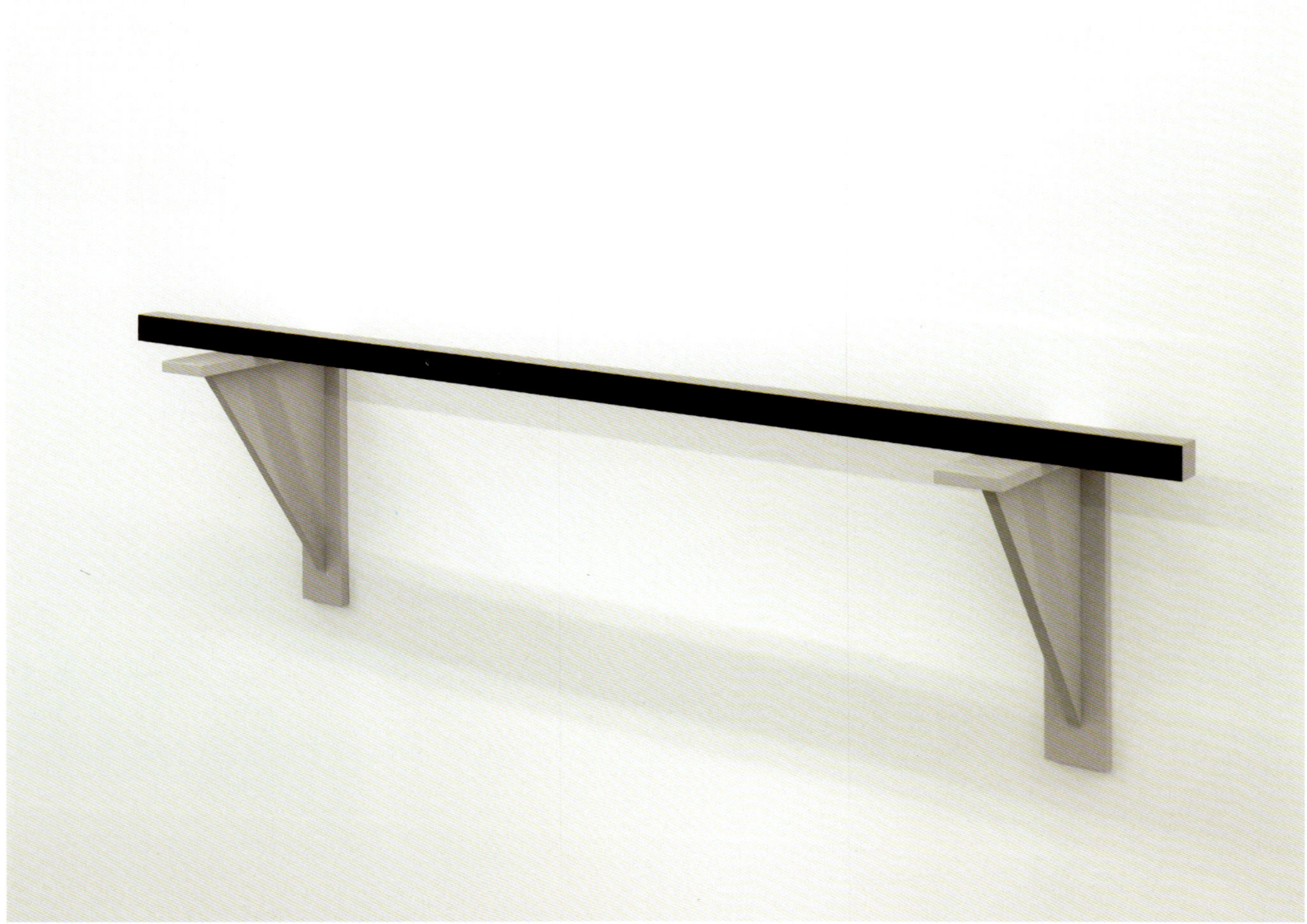

STANDARD METER N° 8 AND N° 3, 2007

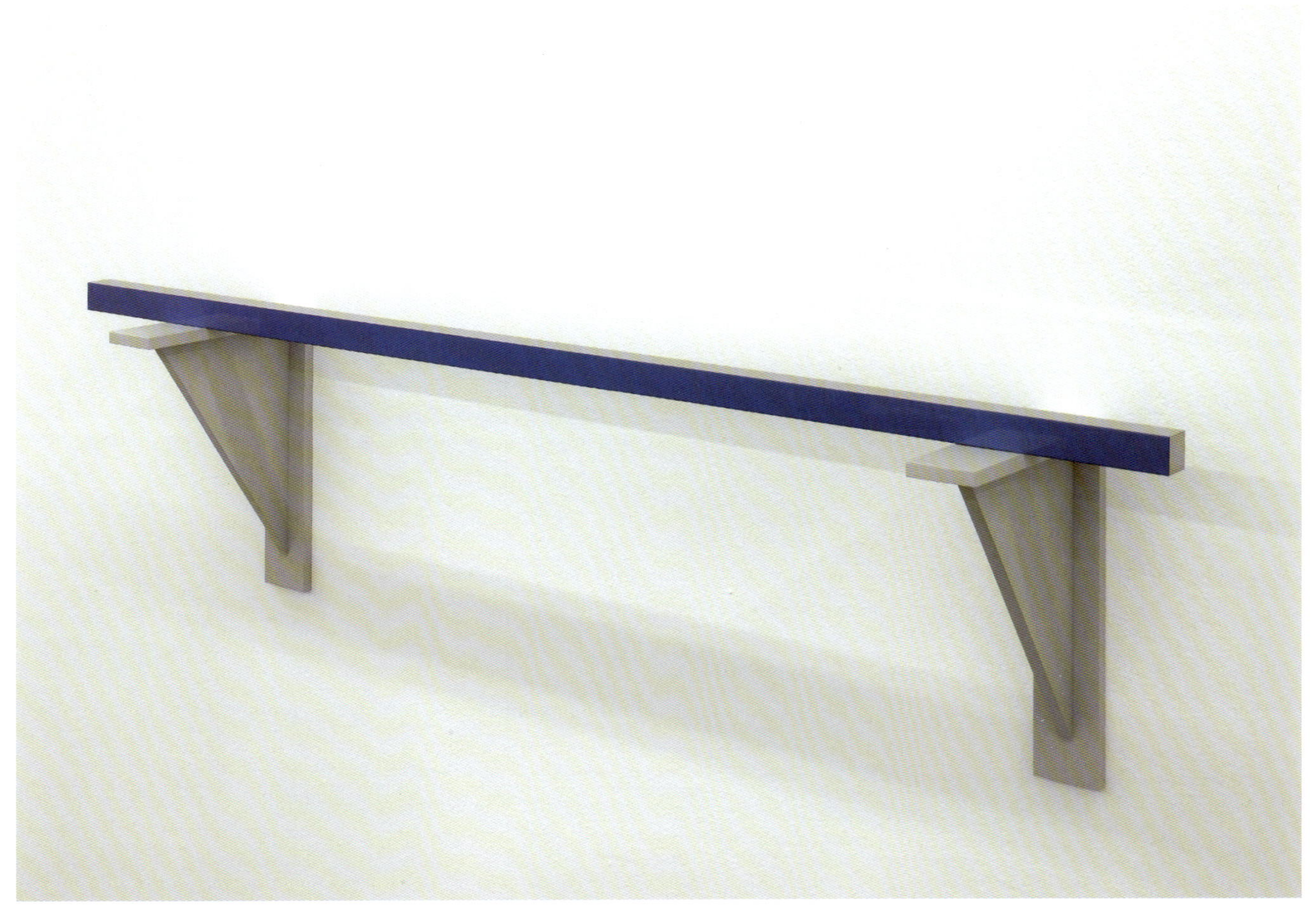

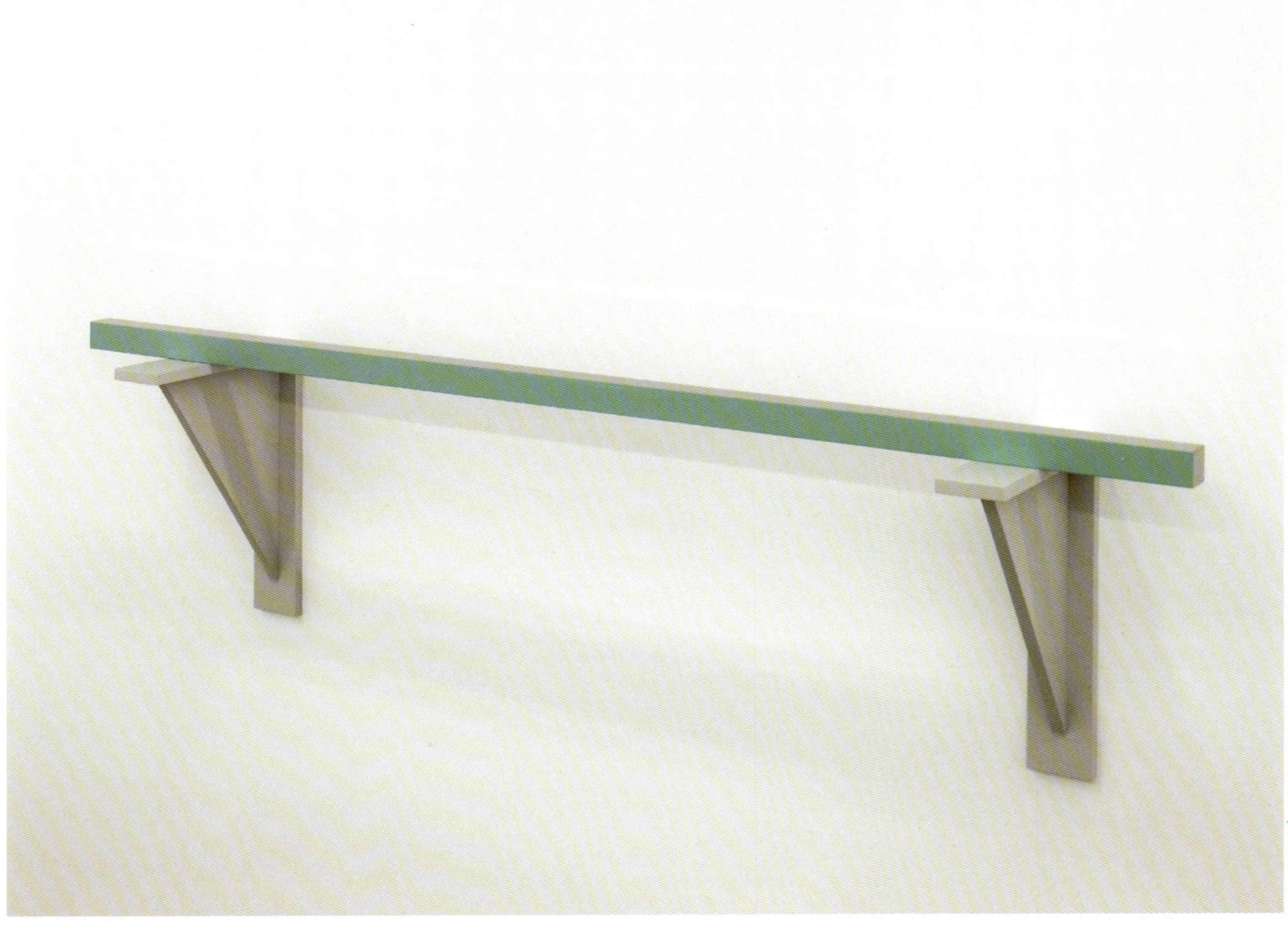

STANDARD METER N° 9 AND N° 7, 2007

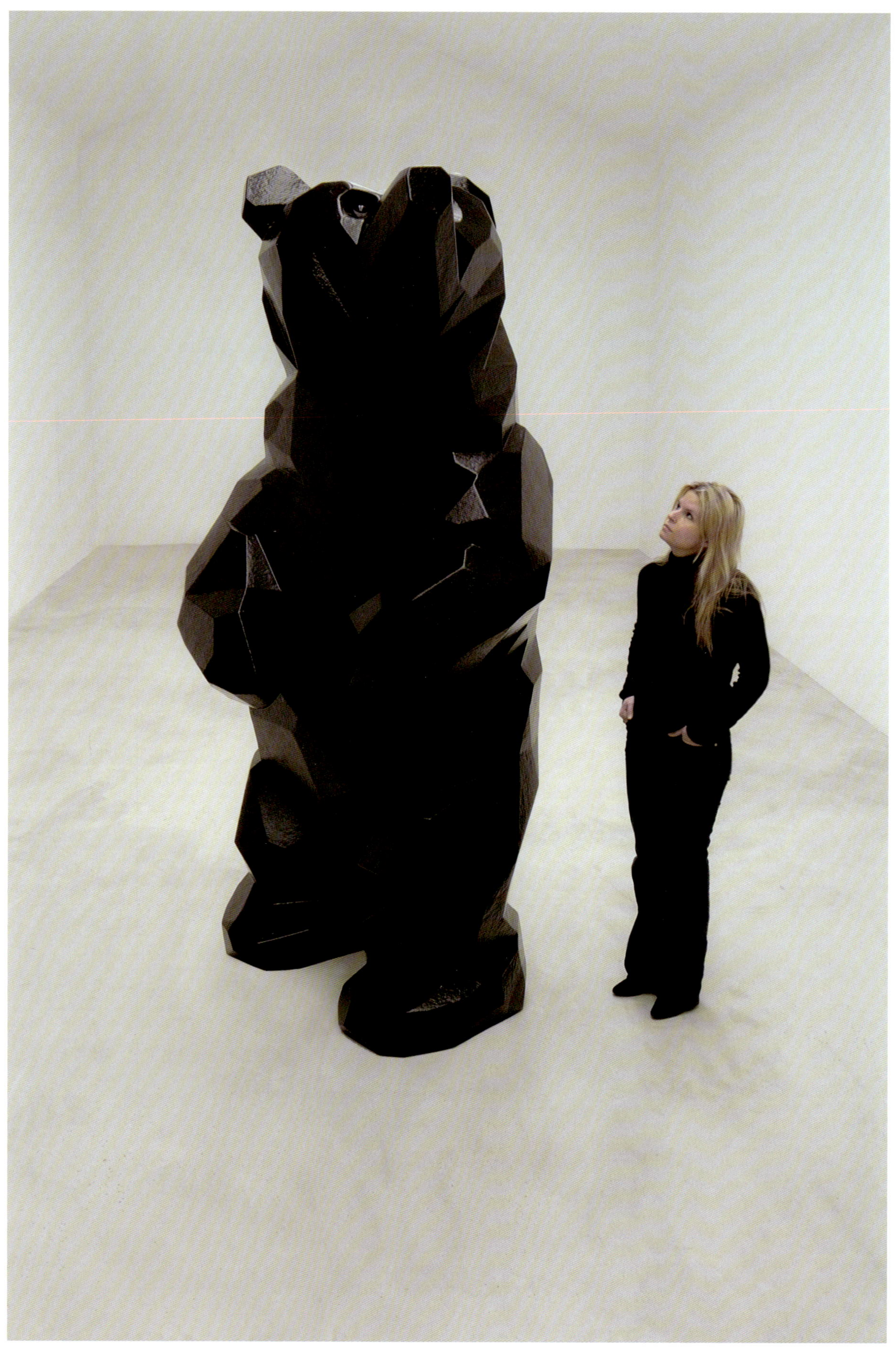

L'OURS (THE BEAR), 2008

MEASURE FOR MEASURE

Jean-Pierre Criqui

The English schoolmaster and theologian Edwin Abbott Abbott, who died in 1926 at a ripe old age, is best remembered for his novel *Flatland*, published in 1884. *Flatland* is a very odd book, rediscovered following the science-fiction boom in the 1950s. The hero is a square who begins by describing his homeland, which gave the book its name. In the second part, the square recounts his travels to foreign climes, beginning with Lineland, whose territory consists (as its name suggests) of a single perfectly straight line. The king of Lineland is very proud of his kingdom and refuses to acknowledge any other form of external reality: "It seemed that this poor ignorant Monarch—as he called himself—was persuaded that the Straight Line which he called his Kingdom, and in which he passed his existence, constituted the whole of the world, and indeed the whole of Space. Not being able either to move or to see, save in his Straight Line, he had no conception of anything out of it […] Outside his World, or Line, all was a blank to him; nay, not even a blank, for a blank implies Space; say, rather, all was non-existent." The Flatlandian square's final journey represents the dialectic counterpoint to his first expedition. He is guided through Spaceland by a sphere, and is astonished by the discovery of three-dimensional space, depth, and volume. Once the narrator has returned home, he finds himself quite unequal to the task of explaining these notions to his fellow countrymen, despite writing an educational treatise entitled *Through Flatland to Thoughtland*, which in fact lands him in prison. In his preface to a recent Italian edition of Abbott's fable, Giorgio Manganelli highlighted the inexhaustible ambiguity of *Flatland* with his usual irony: "His space is located between the *bon mot* and the Apocalypse: it is rather ample, and inhabited by monsters that are as terrifying as they are docile."

Looking back at Xavier Veilhan's oeuvre over the past ten years, it becomes apparent that his art has echoes of *Flatland*. His artistic practice is largely based on playing with the notion of scale and shifting spatial, temporal, and materiological dimensions, placing it at the crossroads of the unusual and the familiar, between memory and premonition. The blend of déjà-vu and the yet-to-come induces a relationship with the audience that makes Veilhan the perfect example of a Pop artist for the 21st century, with an accessible formal vocabulary and referents, while at the same time cultivating a certain air of detachment and reserve in his use of affects, thereby distancing himself from the empathy aroused by direct borrowings from the sphere of commodities and the media. He is overtly cautious in handling the register of passions and identificatory illusions. Although the work of art always dialogues with the viewer on an equal footing, as it were, it nonetheless invariably finds one way or another to tear itself away from the instance of the Now, whether it be the present of the place of display or of the individual encountering it.

The exhibition *Veilhan Versailles*, which continues to explore many of the questions addressed by the artist over the last decade, exemplifies this from the outset. *Le Carrosse*, placed right in the center of the Cour d'Honneur, confronts the viewer with the type of object associated with the spirit of the place and the figure and age of the monarch who commissioned

Versailles—a *Grand Siècle* monochrome. It is a UFO shot through with a shock wave which vibrates clear across the chronology separating us from its origins, or an archetype teleported onto the uneven paving stones at its own risk, like Captain Kirk in an episode of *Star Trek* ("Beam me up, Le Nôtre!"). Physicists would perhaps use the technical term "hysteresis" (which has nothing to do with hysteria, nor with history: the Greek verb *husterein* simply meaning "to be late") to describe such a case where the effect lags behind the cause in impacting the behavior of a body subjected to an action. This suggests the presence of a form of memory, and importantly for the present argument, that *Le Carrosse* "remembers," both literally and metaphorically.

A little further on, *The Naked Woman* is equally, if differently, disconcerting. She is clearly a contemporary human—a small goddess dating from long after the age of the gods. She is also the avatar of an age-old representation—the metal version of the scale model that Claude Lévi-Strauss suggested was the starting point for art in *The Savage Mind*. It is but a short distance from the Willendorf Venus to Yuri Gagarin, as *The Effigy* hints. In this work, Veilhan celebrates space in its most technological dimension, not without a certain hint of mourning, already marked by Yves Klein in *Ci-gît l'espace (Here Lies Space),* another work that seemed to come out of nowhere at almost exactly the same time as the Soviet hero was shot into orbit. As if to echo his larger-than-life cosmonaut, Veilhan has chosen to represent a heavenly body, *The Moon* at almost the other end of the exhibition; it is probably also a nod to the reflective wall sculpture with the same title that Jeff Koons installed at one end of the Hall of Mirrors last year. Veilhan recommends observing *La Lune* from the center of the terrace, where the king stood. Those who feared that Veilhan would conform excessively to the solemnity of the setting should take good note. "Mooning" the Sun King indicates a joyful irreverence which may come at the right moment to lighten the atmosphere, if such a thing were needed.

The belief that there can be no moderation without excess is a thread running through Xavier Veilhan's art from his earliest works onward. Like many of those fortunate enough to see his first solo exhibition in Paris, at the Galerie Jennifer Flay in 1991, I have a vivid memory of the occasion, particularly the evident (and yet paradoxically serene) disturbance that his sculptures caused in our vision of the premises and our own place within them. It featured a suspension bridge, a horse in harness, pigeons, and an electric pylon, all subjected to different variations in scale, and all in one single color, chosen with a complete lack of regard for realism. His subsequent works have confirmed that Veilhan is one of the great modern sculptors of human and animal figures, like his (slightly older) contemporaries Charles Ray, Katharina Fritsch, and Stephan Balkenhol. The period beginning in 2000 is particularly rich from this point of view. Veilhan has released a whole host of statues (he does not shy away from the term) into cities, museums, and galleries, from the huge man with a mobile phone and the pizza delivery man in the public square outside the Museum of Contemporary Art in Lyon and the surrounding architectural complex, to the recent characters, often simply referred to by a forename (sometimes the artist's own), which represent various stages of a process of geometricization. Animals occupy a place roughly equal to humans: his bears, penguins (both on public display in Lyon, with other variants and sizes on display within walls), and lion (in a public square in Bordeaux), as well as a brightly colored rhinoceros and a silvery shark, are some of the most familiar creatures in the bestiary of contemporary art. Veilhan takes them as an opportunity to pay more or less explicit homage to earlier artists working in the tradition of animal art, not all of whom are leading lights honored by modern art; they include Barye (described by Théophile Gautier as the "Michaelangelo of the Menagerie"), Bartholdi, and Pompon, among others. Given Veilhan's penchant for colossi, which sometimes tips over into monstrosity (one of his biggest successes, *Le Monstre*, which now looms threateningly over the Place du Grand Marché in Tours, is like something straight out of a Marvel comic), it is tempting to include in this brief list of influences Gutzon Borglum, who sculpted the famously imposing faces of four American presidents—each eighteen meters in height—in the side of Mount Rushmore (South Dakota) from 1927 to 1941.

But Veilhan would not be what he is—one of the most significant artists of the period— if he hadn't always combined this gently ironic neo-classical tendency with a broad range of works drawing on a wide variety of media, some completely innovative, and with experiments designed to take the figure of the artist into less familiar territory. These include the *Light Machines*, a new one of which was shot at Versailles and is now on display there. These are an example of the former register, if we imagine that our age of HDV and downloadable films had an unlikely ancestor in the form of an exquisitely lo-fi cinematograph, its screen of a thousand or so electric lightbulbs of various intensities displaying a few short scenes whose rather stuttering repeti- tion can be seen as a form of hypnagogic hallucination, rather like a mist consisting of distance (the blur that characterizes reminiscences) and closeness (the way our body is absorbed by the colored halo). The latter register of this attempt at general diversification includes the curating of works by other artists (the *Projet hyperréaliste* or *Baron de Triqueti*, for example) and the shows, performances, and concerts (with musicians such as Air) that he has organized. Then there are his films, of course, including *Furtivo*, his latest and most ambitious. *Furtivo*, which has a soundtrack but no dialogue and lasts nearly half an hour, is the account, or rather mirrors the reflections of the twin odysseys of an ultra-modern, "stealth" sailing boat, crewed by Veilhan and his friends and family, and of a character acted by Sébastien Tellier, who also composed the music. Shaken by visionary flashes and demiurgic impulses, Tellier—a Nobodaddy in a white suit and dark glasses—appears clearly as an allegori- cal representation of the artist-creator. The seriousness of Veilhan's belief in this romantic image is not easy to measure (as we have seen, he only features on screen himself as part of the crew), but by crossing aesthetics that are heterogeneous to say the least (quasi-Blakeian prophetism and a feel for cinematography that is some- times reminiscent of the finest advertising films), *Furtivo* achieves a singularity that is as true as it is enigmatic. The present book draws on literary fiction, essays, and inter- views in an attempt to give an account of Veilhan's work.

35

THE WHO, "GOING MOBILE," 1971

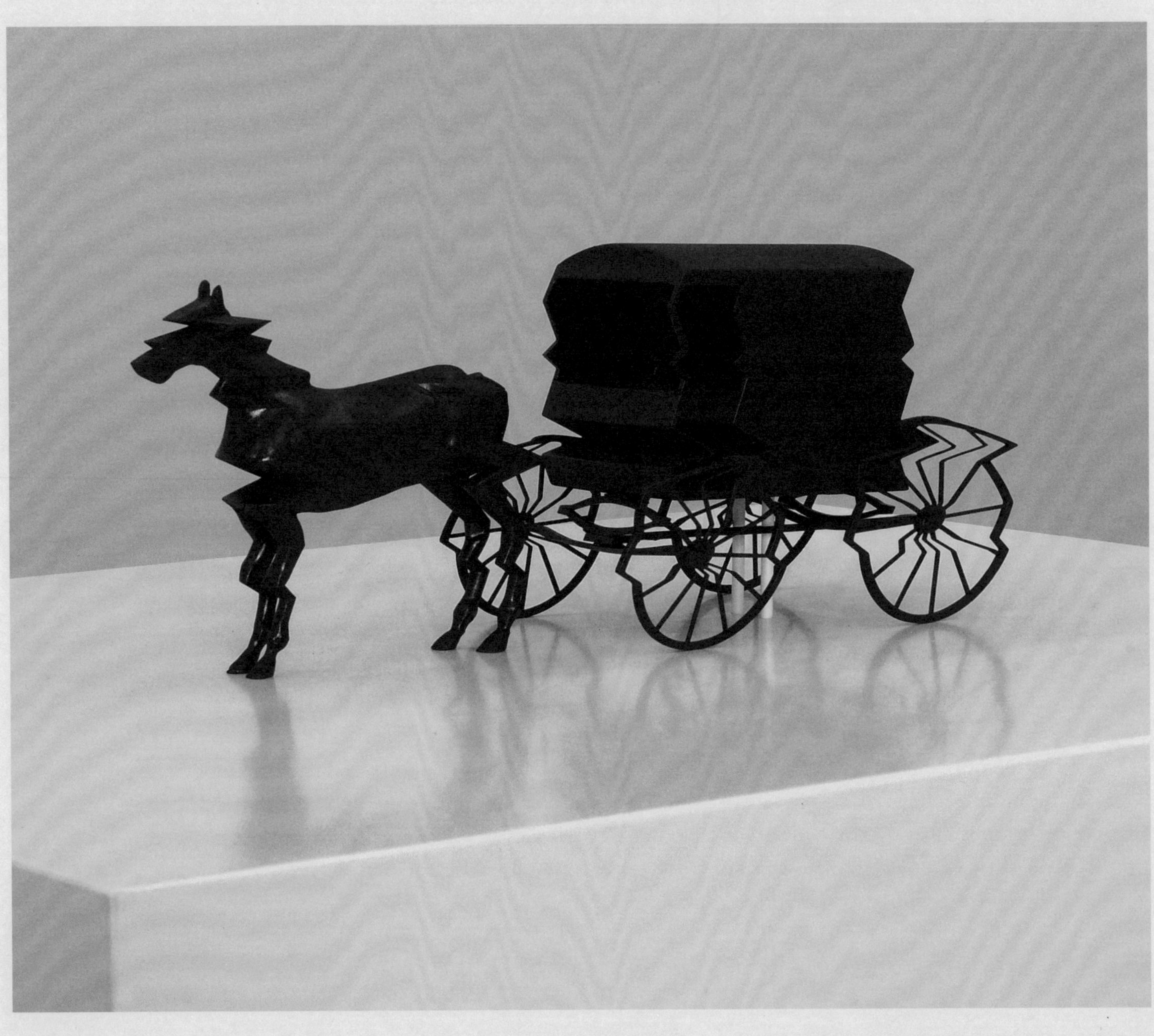

AMISH VIBRATION, 2008

GOING MOBILE
KINE-VISION THE MAGIC OF SPEED AND OTHER ARCHAEO-MODERNIST PHANTASMAGORIAS

Arnauld Pierre

A carriage drawn by powerful horses sets out from the Château de Versailles at great speed, echoing Louis XVI's failed attempt to escape from the Tuileries during the Revolution. The work is Xavier Veilhan's *Carrosse*, the last of a series of such vehicles inaugurated by *Amish Vibration* at the *Furtivo* exhibition at the Galerie Perrotin in spring 2008, and including three further works for the screening of his eponymous film at the Pinacoteca Giovanni e Marella Agnelli in Turin a few months later. As its name suggests, *Le Carrosse* is much larger than the earlier works, and also creates the impression of much greater speed. The six horses drawing the carriage are no longer immobile, but rather captured at different points of a full gallop, in reference to the photographic procedure perfected by the American Eadweard Muybridge in the late 19th century, which fragmented movement into a series of poses. Although the horse and carriage in *Amish Vibration* are shown at rest, they are by no means visually immobile; the image was blurred by a wave that deformed its outline, making the work tremble like the picture on a badly adjusted TV set.[1] The same phenomenon is at play in *Le Carrosse*, accentuating the impression of accelerating speed as it rattles across the cobblestones of Versailles. The effect of speed appears to create a frayed trail behind the uniformly featureless purple shapes, somewhat reminiscent of the surging movement suggested by the Futurist sculptor Umberto Boccioni's *Forme uniche della continuità nello spazio*, which celebrates a new, energetic unity of matter, space, and time, created through the intensification of movement. This source is confirmed by the choice of titles for one of the works in the Amish Series, *Amish Boccioni*, and by the shapes, streamlined yet somehow disjointed. Veilhan's works, like those of Boccioni, are frozen in unchanging immobility, while still achieving a state comparable to the "new stasis, the new superior pause of movement that cannot be subdivided,"[2] which the great art historian Roberto Longhi saw as the key characteristic of Boccioni's work.

Applying such Boccionian stylization to such an un-Futuristic object as a horse-drawn carriage is rather surprising—as is the oxymoron of the title *Amish Boccioni*. The language of one of the most technophile of all avant-garde artists modifies the appearance of a vehicle whose archaism is underscored by reference to the American Anabaptist community famous for its fierce opposition to the modern way of life. However, it should be noted that Carlo Carrà worked on a similar theme as long ago as 1911, in one of the most frenetic and chaotic of all Futurist paintings, *Sobbalzi di carrozza*, where the outlines of two white horses and fragments of spoked wheels emerge from the composition's lines of force. Likewise, Boccioni himself often used the motif of the horse as an allegory of the gathering might of the modern world (*The City Rises*, 1910–1911).[3]

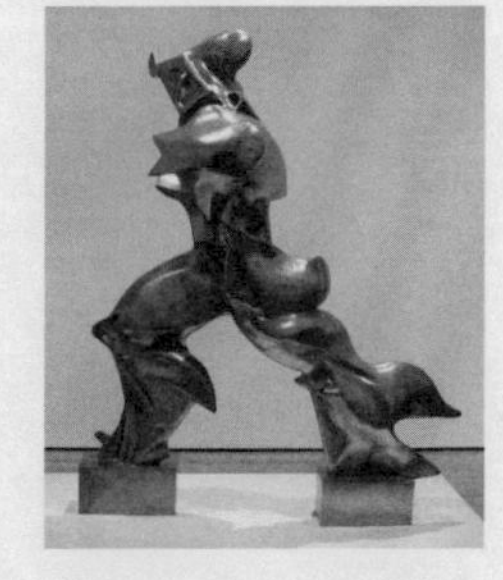

↗ Umberto Boccioni (1882–1916)
Forme uniche della continuità nello spazio, 1913
Bronze, 111.2 × 88.5 × 40 cm

1 I have borrowed this image from Éric Troncy, "Xavier Veilhan, *Furtivo*, galerie Emmanuel Perrotin, Paris," *Frog* 7, 2nd semester 2008, p. 44–47.

2 Roberto Longhi, "La sculpture futuriste de Boccioni" [1914], *Les Cahiers du Musée national d'art moderne* 47, spring 1994, p. 43.

3 Claude Quiguer rightly notes that the horse is one of the four great metaphors of machinery, along with storms, women, and monsters. See Quiguer, *Femmes et machines de 1900. Lecture d'une obsession Modern Style*, Klincksieck, Paris 1979, p. 207 & 217 ff.

It should also be borne in mind that families of technological objects sometimes seem to transmit their genes from generation to generation, and that no progress can be accomplished without preserving a hereditary trace of the preceding stage. Veilhan is fully aware of this; his three *Bicycles* (2000) demonstrate how the most sophisticated bicycle design echoes the shape of the earliest pedalless velocipedes. It has often been noted that the earliest railway carriages and automobiles looked like coaches, simply stripped of their horses and placed on rails or the road. Even language sometimes bears such traces: in Italian, the Futurist movement's mother tongue, "carrozza" means both "car" and "railway coach," as well as "carriage." It should also be borne in mind that the first literary evidence of the effects of speed on perception came from a passenger not in a car or train, but a horse-drawn carriage—the mail-coach that whisked Gérard de Nerval off on a journey recorded in the poem *Le réveil en voiture* (1832): "This is what I saw: Trees along the road / Fleeing in confusion, like a routed army"—the first of many such kinetic images throughout the poem. All were destined for a bright future, but this particular example was transcribed word-for-word by Nerval's friend Théophile Gautier on board the train to Brussels in 1836 and by Octave Mirbeau in a 15-horsepower car, the CGV 628–E8, which became the "heroine" of his 1905 novel of the same title.[4] Whether prompted by the mail-coach, train, or car, observations from such traveling vision machines led to the same hallucinatory images of dissolving and disappearance, all bearing the symptoms of speed's power to literally deform. As Victor Hugo wrote in a letter in 1837, later incorporating the observation into his *En voyage*, the speed of such journeys was unprecedented: "the flowers by the side of the road are no longer flowers but flecks, or rather streaks, of red and white; there are no longer any points, everything become a streak."[5] Such accounts reflect the emergence of a sort of Impressionism avant la lettre, adumbrating the evanescence of appearance characteristic of modern painting, to the point where it has been claimed that Impressionism was born from the door of a train traveling at fifty or eighty kilometers an hour.[6]

The list of vehicles featured in Veilhan's work has already been compiled. It is extensive, and reflects his statement that an object with wheels is of necessity beautiful, and a handsome bicycle is worth any number of sculptures.[7] The link between machines and beauty is one of the surest signs of the renewal of Modernism in his oeuvre, which is filled with cars and motorbikes, airplanes and airships, ships and submarines, in paintings, sculptures, photographs, and films. *The Vehicle* (1995) is the quintessential example: a simple tubular chassis on four spoked wheels, with no steering system or brakes, equipped with a pulse reactor motor that makes it

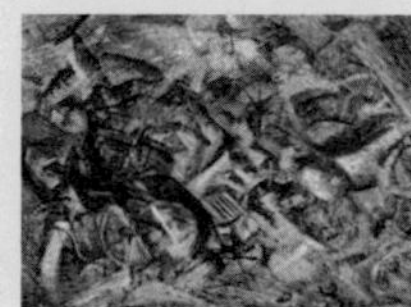

↗ Carlo Carrà (1881–1966)
Sobbalzi di carrozza [Jolts of a Cab], 1911.
Oil on canvas, 52.3 × 67.1 cm

4 Claude Pichois discusses these examples in an essay that is still astonishingly fresh and relevant, *Vitesse et vision du monde*, La Baconnière, Neuchâtel 1973, p. 11 ff.

5 Quoted in Wolfgang Schivelbusch, *The Railway Journey: The Industrialization and Perception of Time and Space in the Nineteenth Century*, trans. Anselm Hollo, Berg, New York 1986, p. 55.

6 Henri Vincenot, *L'Âge du chemin de fer*, Denoël, Paris 1980, p. 136. Vincenot's assertion is based on an evocative memory described by Johan Barthold Jongkind: "I saw thousands of successive paintings flashing in the frame of the train window at lightning speed, but I only glimpsed them, as each was very quickly erased by its successor [...] And I understood that that was how one had to paint: simply grasping the essential of the light caught in a second at different moments." This extract is also quoted in Clément Chéroux's interesting article "Vues du train. Vision et mobilité au XIXe siècle," *Études photographiques* 1, November 1996, p. 75.

7 Veilhan, interview with Timothée Chaillou, "La réalité n'est que mouvement," *Intersection* 2, spring 2008, p. 91–99. As Marinetti wrote in the famous *Futurist Manifesto* of 1909, "We affirm that the world's magnificence has been enriched by a new beauty: the beauty of speed. A racing car whose hood is adorned with great pipes, like serpents of explosive breath—a roaring car that seems to ride on grapeshot is more beautiful than the Victory of Samothrace." Trans. R.W. Flint, in Umbro Apollonio, ed. *Documents of 20th Century Art: Futurist Manifestos*, Viking, New York 1970, p. 19–24.

an object purely and intransitively designed for speed. However, the list does not leave much room for the train, which was the emblematic means of transport of the high Modernist period; its rare appearances confirm its key status as a manipulator of vision. A TV set broadcasting images of working scale models of trains was at the heart of the kinetic installation *The Cranes* at the Galerie Jennifer Flay in 1993. Veilhan has always described the various updated versions of the work as mechanistic metaphors of the gaze. The viewer set the cranes rotating and launched a steel ball rolling along a rail simply by opening the door to the space, thereby becoming a participant in his own perception of movement. In the photographic series *Les Bars de TGV* (1995), the lengthwise perspective of the train carriage is captured with flawless clarity, while the landscape is blurred through the frames of the side windows. This is a constant feature of the modern gaze: it is not the train that appears to be moving fast, but the landscape it is traveling through, onto which the traveler projects his own mobility. Of all Veilhan's works, those that take the most account of the deformation imposed on subjects by speed are without doubt the *Ghost Landscapes*. These are lacquered aluminum panels reproducing digitized copies of photographic images, reduced to a set of pixels that blur their legibility. This cybernetic Impressionism—the Impressionism of the age of the pixel and information theory[8]—should be read in terms of the abstraction of speed, as attested by the place taken by *Ghost Landscapes* in the setting where they were first shown, the exhibition *Vanishing Point* at the Pompidou Center in 2004. They were displayed on either side of an inflatable dinghy at full throttle, its nose lifted up by the speed, seeming to roar out of a space artificially extended behind it by a decorative backdrop. The perspective suggested by the installation's title is thus deepened by the speed of the moving object; it is not so much the result of a scopic operation as of a commitment to kinesthetics. This meaning was adumbrated by a road movie by Richard Sarafian, also entitled *Vanishing Point* (Twentieth Century Fox, 1971), in which Kowalski (Barry Newman) represented "the last American hero to whom speed means freedom of the soul."[9] But while the perspective grows deeper in the lengthwise axis of the moving object, the lateral view only records flattened, deformed images of the landscape, reduced by speed to the spectral state suggested in the title. The image of pictures obliterated by the effects of speed was already present in the heroic period of Modernism, in the works of Octave Mirbeau. In *La 628–E8*, Mirbeau—both driver and writer—makes a contradictory observation. On the one hand, the acceleration of modern life makes the books and paintings that cover his walls appear dead to him, while on the other, visiting a museum straight after getting out of his car, the works of art seem to share the intoxication of the moment: "Rooms, rooms, rooms, in which it seems to me that I am motionless and it is the paintings that are moving past me at such speed that I can hardly glimpse their blurred, confused images ... "[10] This echoes the group of friends visiting the Louvre at a run in Jean-Luc Godard's film *Band of Outsiders* (1964), as well as the way Veilhan describes his own typically modernist, scopic vision: "I like crossing through things to see them better, rather than looking at them without moving."[11]

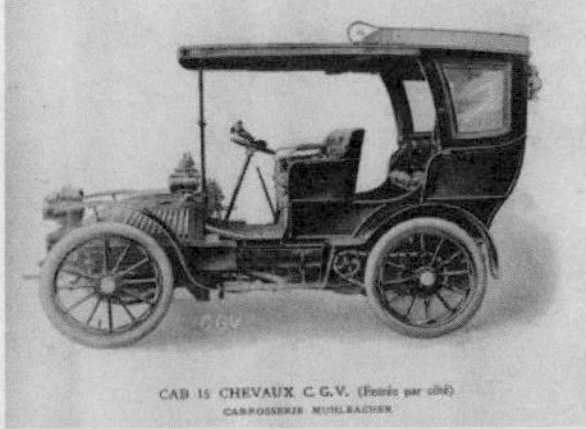

↗ The *628–E8*, 1907, Octave Mirbeau's (1848–1917) eponymous novel's heroine.

8 I discuss this artistic lineage in my essay "De la touche au pixel. François Morellet, l'abstraction systématique et la tradition impressionniste," *Correspondances: Claude Monet / François Morellet*, exh. cat., Musée d'Orsay, Paris 2006, p. 15–30.

9 This is how he was introduced by DJ Supersoul, who followed his Modernist epic on a pirate radio station. There is also an interesting comparison to be made with one of the masterpieces of American Precisionist painting, Ralston Crawford's 1939 *Overseas Highway* (The Regis Collection, Minneapolis), which suggests the same idea of a spatio-temporal perspective given depth by a moving body by using the verges of the freeway as convergence lines.

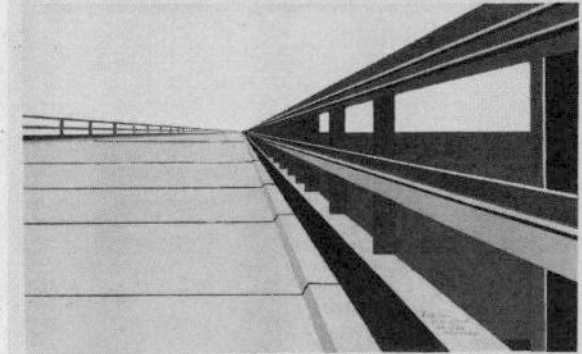

↗ Ralston Crawford (1906–1978) *Overseas Highway*, 1939 Oil on canvas, 76.8 × 92 cm

10 Octave Mirbeau, *La 628–E8* [1905], 10 / 18, Paris 1977, p. 54.

11 Veilhan, interview with T. Chaillou, *Intersection*, p. 98.

The *Ghost Landscapes* share another point of contact with Modernist kine-vision. They are clearly not totally abstract: the image is always there, latent, reappearing once the gaze becomes distanced; when the visitor steps back, the mosaic of pixels re-forms identifiable images, alternating between current urban scenes and traditional Impressionist settings: the countryside outside Paris, the beach at Etretat, a crashing wave, and so on. As Michel Gauthier noted, "from abstraction to representation it is but a step (or two)," the two being simply "possible states for a single object, depending on the standpoint."[12] This experience is characteristic of those reported by travelers in the early days of train and car travel: seen from a moving vehicle, things in the distance seem to move more slowly and are thus more legible, while those in the foreground are more affected by speed, become blurred, and drop below a minimum level of visibility.[13] A few generations later, the writer Paul Morand noted, "Speed kills shapes. What remains of a landscape seen at 500 km an hour? Nothing. The foreground and middle distance are suppressed. Below one three-hundredth of a second, even cameras fail."[14] The lesson of *Ghost Landscapes* today is thus the same as that taught by trains in the past: up close, images vanish, but a more distant viewpoint restores the faculties of the gaze. In fact, the *Ghost Landscapes* are not Veilhan's only visual structures to explore the consequences of mobile vision. For example, he deliberately introduced a reference to vision from the standpoint of a train into another series of pixilated images. The *Light Machines* are a series of large vertical screens, covered in hundreds of lightbulbs which blink on and off, recreating short films which the artist declared were "pleasant to look at, like a landscape or the view from a moving train"[15]; one of them (*Light Machine n°4 : La Route*, 2001) was indeed filmed from a car door. Veilhan's corpus also includes two panoramas (*The Clearing*, 1998, and *The Beach 2000*, 2000) which should also be read in this context. Not simply because their pixilated structure raises the same question of point of view as *Ghost Landscapes*, but also because their environmental format raises the additional issue of peripheral, lateralized vision, stripped of depth. The retrospective study of 19th-century panoramas and dioramas has clearly demonstrated that such installations were deeply influenced by the traveler's vision. Dolf Sternberger, whose pioneering analysis was based on numerous accounts from the period, wrote that the railway "transformed the world of lands and seas into a panorama that could be experienced."[16] Conversely, the form of kinesthesic vision implied

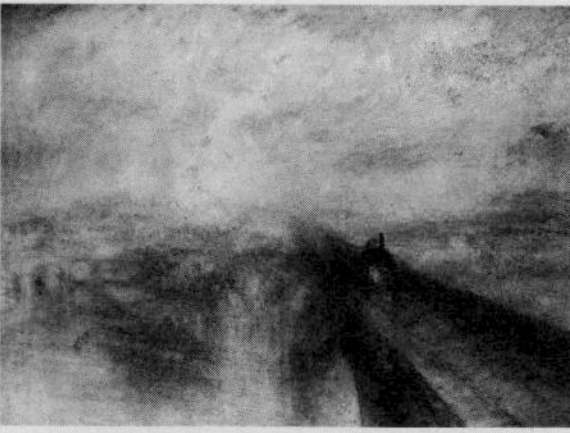

↗ Joseph Turner (1775–1851)
Rain, Steam, Speed–The Great Western Railway, 1844
Oil on canvas, 91 cm × 121.8 cm

12 Michel Gauthier, trans. S. Welch, "Oh Monsters, Oh Studio!" in *Xavier Veilhan. Le plein emploi*, exh. cat., musée d'Art moderne et contemporain, Strasbourg 2005, p. 52–53.

13 See Schivelbusch, *The Railway Journey*, p. 55–56 and 63–64 for an interesting discussion of the way the invisible foreground cuts the traveler off from a concrete relationship with the landscape, which is thereby transformed into a series of paintings.

14 Morand, *Papiers d'identité*, 1926. Quoted in Pichois, *Vitesse et vision du monde*, p. 116.

15 Veilhan, quoted in David Perreau, trans. C. Penwarden. *Xavier Veilhan*, Hazan, Paris 2004, p. 14. Emphasis added.

16 Sternberger, *Panorama, oder Ansichten vom 19. Jahrhundert*, Hamburg, 1955, p. 50, quoted in Schivelbusch, p. 62.

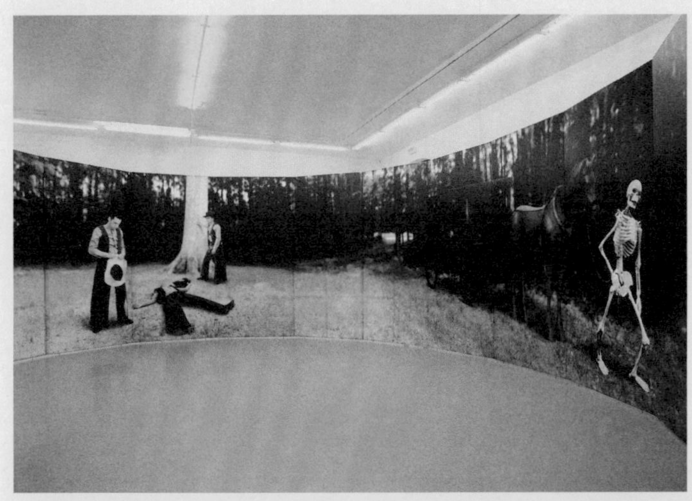

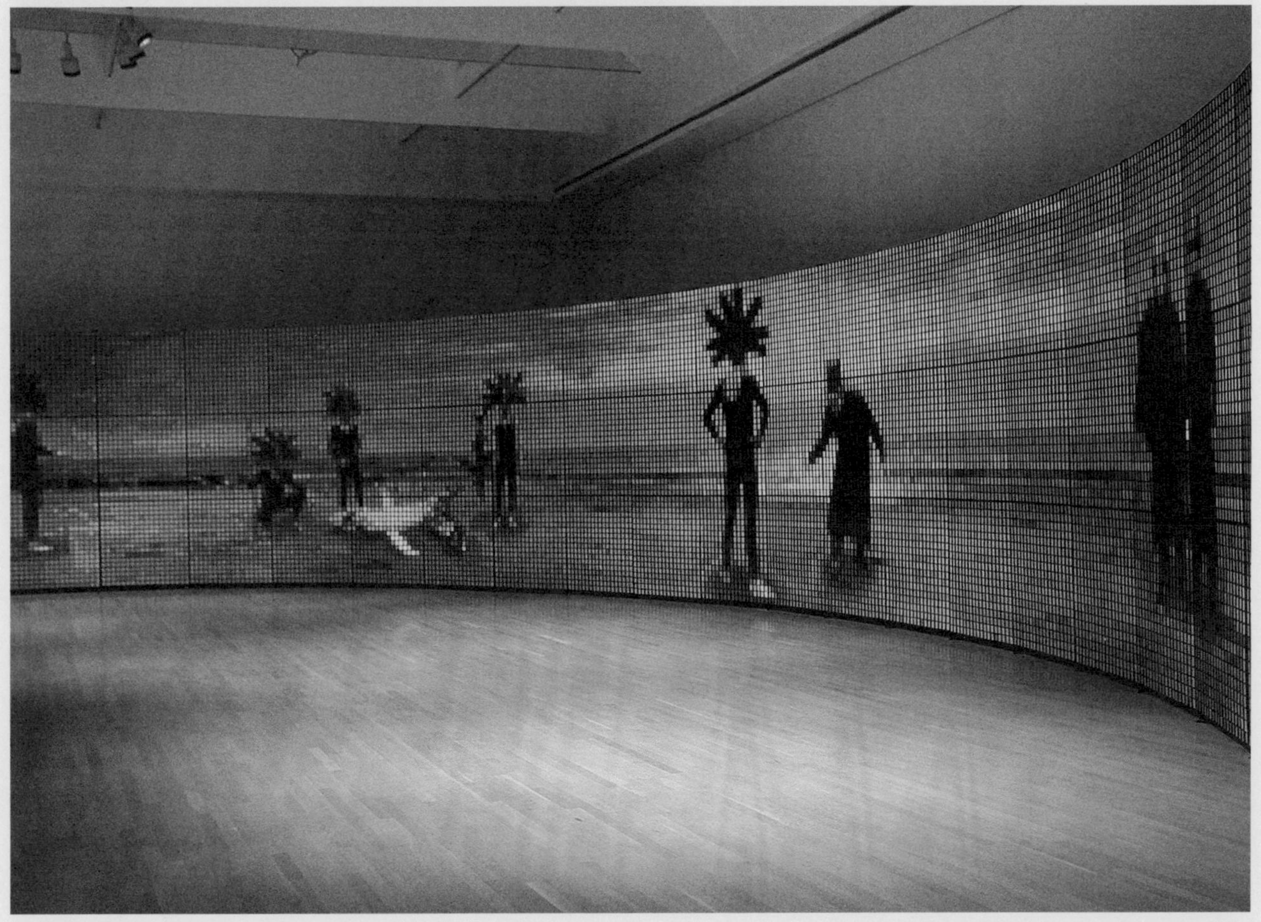

[ABOVE] **LA CLAIRIÈRE (THE CLEARING)**, 1998; [BELOW] **THE BEACH 2000**, 2000

by the panorama recreated something of the traveler's kinetic experience. For Benjamin Gastineau, author of the serial novel *La Vie en chemin de fer* (1861), railways were like the machinery of a panorama that "throws the switches, changes the decor, and shifts the point of view every moment."[17] One of the most spectacular of these vision machines was the famous Trans-Siberian Panorama shown at the Universal Exhibition in 1900, but this was just the last of a series of panoramas whose painted lengths of canvas unfurled landscapes from around the world for an audience sitting in imitation train carriages. The sets representing the foreground were unrolled faster so as to increase the kinetic illusion.[18]

Xavier Veilhan first explored the link between visuality and mobility in an earlier, less technically ambitious exhibition. He showed his sculptures and paintings at the Galerie Jennifer Flay in Paris in 1994. The former were geometrically simplified scale reproductions of the columns in the Place de la Bastille and Place Vendôme and the obelisk in the Place de la Concorde in Paris. The latter were silhouettes of statues of famous men on their plinths. The overall effect was clearly a reference to 19th-century Paris and its love of statues and monuments placed to best advantage in long urban vistas. One of the paintings was remarkable for its subject: *Haussmann* (1994) commemorated the man who designed the modern-day city and planned the broad avenues not simply as the repressive space that has so often been criticized, but also as the urban equivalent of the visual spectacles that held great fascination for the period (such as panoramas), while at the same time extending modern transport routes into the city itself. As Wolfgang Schivelbusch has written, the train station acts as an intermediary space, transforming the railway into a boulevard, thereby taking part in the same phenomenon of accelerating both transport and modes of perception as the railway lines themselves.[19] In Veilhan's space, the circulatory function of Haussmann's city is clearly indicated by the obvious presence of a soundtrack broadcasting a journey made by moped between the three points, recorded on an aluminum and acetate disc bearing a silk-printed image of the columns and obelisk. The soundtrack accompanied visitors on their tour of the three monuments, enabling them to imagine themselves riding pillion on the noisy moped for a tour of the highlights of Paris. What did visitors see and what really made an impact on them? The very form of Veilhan's works answers the question: shapes that give a general idea of the thing, glimpsed too briefly to give any more detail, and the memorials of great men stripped of their eyes and their relief, reduced to spectral outlines by an all too fleeting gaze. The monuments were a metonym for the urban setting itself, suggested by numerous other paintings and several panels cut into simplified silhouettes of urban or industrial buildings, produced at around the same time. The 1994 installation *Sans titre (Les Silhouettes)*, reminiscent of props backstage, seemed to take the idea of transforming the modern street into a simple stage set or a life-size panorama even further, through the impact of a new, accelerated intensity of street movement. Veilhan thus draws on two sorts of spectral image: the *Ghost Landscapes* proper—fragmented images subjected to the invisibility that results from speed—and more stable, synthetic images or silhouettes,

17 Quoted in Schivelbusch, *The Railway Journey*, p. 61.

18 Cf. Patrick Désile, *Généalogie de la lumière. Du panorama au cinema*, L'Harmattan, Paris 2000, p. 84.

19 Schivelbusch, *The Railway Journey*, p. 181 ff.20. The various objects included in the exhibition at Galerie Jennifer Flay in 1991—a bridge, an electric pylon, a sulky, a submarine, and so on—could similarly appear to be three-dimensional signs or logos because of their simplified shapes and pure monochrome colors. One of the objects was indeed a signpost, pointing in three different directions.

which survive kinetic deformation by accepting the reduction of the thing seen to a sign or pictogram.[20] The simplification which has been a constant feature of Veilhan's various figurative series since the late 1980s, whatever the medium, is thus not merely to be understood in its most widely accepted interpretation, as an essentialist search for generic type and form,[21] but also—and above all—as the result of a visual strategy comparable to those of communication and signage. These are reduced to plain, flat geometric shapes and pure colors by the necessity of achieving rapid, thorough understanding, and of catching the eye of an audience suffering from the shock of speed and the abundance of demands on their attention. As Fernand Léger noted, "Speed is the law of the modern world. The eye must 'be able to choose' in the fraction of the second when it risks its existence, whether it be driving a car, in the street, or behind a scholar's microscope."[22]

The acceleration of the modern world should thus promote the emergence of a form of super-nature through evolutionary adaptation to the new conditions of the human gaze. In fact, it is the supernatural that regularly returns, as Veilhan's use of the expression "spectral images" well suggests. The term should be understood literally, for the modern subject is also permanently exposed to hallucinations by the shocks of a mechanized life, and his consciousness is regularly haunted by fantastical visions, born from the magic of speed. The first experiments with mechanical locomotion gave rise to the first kinetic impressions, verging on the oneiric, such as those of the British writer Charlotte Stanley, traveling on the Manchester to Liverpool train in 1829: "I never felt so strange, so much in a state of magic, of enchantment, as if surrounded by new powers and capabilities."[23] Modern machines, the products of technological rationality, engendered visions that converted reality into a phantasmagorical spectacle. The French writer Paul de Kock described railways as "nature's genuine magic lantern"[24] in 1842, while the German Joseph von Eichendorff saw them as "like a kaleidoscope."[25] The same image is found in the writings of Marcel Proust, who describes the "magic coach" whisking him off to Florence, and Maurice Maeterlinck, who described a car as a "magical machine."[26] What happens to the landscape when it is seen from these new machines of vision and enchantment? It becomes an unreal, archaic, shadowy world of specters. Gerhart Hauptmann looked out of a train window at night and saw the plume of steam and smoke blending with the shapes of the landscape as a "domain of ghosts."[27] Benjamin Gastineau saw the railway as the machinery of a panorama, showing "skeletons and lovers, clouds and rays of light, happy vistas and somber views, nuptials, baptisms, and cemeteries"—the whole of life, with "its happy scenes, sad scenes, burlesque interludes, brilliant fireworks."[28]

20 The various objects included in the exhibition at Galerie Jennifer Flay in 1991—a bridge, an electric pylon, a sulky, a submarine, and so on—could similarly appear to be three-dimensional signs or logos because of their simplified shapes and pure monochrome colors. One of the objects was indeed a signpost, pointing in three different directions.

21 Cf. Marie-Ange Brayer, "Xavier Veilhan, l'image générique," *Artpress* 171, Paris, July–August 1992, p. 39–42.

22 Léger, "Le spectacle: lumière, couleur, image mobile, objet-spectacle," *Bulletin de l'Effort moderne*, Paris, 1924; translation adapted from F. Léger, *Functions of Painting*, trans. A. Anderson, Viking, New York 1973, p. 35. See also "Les réalisations picturales actuelles" (Les Soirées de Paris, 1914, translated in ibid., p. 11–12): "When one crosses a landscape by automobile or express train, it becomes fragmented; it loses in descriptive value but gains in synthetic value. The view through the door of the railroad car or the automobile windshield, in combination with the speed, has altered the habitual look of things […] The compression of the modern picture, its variety, its breaking up of forms, are the result of all this. It is certain that the evolution of the means of locomotion and their speed have a great deal to do with the new way of seeing."

23 Quoted in C. Pichois, *Vitesse et vision du monde*, p. 18.

24 Ibid.

25 Quoted in Schivelbusch, *The Railway Journey*, p. 62.

26 Cf. Pichois, *Vitesse et vision du monde*, p. 81 & 93.

27 Quoted in Quiguer, *Femmes et machines de 1900*, p. 262.

28 Quoted in Schivelbusch, *The Railway Journey*, p. 61.

This echoes the fantastical world of Veilhan's own panoramas, with his explorers and hyperbolically attired natives inexplicably gathered round the corpse of a shark, his dead cowboys and—echoing Gastineau—his skeleton leading a horse-drawn hearse (the direct forebear to the *Amish Series*) to some unknown graveyard. Claude Quiguer noted the widespread presence in iconography from the dawn of the 20th century of "the figure of death in danses macabres serving as a grotesque emblem for the motorized procession of the new century."[29] This also explains the presence of such funereal—but not excessively tragic—motifs as *The Skulls* and *The Effigy* in the explosive exhibition at Galerie Jennifer Flay in 1994, and *The Minuet* (2000)—a ring of skeletons built from sheets of aluminum slotted together using halved joints—placed alongside a reconstitution of *The Model T Ford* (1997–1999) at an exhibition at Le Magasin Art Center in 2000. Ghosts and skeletons were the classic—in fact almost the sole—subject of the phantasmagorias that amazed drawing rooms throughout Europe at the dawn of the 19th century, thanks to Dr Robertson's invention of the fantascope, a magic lantern on a movable cart that meant the image could be enlarged, as if the object were rushing toward the terrified spectator. Was the fantascope a sort of small locomotive? Once again, Charlotte Stanley's impressions were strikingly just: "The effect of the velocity is that when you stand on the railroad and watch the machine coming, it seems not to approach, but to expand into size and distinctness like the image in a phantasmagoria."[30] Other of Veilhan's images borrow the trembling, quivering light of such phantasmagorical performances, evoking the same surreal atmosphere. The *Lithophanies* are screens of resin and wood that use the line screen system to deconstruct an image that is given the illusion of life by candles shining behind it.[31] It is significant that the images are of clouds, the very stuff of dreams and reveries, in terms of the emotions aroused by these small images that stage the mysterious epiphanies of ghostly shapes.

Speed and dreams go together. Claude Pichois noted that Nerval experienced his kinetic impressions just as he awoke from sleep, in a state where consciousness has not entirely reclaimed its empire. But can it in fact do so? Speed hinders it, artificially prolonging the fogs that dim our understanding and placing us in a somnambulic state where our attention is suspended, slipping into daydreams and hypnagogic hallucinations. Veilhan has stated that such oneiric stimulation is not totally foreign to his photographic tableaux of the late 1990s, which staged bears and penguins in incongruous situations, with men and animals going about their daily lives alongside each other.

Exploring the role of visionary projections in Veilhan's creative process would require an in-depth analysis of some of his indefinably atmospheric films, such as *Keep the Brown* (2003), also featuring bears, and *Drumball* (2003),

29 Quiguer, *Femmes et machines de 1900*, p. 317.

30 Augustus Hare, *Memorials of a Quiet Life*, Strahan, London 1872, p. 281. This echoes reports of the terror expressed by cinema goers at a screening of one of the first films in history, the Lumière Brothers' *Train arriving at La Ciotat Station* (1895).

31 Lithophany is a technique for impressing figures on porcelain, which become visible when lit from behind, patented by Baron de Bourgoing in 1826. Various forms of line screen systems were used in around 1900 to experiment with 3-D effects and moving images. See Kim Timby, "Images en relief et images changeantes. La photographie à réseau ligné," *Etudes photographiques* 9, May 2001, p. 125–147.

a series of silent, unconnected, autarkic actions like those experienced in dreams. Silently gliding circles, such as the pucks in *Air Hockey Table* (2005) and the nighttime skaters in *Boucle* (2006), frequently appear in his stagings, the fluidity of their movements capturing the viewer's gaze to the point of hypnosis. The most explicit reference to the generative role of dreams is in the film *Furtivo* (2008). The main protagonist, the musician Sébastien Tellier, is asleep, engendering the Futurist objects that appear in the film in turn—a car, a racetrack, a ship's wheel, a racing yacht, a sleek-bodied shark. The entire film seems to be nothing but a dream-like parenthesis between the moment when the objects are first seen as white lines against the black screen of Tellier's visions, and the moment when some of them, such as *The Shark* (2008), actually take on real existence, first at the exhibition *Furtivo* in Paris, then later in Turin. Whatever angle we take to look at Veilhan's kine-vision, it can thus easily be connected to a realm of imagination where phantasmagorias and positivity share a mutual influence, like at the peak of High Modernism.

I use "High Modernism" to refer both to the long period of transition that saw a process of failed experiments and technological dead ends eventually leading to the development of a set of tools used by modern perception, and to the techniques of observation that draw on them. This is the matricial moment of modernity referred to in Veilhan's late-1990s photographic tableaux, nicely defined by Liam Gillick as "neo-fictional" works, evoking key moments of the Industrial Revolution.[32] Their themes are the Eiffel Tower (*The Eiffel Tower*, 1999) and the dirigible (*The Dirigible*, 1999); they are inhabited by characters whose clothing identifies them as contemporaries of these major technological achievements. Other works in the series eulogize key figures in the 19th-century ideology of progress—*Mechanics* (1997) and *Engineers* (1998). In Veilhan's artistic vision, the latter are clad in curious geometric garb combining Malevitchian and Assyrian influences, reflecting the subtle dosage of modernity and eternity in Baudelaire's definition of beauty. The obvious historicism of these works raises an insistent question: does their return to the matrix of modernity simply represent yet another simulacrum in the vast postmodernist interplay of quotations, as Gillick seems to suggest when he asks if Veilhan may be "the last great 19th-century artist, reclaiming the two debatable yet central contributions of that century, engineering and history painting"?[33] But if postmodernity is best defined, as such an eminent thinker as Fredric Jameson has suggested, as the abolition of past and future in the anomy of a present which slips from the grasp of chronology,[34] then we must acknowledge that Veilhan's old images of progress are examples of a far more complex temporal construction. For Veilhan's attraction

32 Liam Gillick, "'Eastworld.' Xavier Veilhan's mirrored context," *Xavier Veilhan*, exh. cat., Le Magasin, Grenoble 2000, p. 27.

33 Ibid., p. 28. In the same work, Dan Cameron reads the anachronistic nature of Veilhan's characters as a veiled commentary on the function of historicism in postmodern art, although he then concludes that the system of references "has much more to do with confronting the place of history in the present than with quoting the past as a way of preserving it." Cameron, "Keeping up appearances," in ibid., p. 10.

34 Fredric Jameson, *Archaeologies of the Future: The Desire Called Utopia and Other Science Fictions*, Verso, London / New York 2005, p. 185.

for modern times could have simply have led him to adopt a straightforward neo-Modernist stance—just another "neo," no more and no less respectable than any other. Yet it seems that he preferred a somewhat different attitude—archaeo-modernism, which could be defined as becoming aware of modernity once it acknowledged itself to be in possession of a long, detailed history. The archaeo-modernist no longer sees himself at the cutting edge of historical time, but rather builds on the depth of his own past, just as Veilhan does when, by claiming to belong to modernity, he embraces its history and any failures it may have experienced: "The way the notion of progress comes across in my work is [...] accompanied by a critique which is expressed through the use of images that are both positive and obsolete, and even degraded. That is the case of the dirigible, for example. In the history of the technological evolution of transport, the dirigible represents a kind of dead end. In those days, everyone thought it would be possible to travel around in balloons, but all it took was a few accidents for the development of this mode of transport to come to an end."[35] In so doing, the archaeo-modernist remains faithful to his duty of Modernist self-reflexivity, while introducing a new element, the historical dimension, which he uses to find his way out of the temporal anomy of postmodernism, while avoiding falling into the illusion of Futurism. His method is not so much extrapolating the future from the data of the present as interpolating the future into the past, in a sort of future anterior tense. Archaeo-modernism is thus not a question of anticipation (an avant-gardist projection into a world to come) but rather retrocipation (a retro-futurist projection into a Utopia that will have been). As a result, Veilhan's modernism, far from returning to predictions from the past, is perhaps the first of the recent generation of artists to launch the excavations of the archaeology of the future.

35 Veilhan, quoted in Perreau, *Xavier Veilhan*, p. 16.

ARNAULD PIERRE

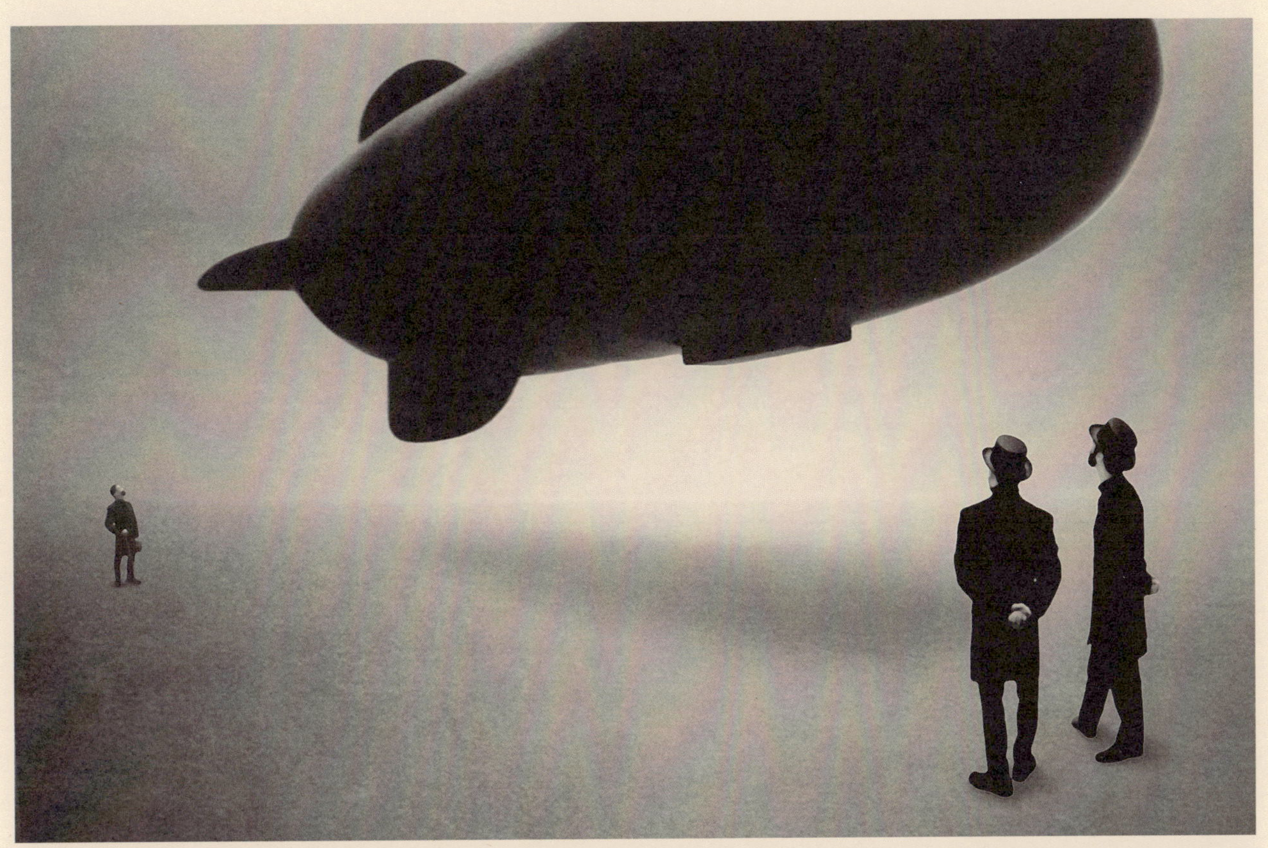

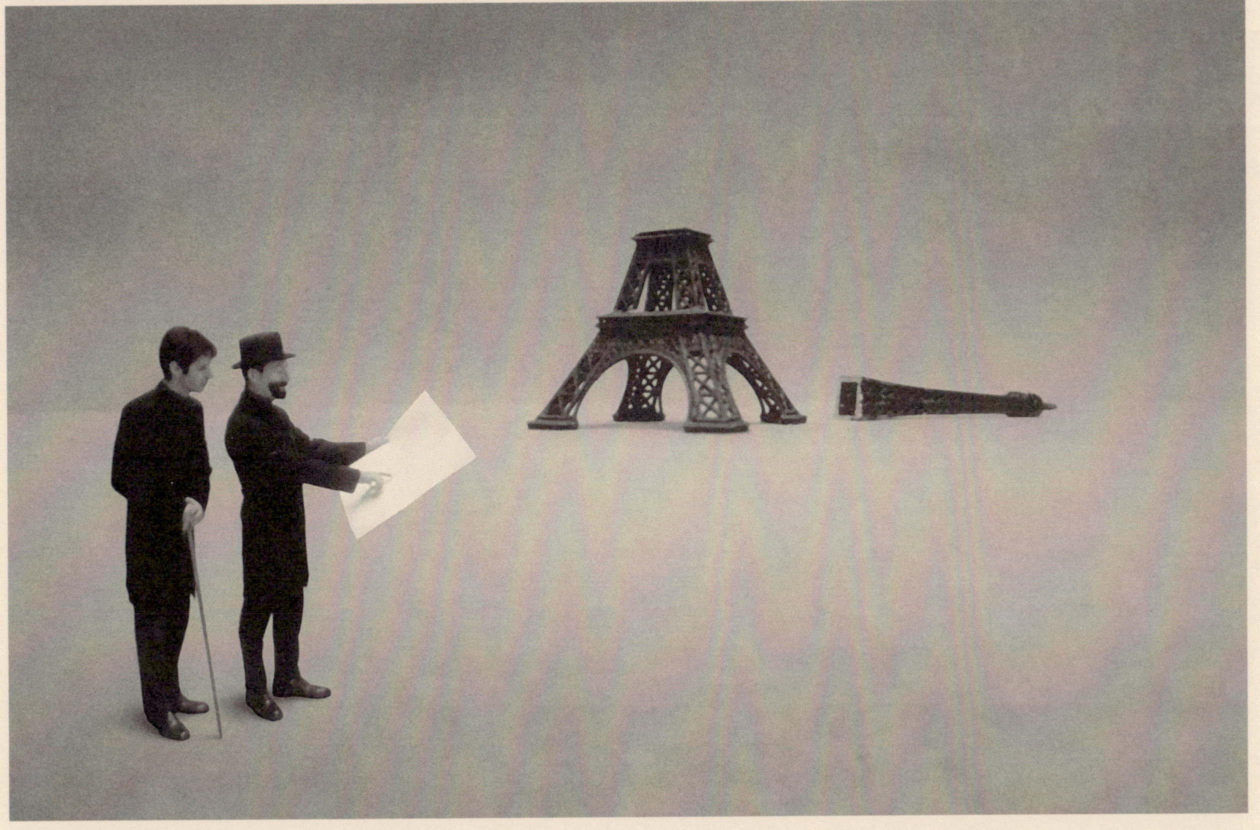

[ABOVE] **LE DIRIGEABLE (THE DIRIGIBLE)**, 1999; [BELOW] **LA TOUR EIFFEL (THE EIFFEL TOWER)**, 1999

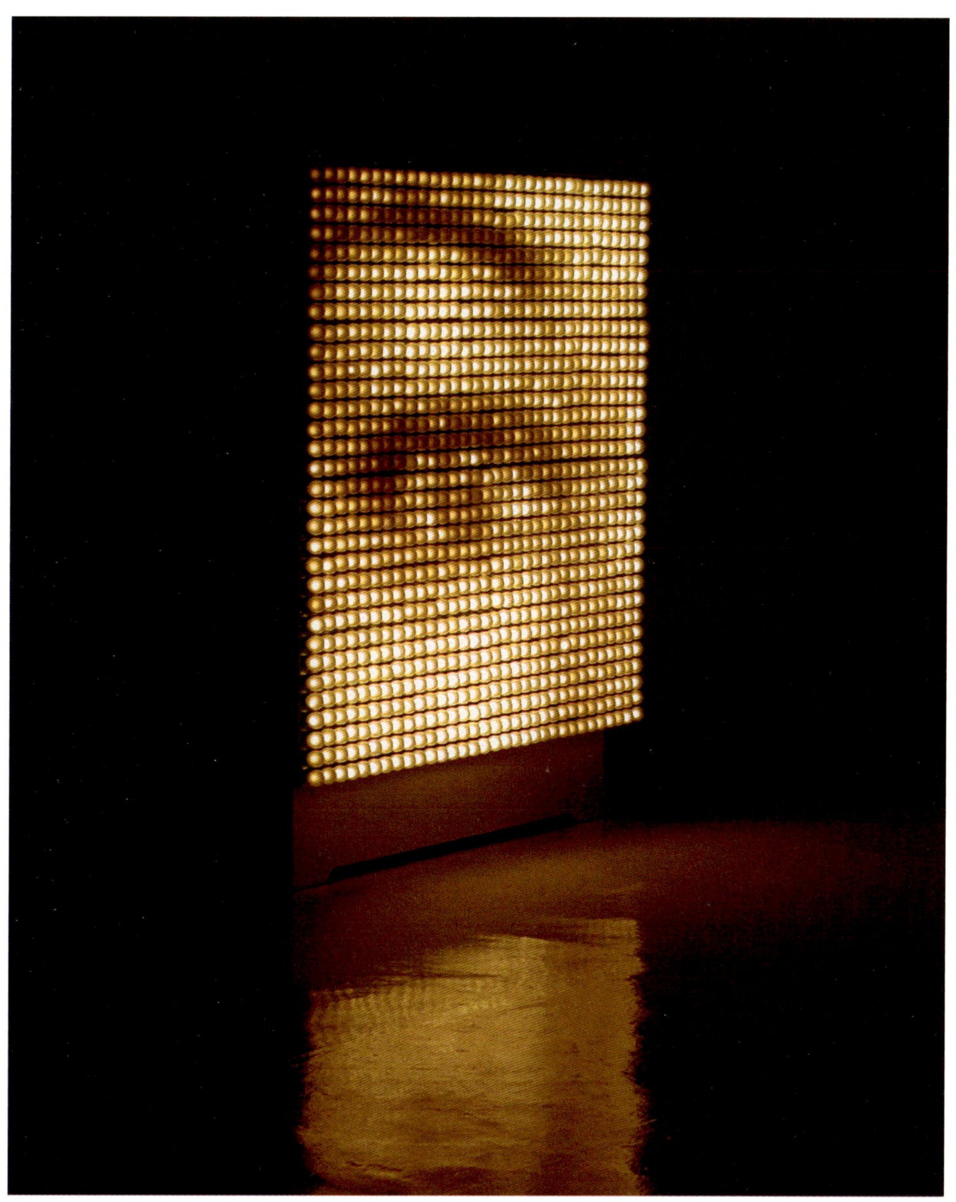

LIGHT MACHINE N° 3, THE EYE, 2001

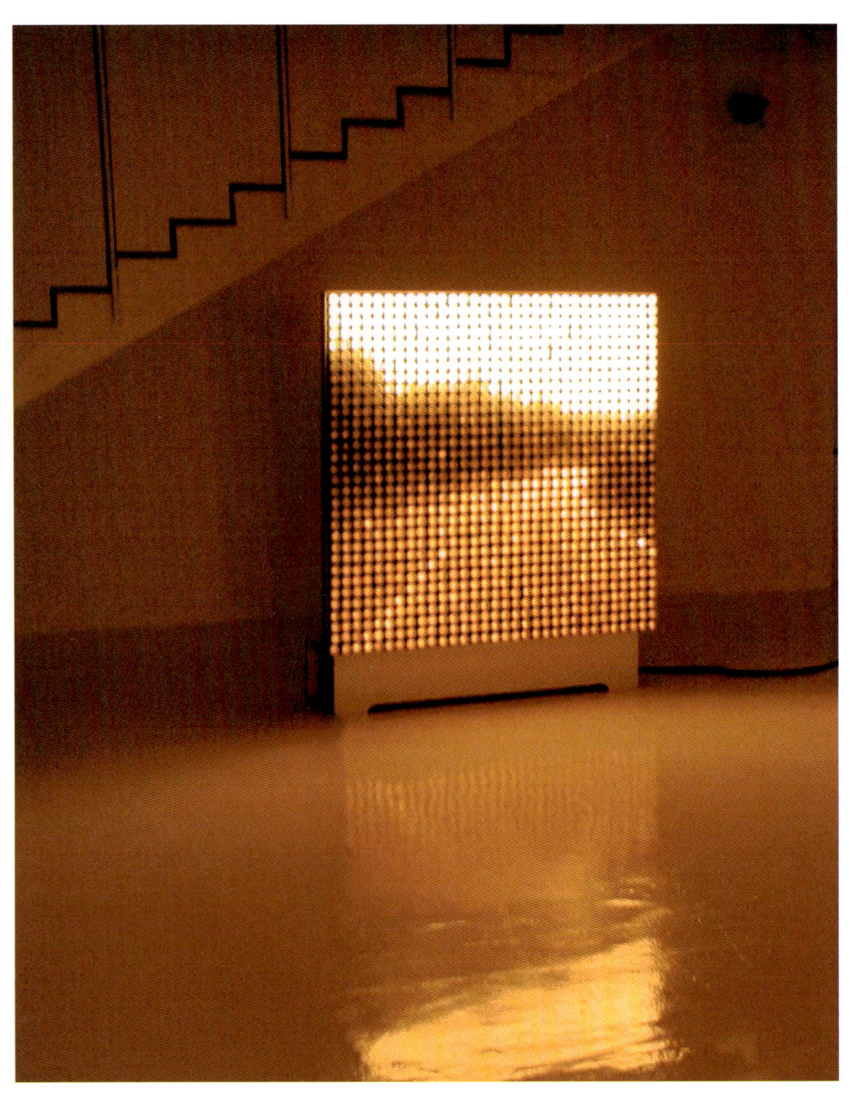

LIGHT MACHINE N° 4, THE ROAD, 2001

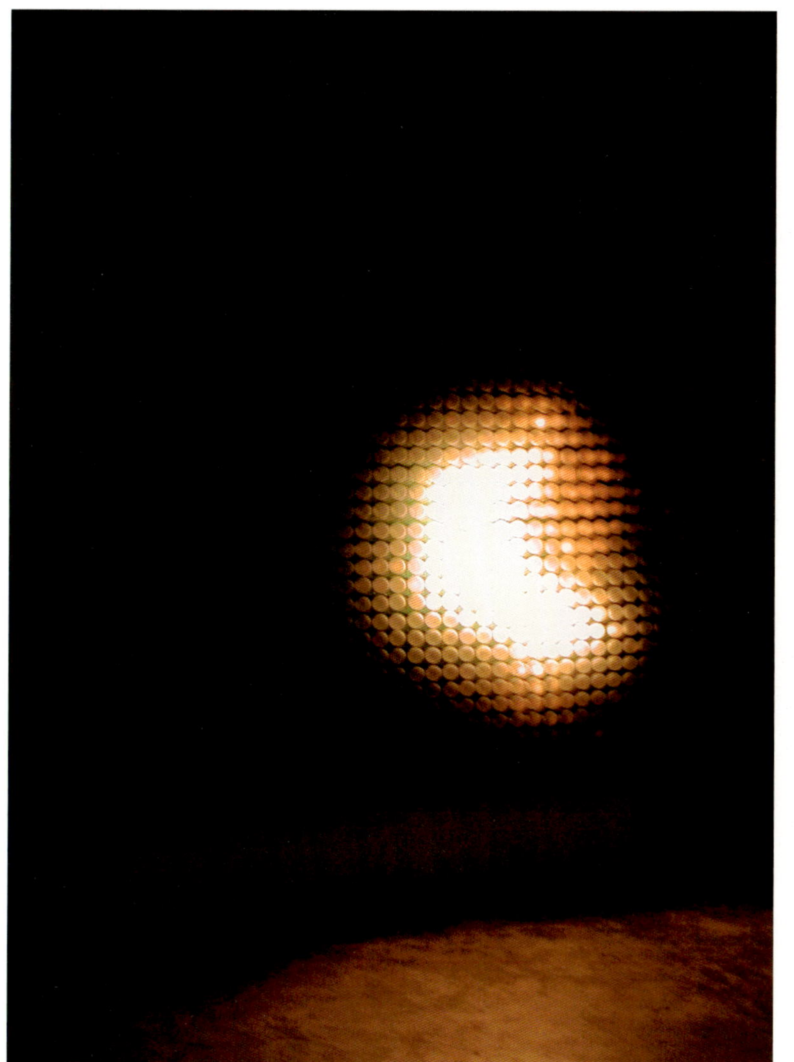 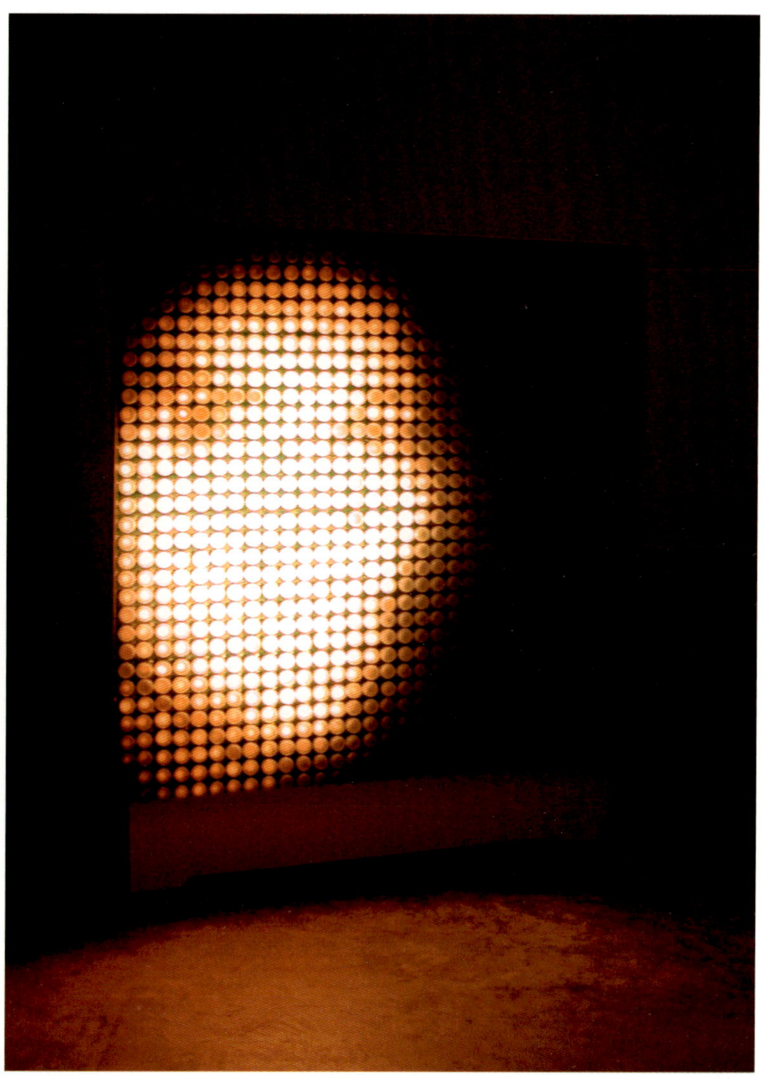

LIGHT MACHINE N° 3, THE EYE, 2001

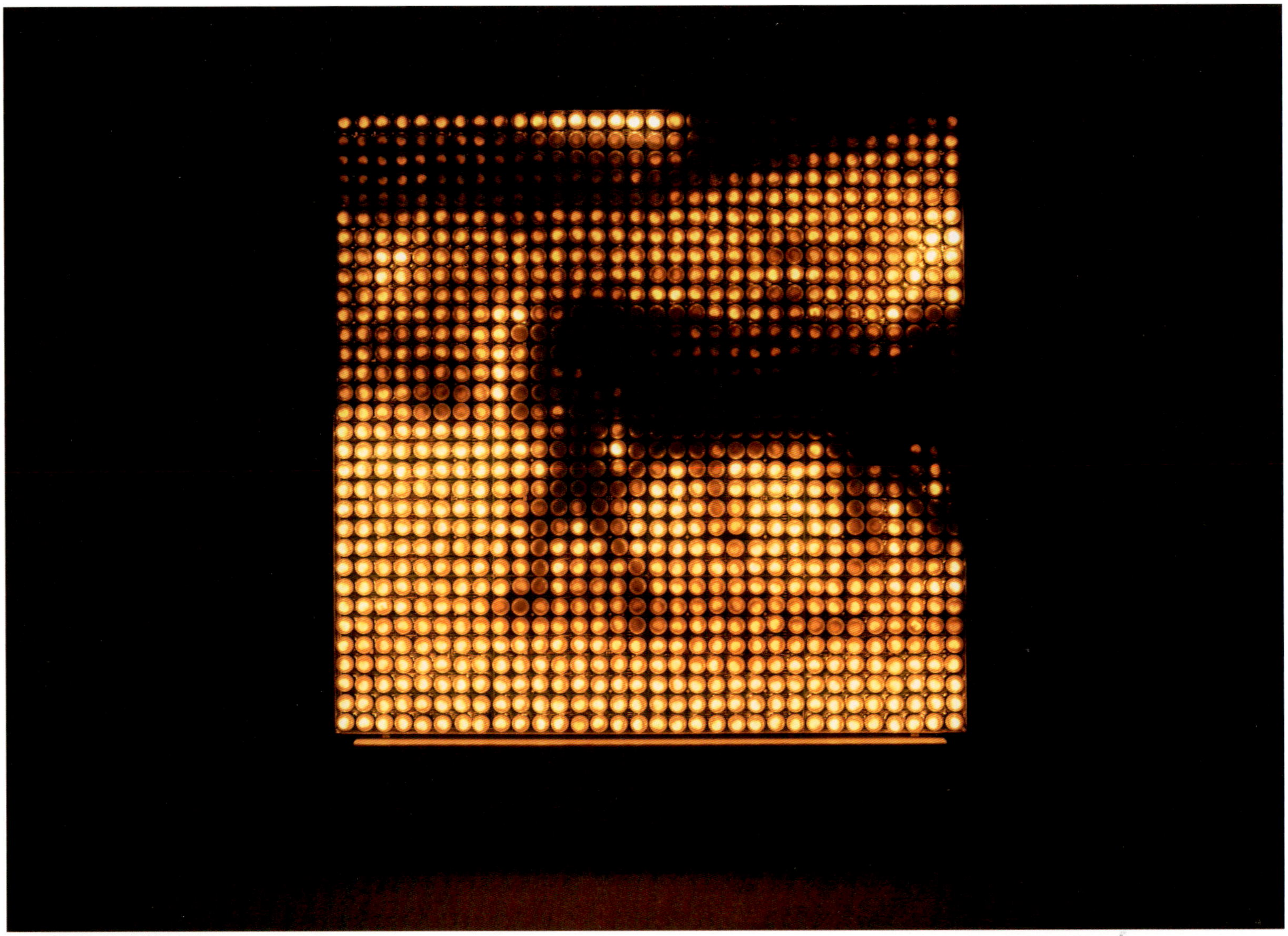

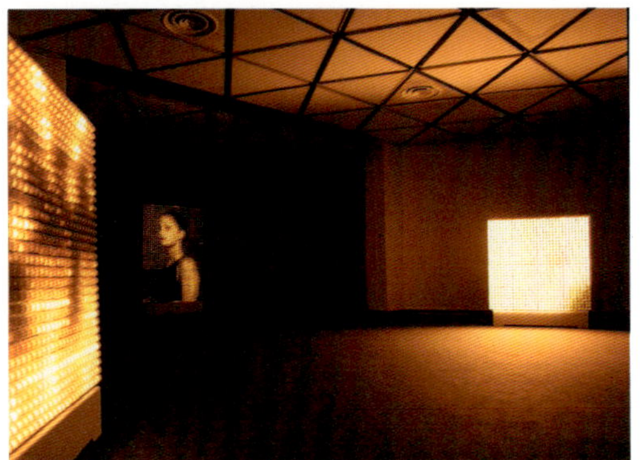
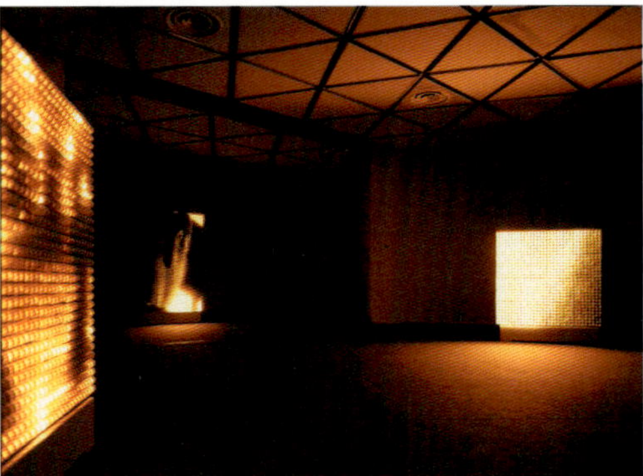
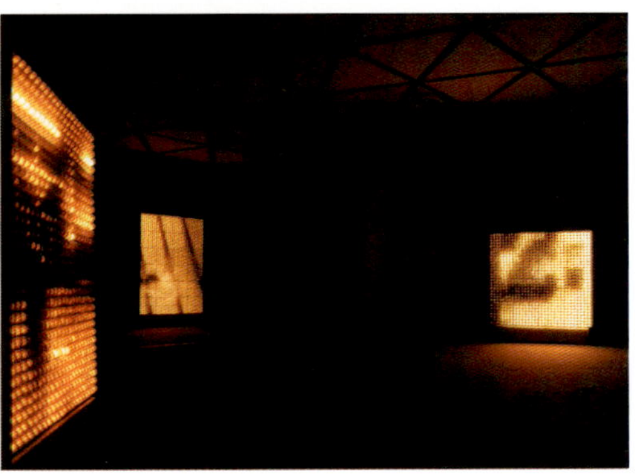

52

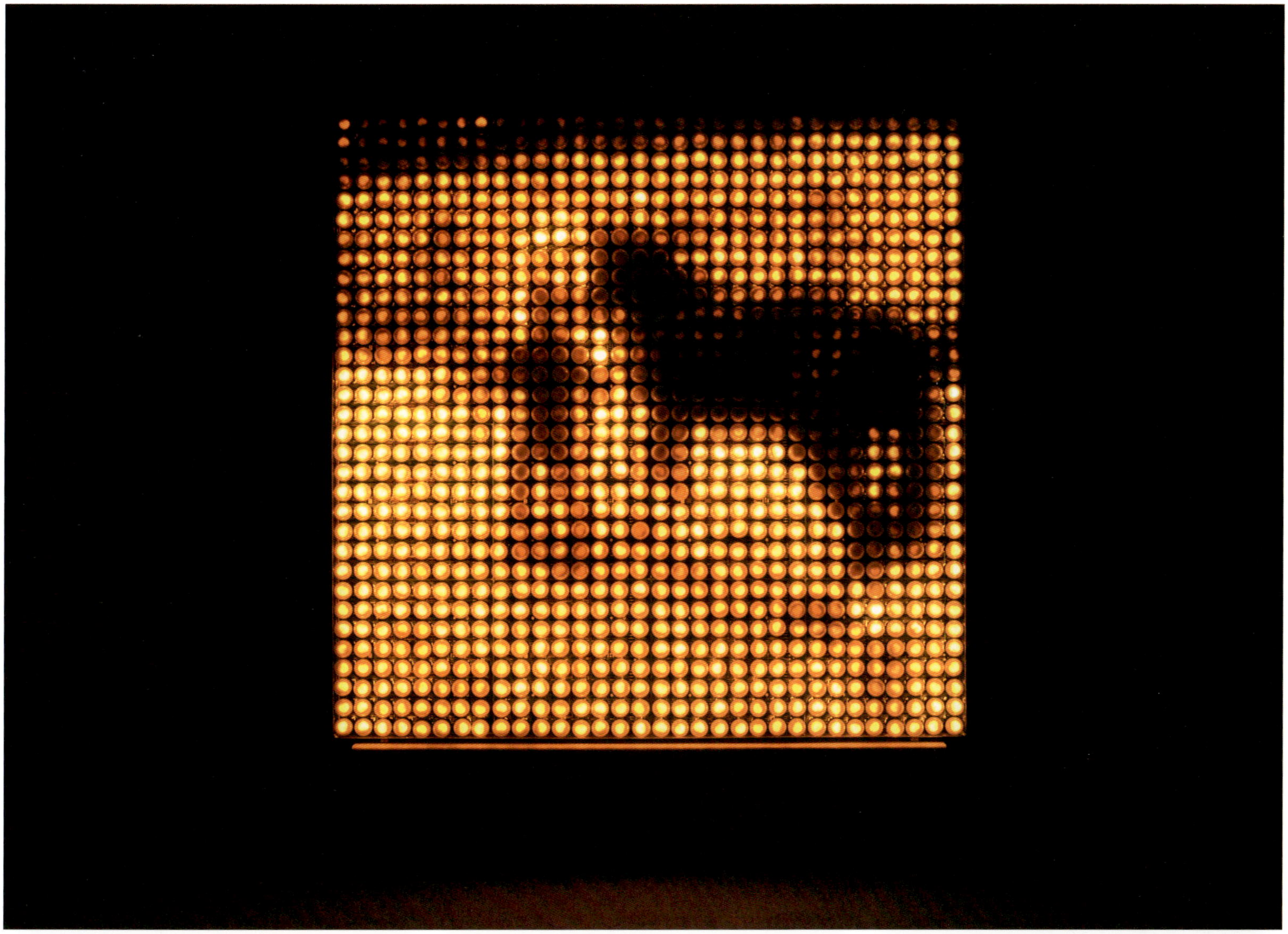

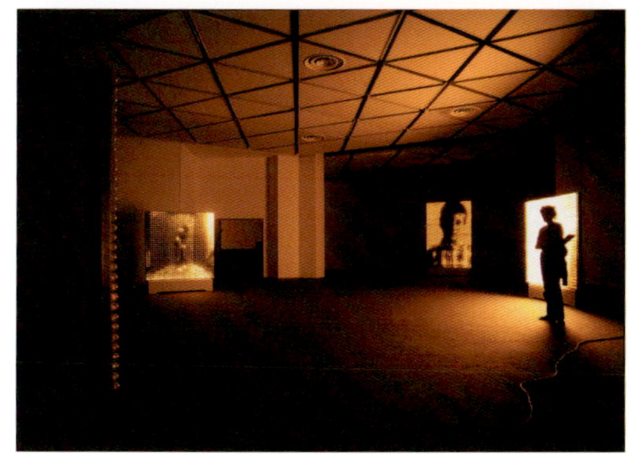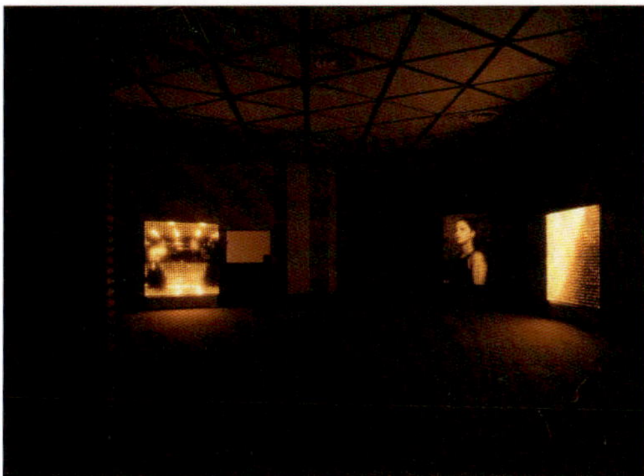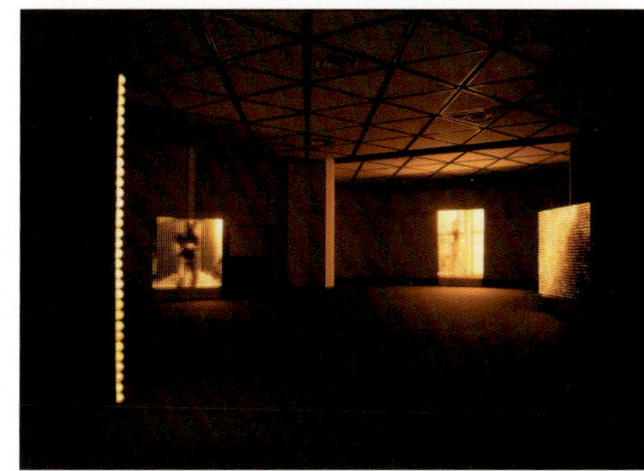

[BELOW] VIEWS OF THE EXHIBITION *LIGHT MACHINES*, FONDATION VASARELY, AIX-EN-PROVENCE, 2004

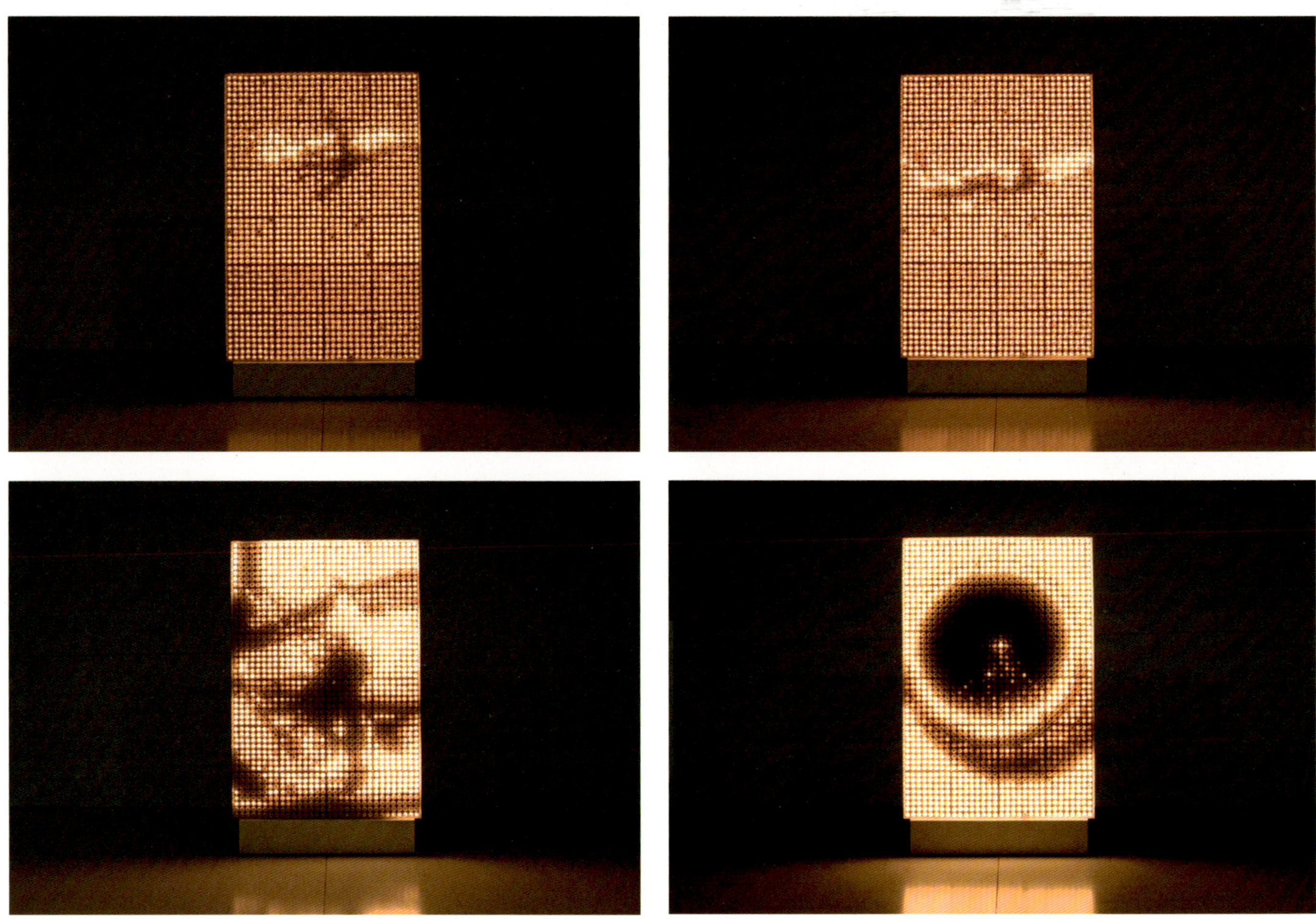

BIG LIGHT MACHINE, JET, 2004

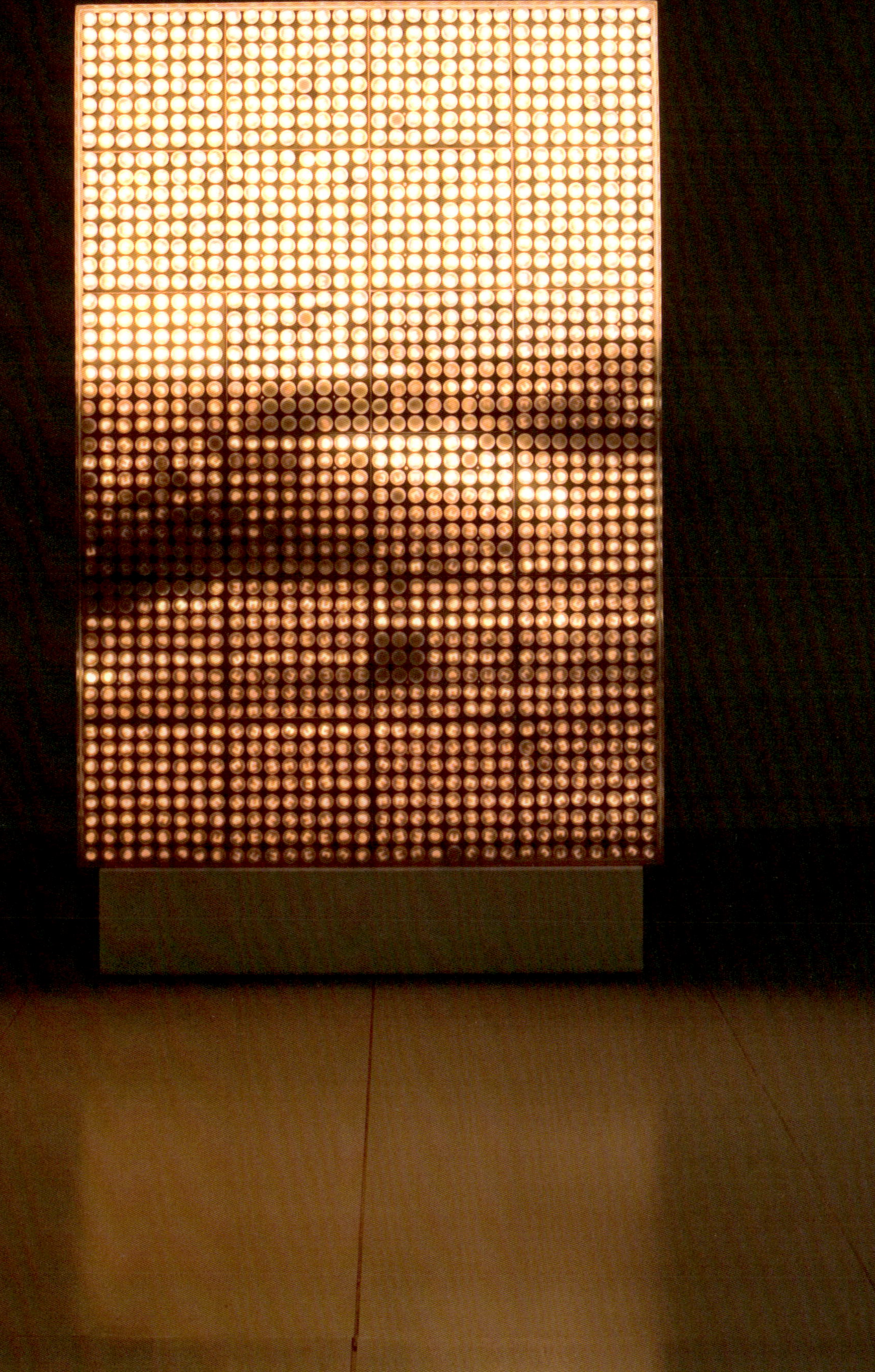

FURTIVO

FURTIVO

XAVIER VEILHAN

[→ P. 56–64] **FURTIVO**, 2008, FILM STILLS

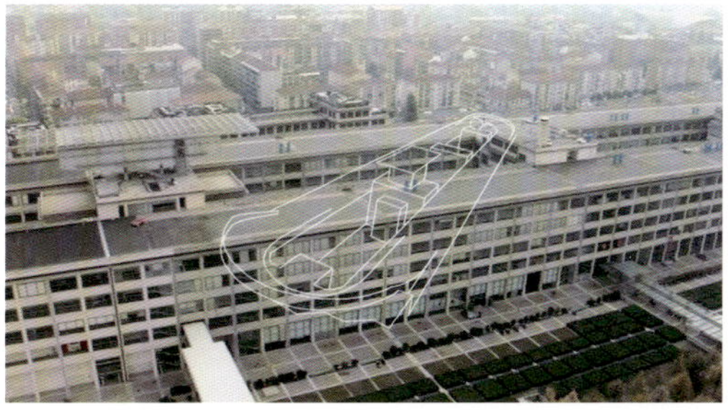

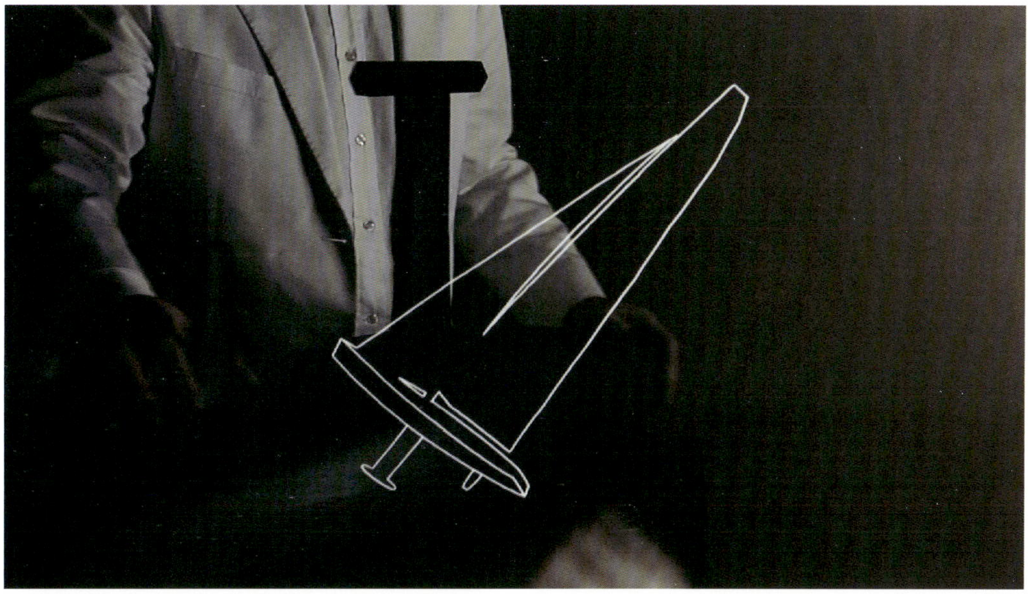

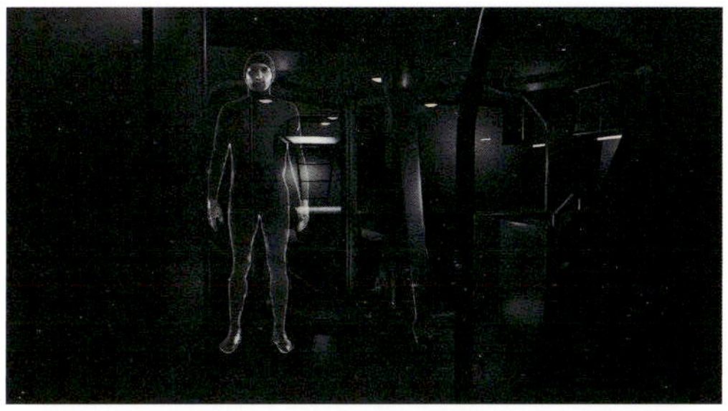

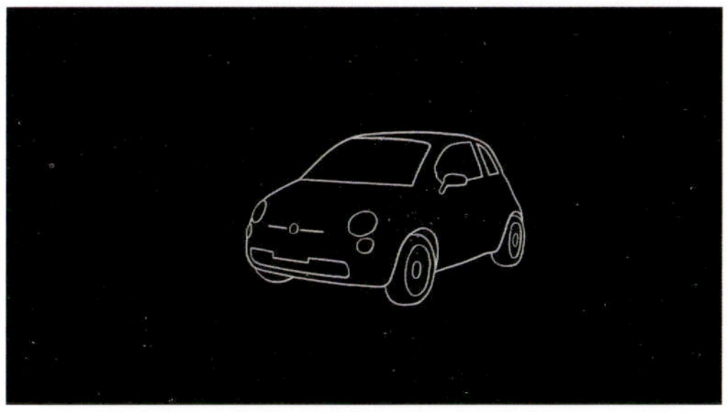

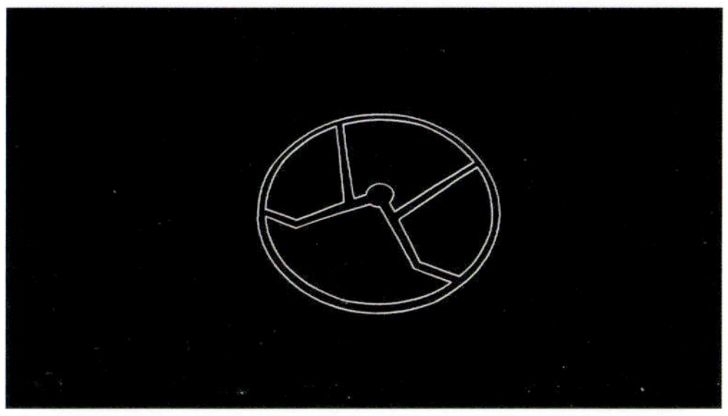

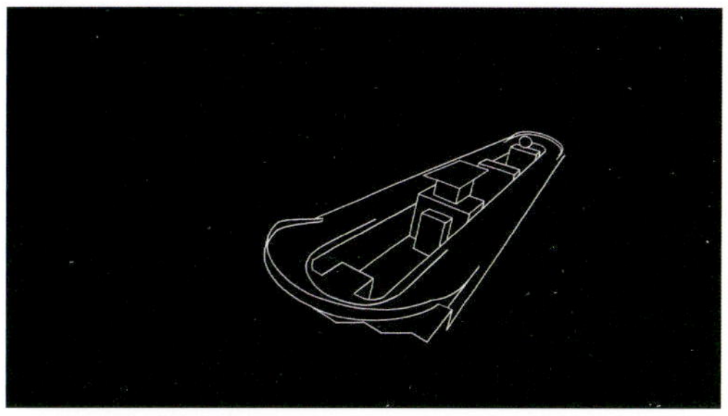

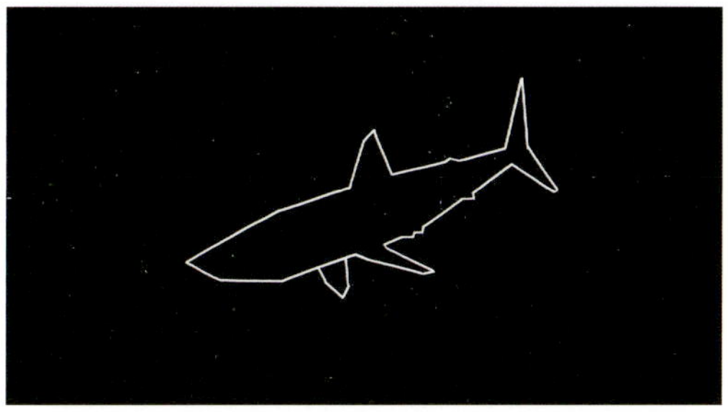

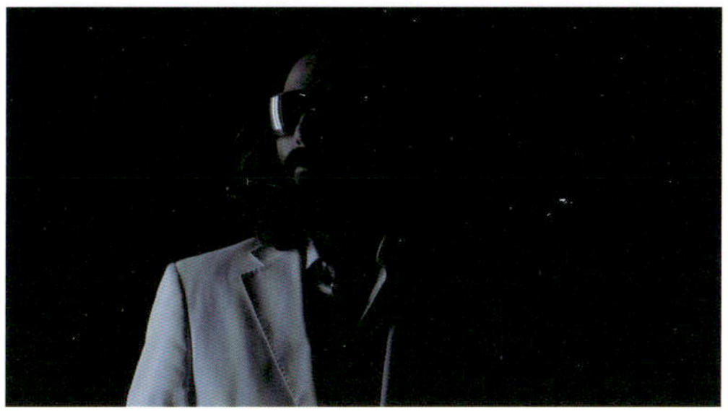

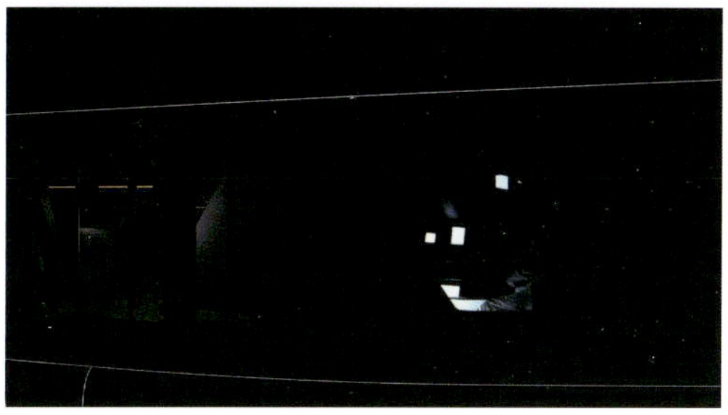

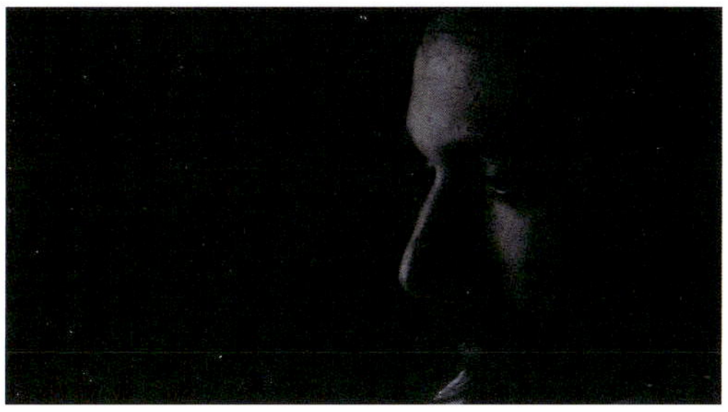

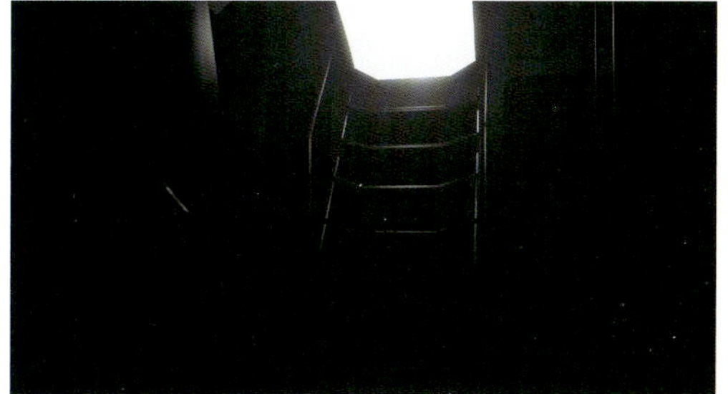

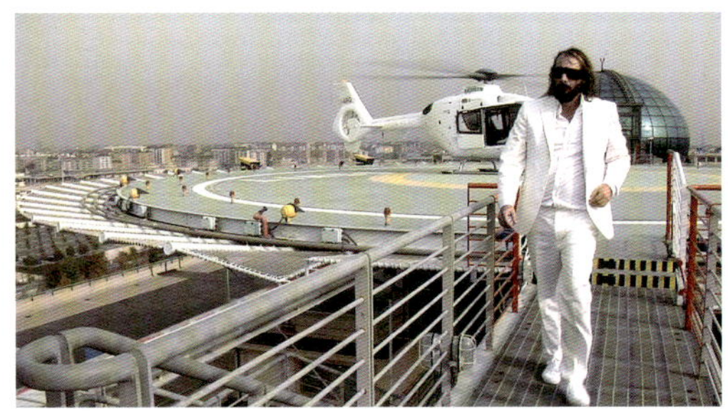
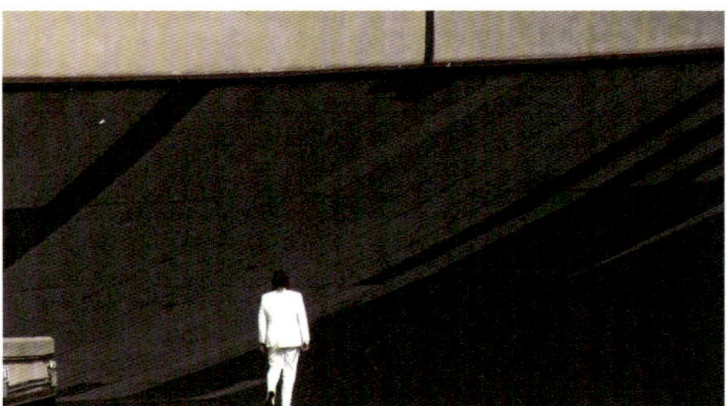
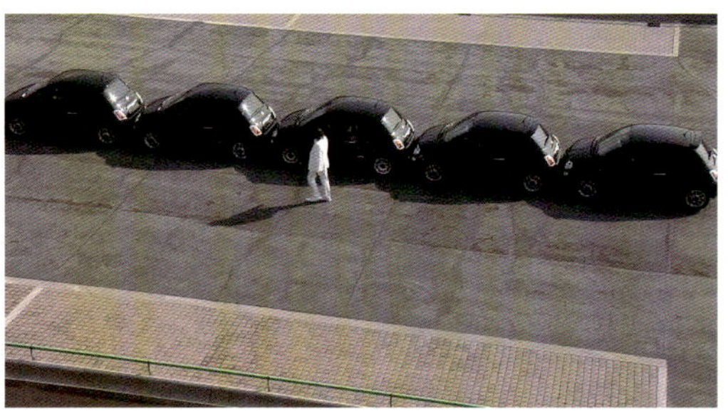
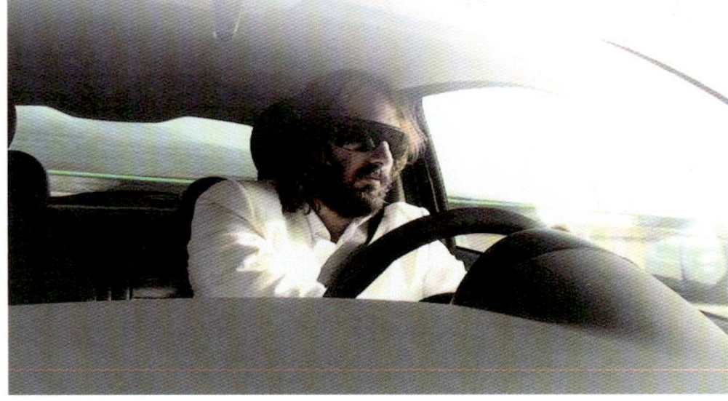
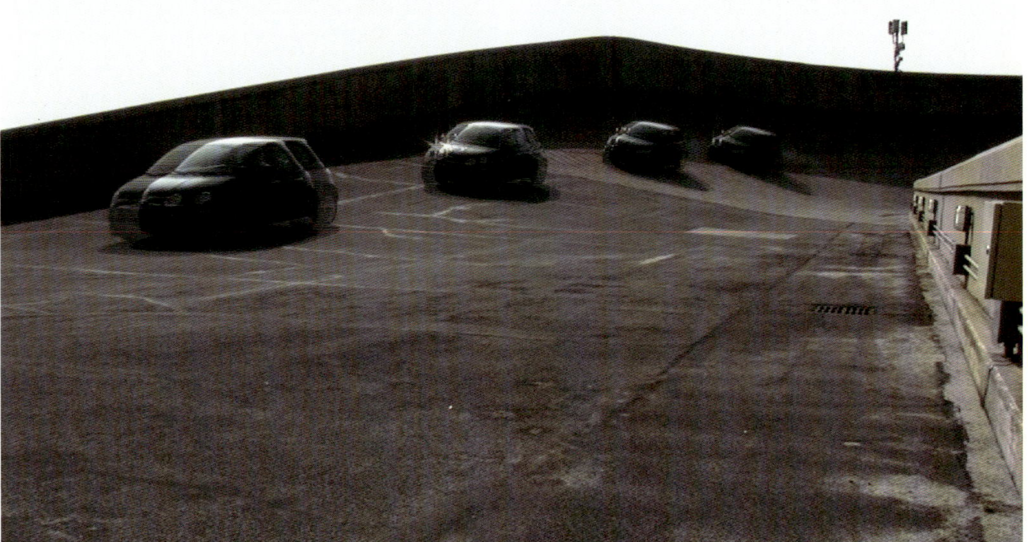
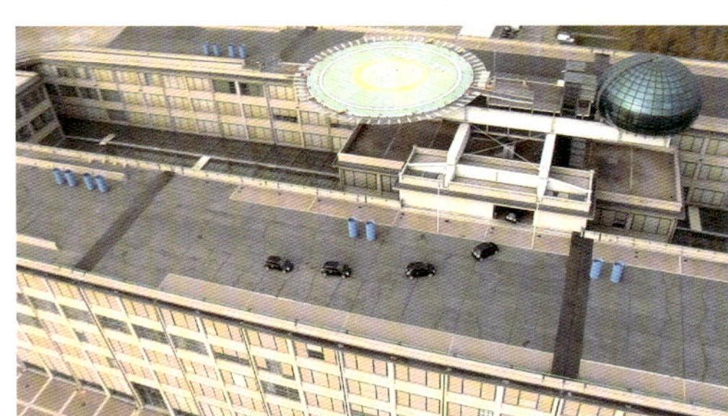
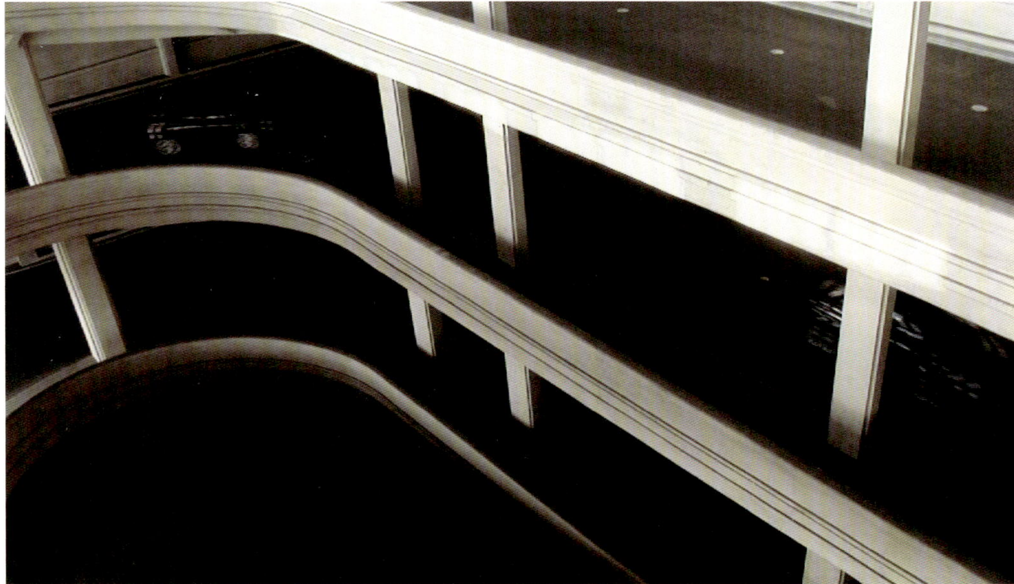
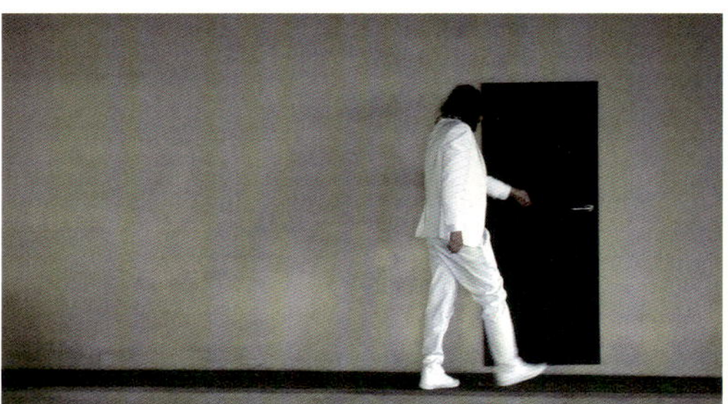

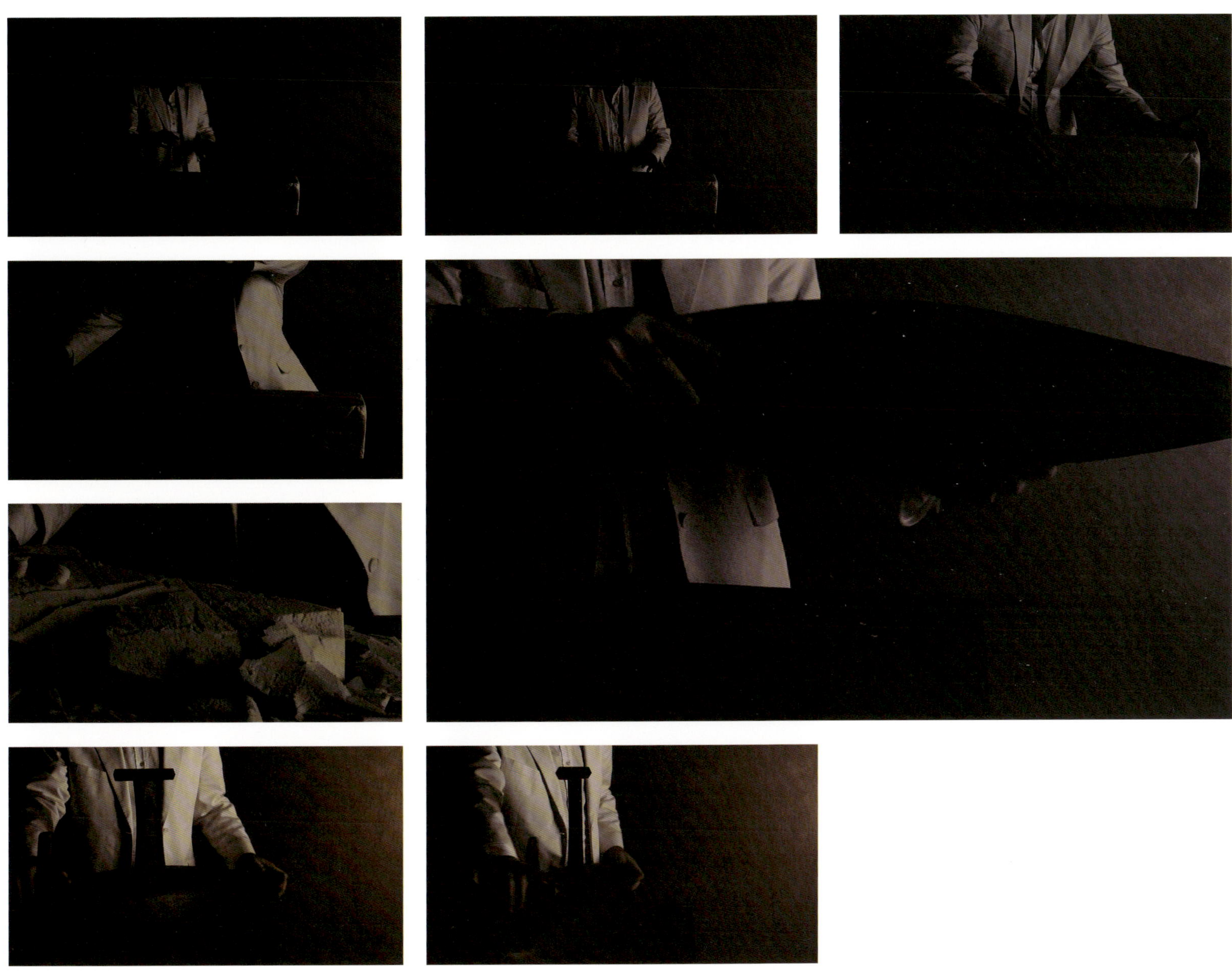

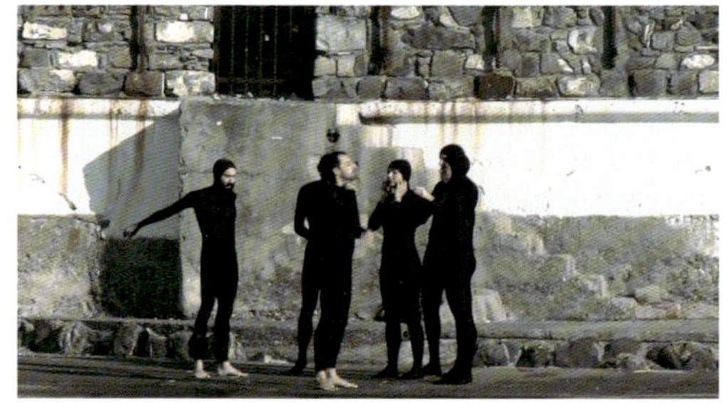
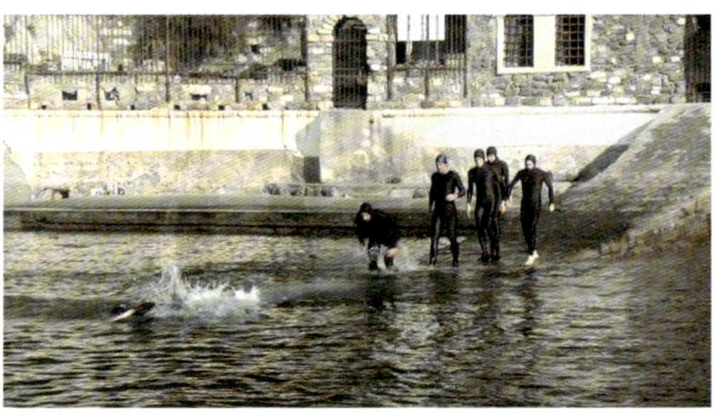
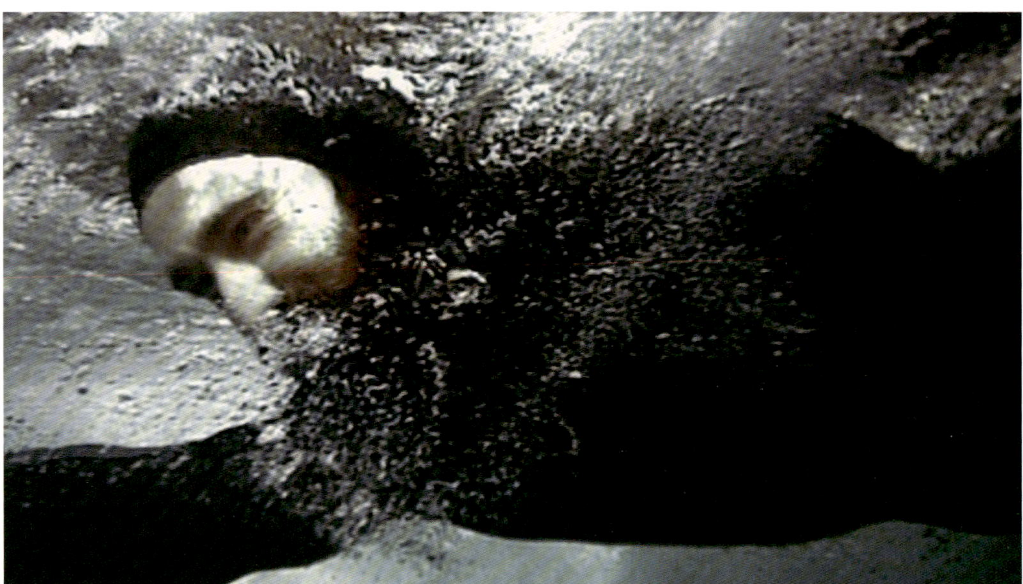
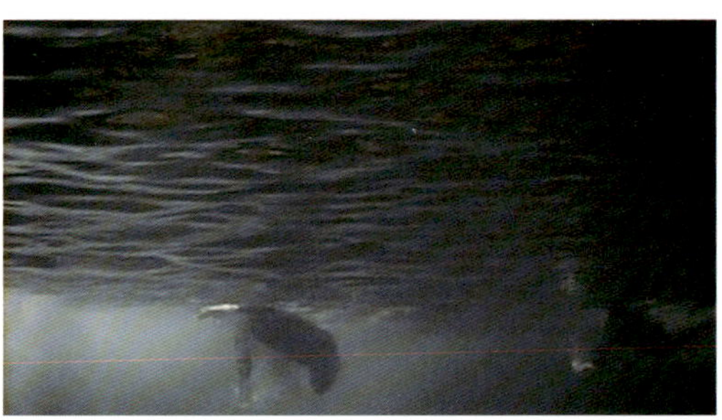
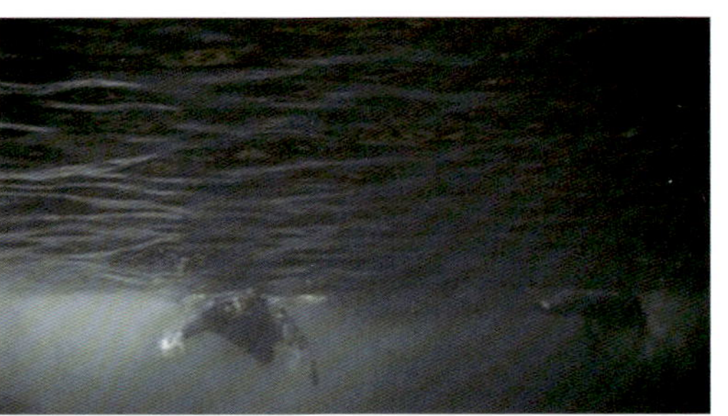
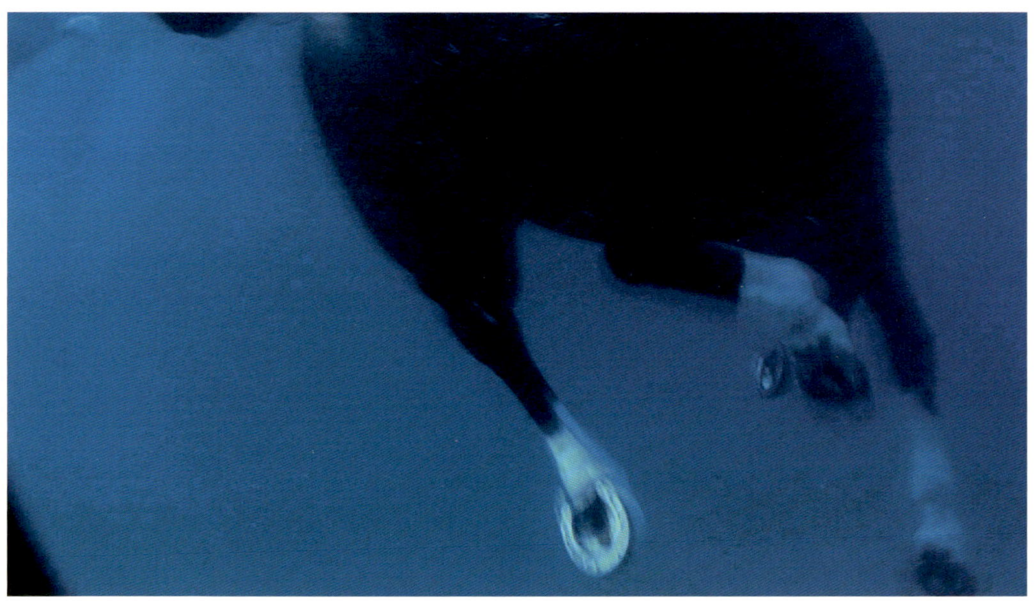

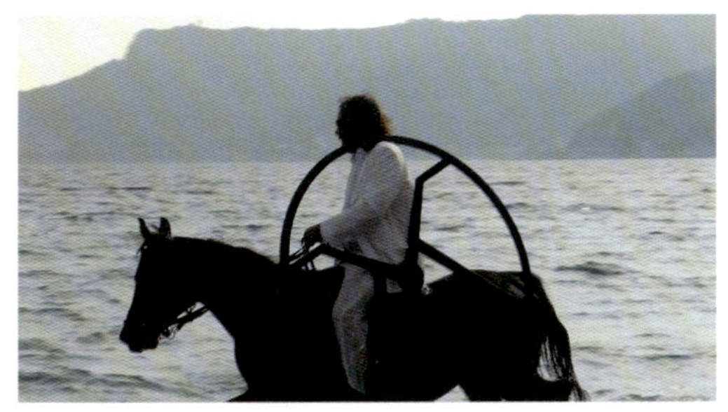
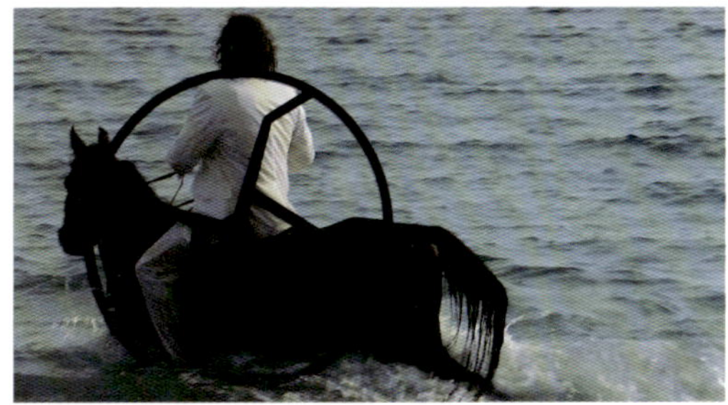
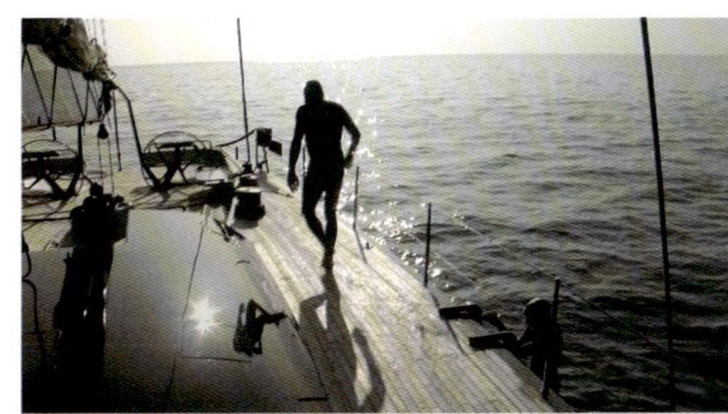
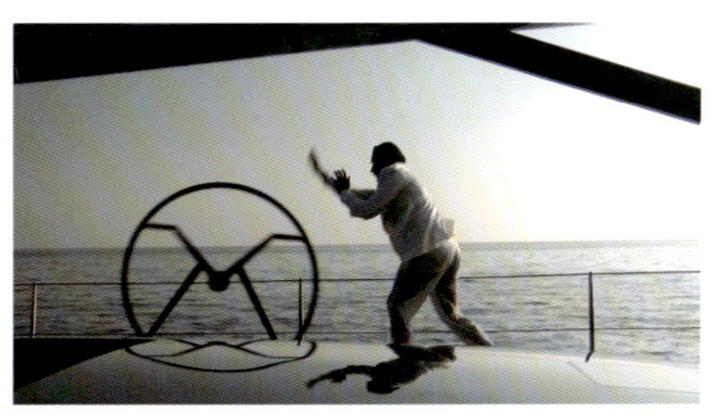
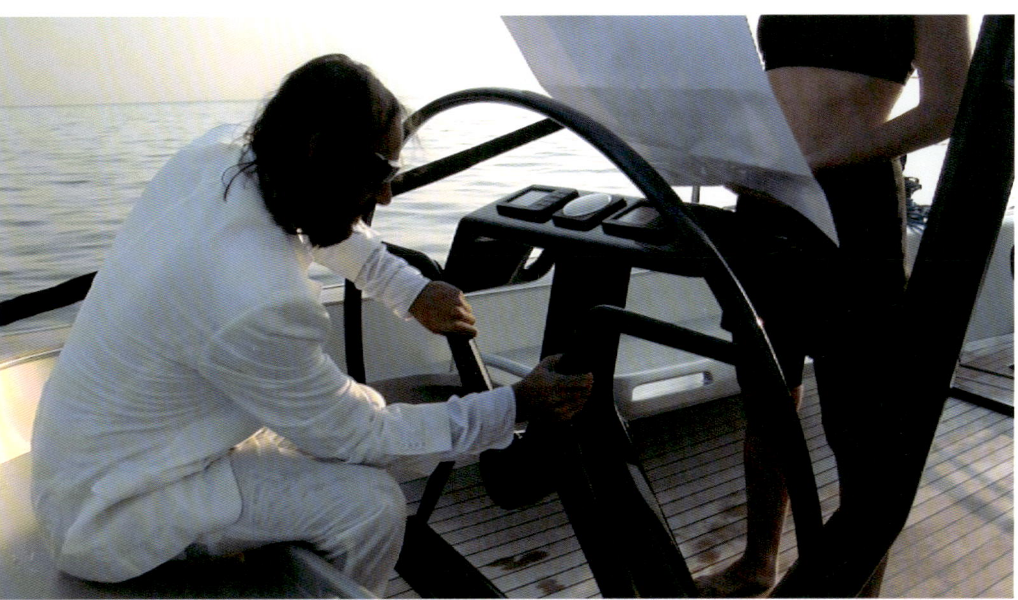

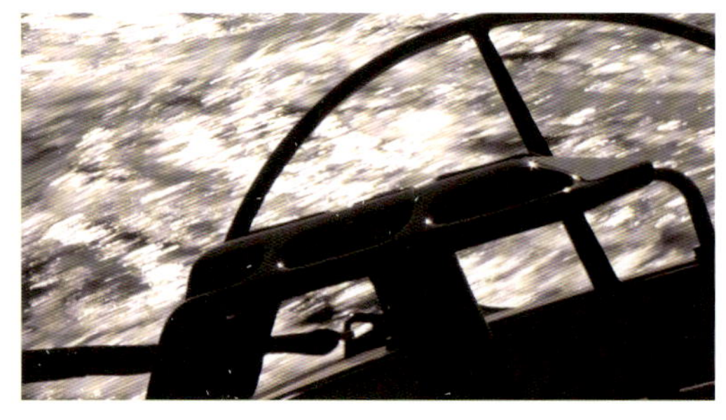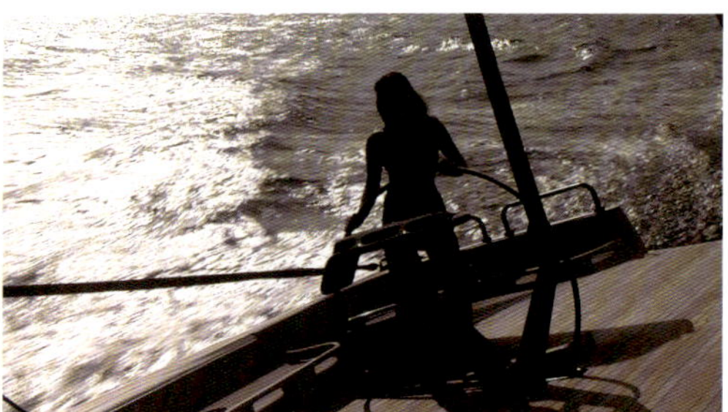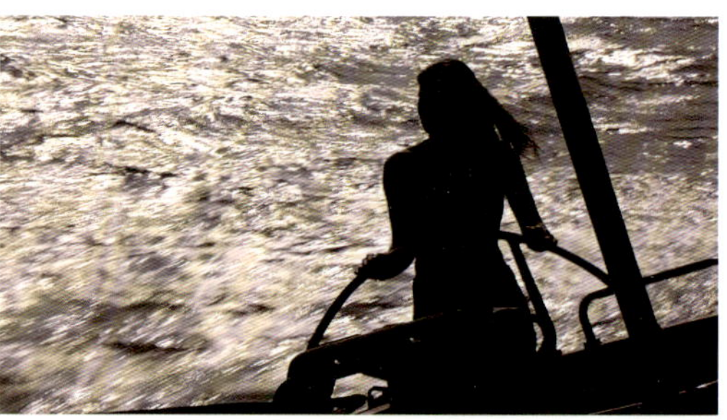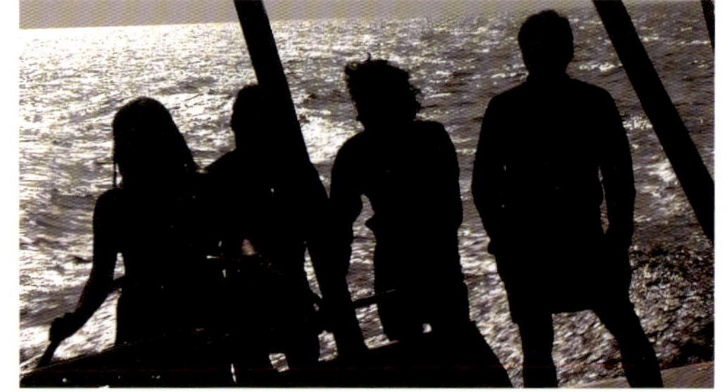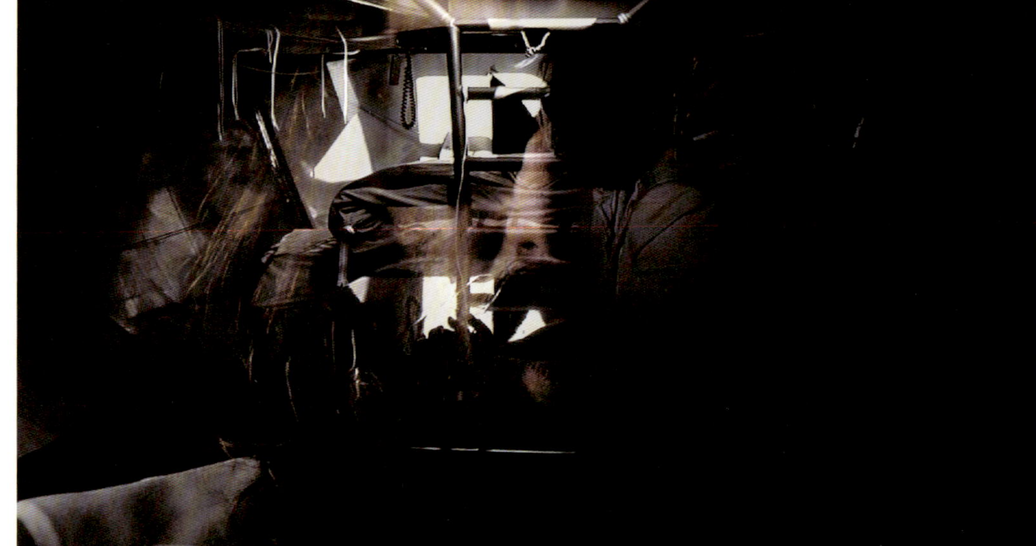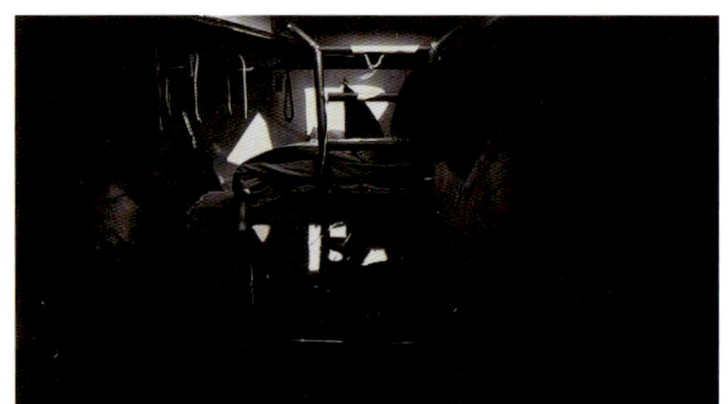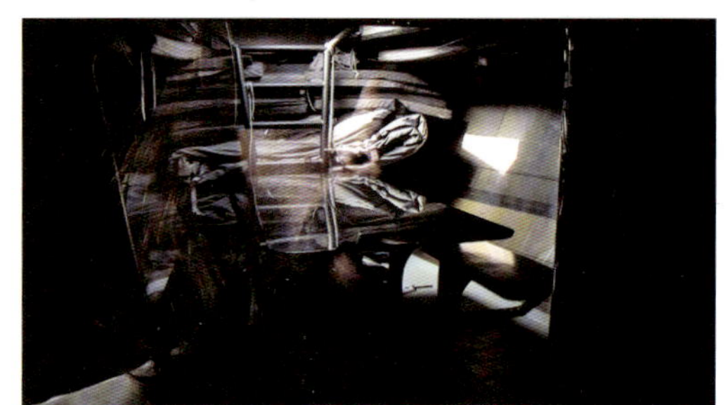

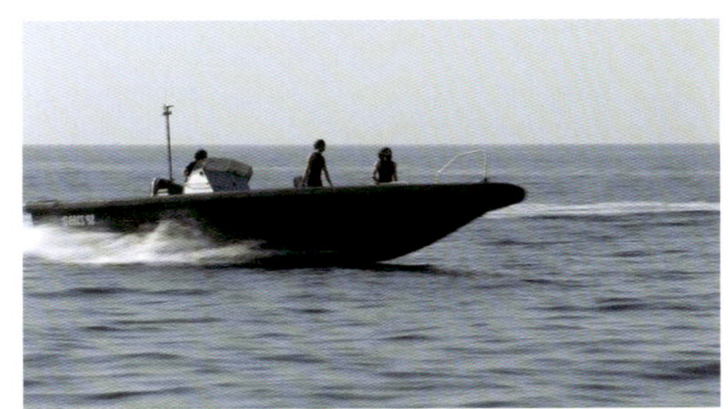

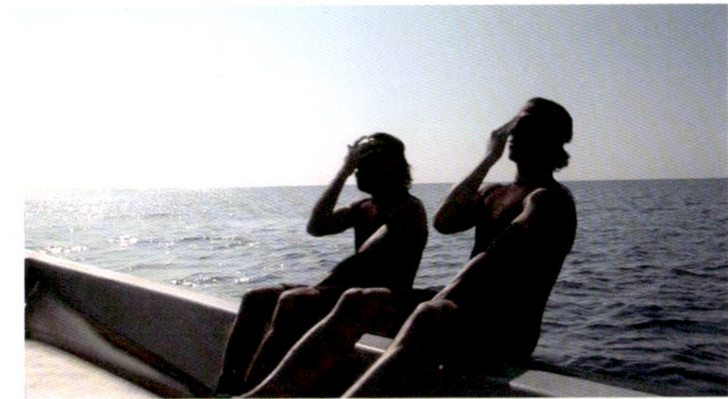

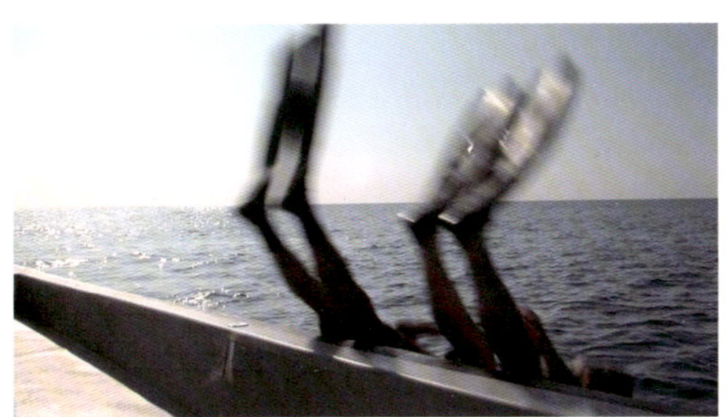

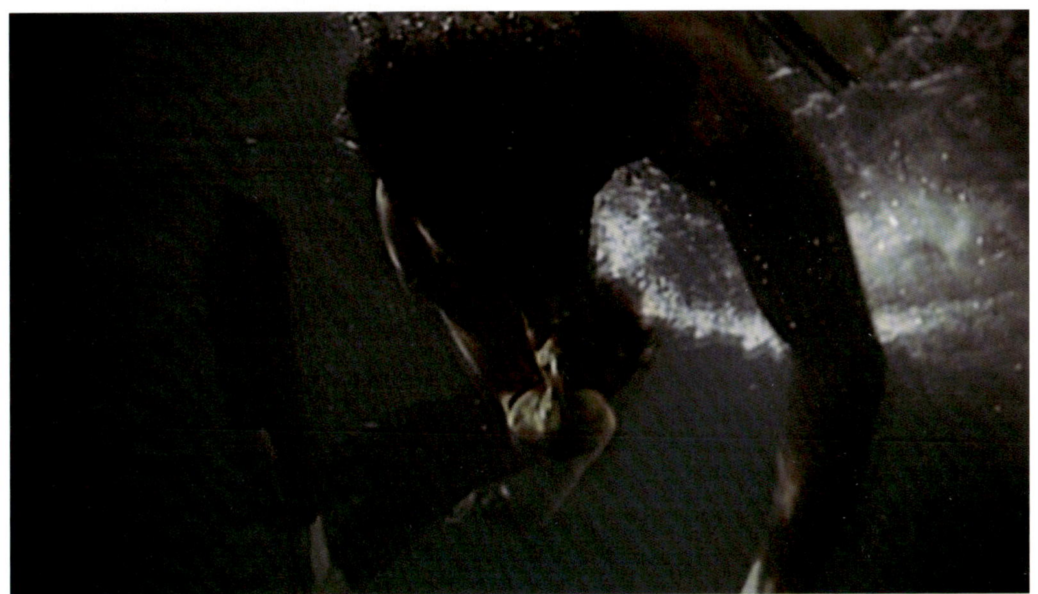

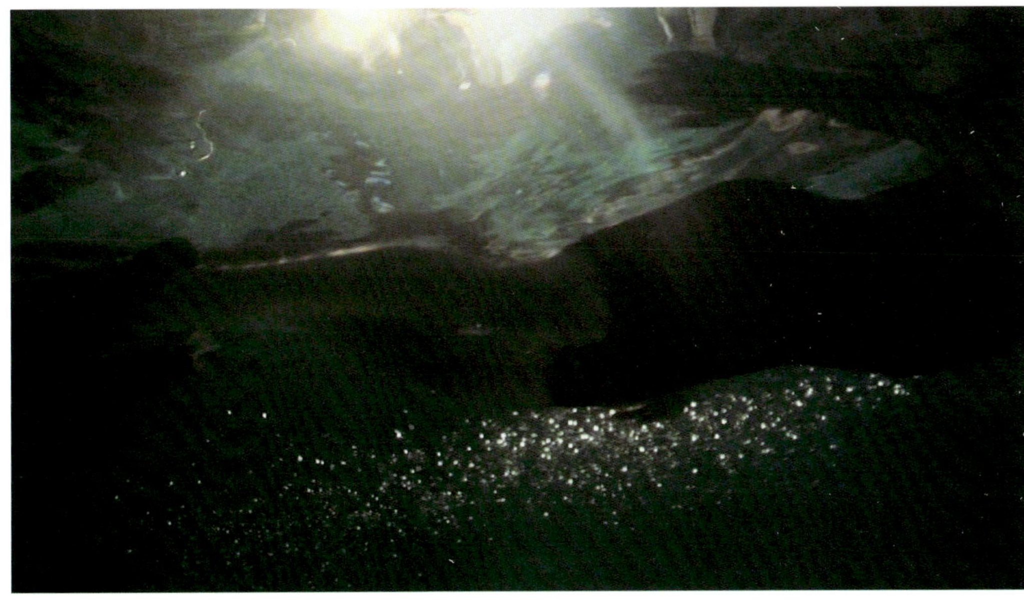

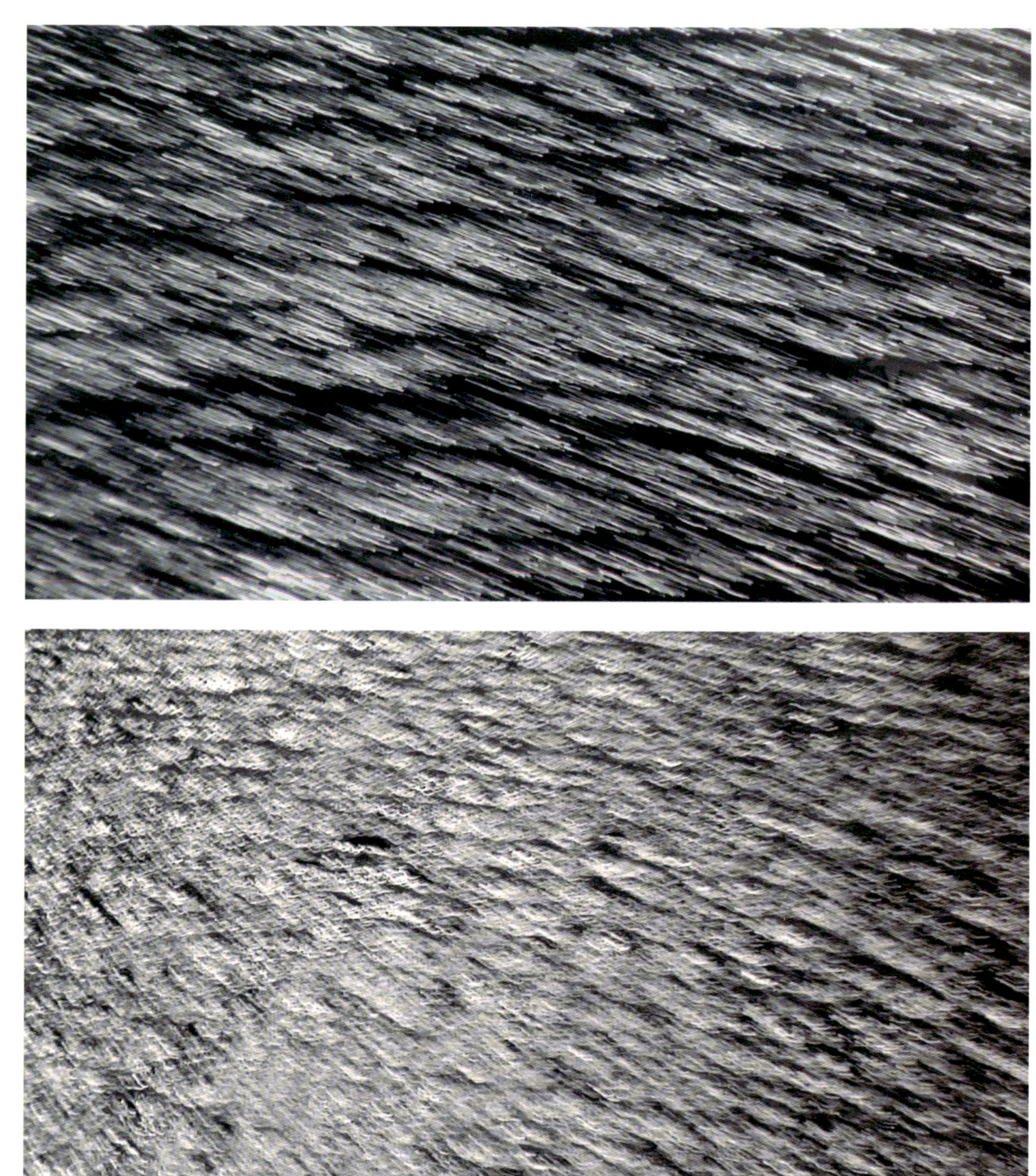

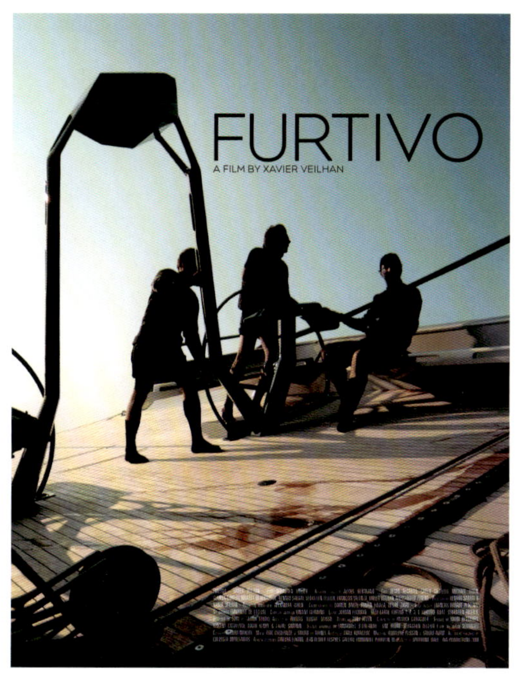

FURTIVO, 2008, POSTER

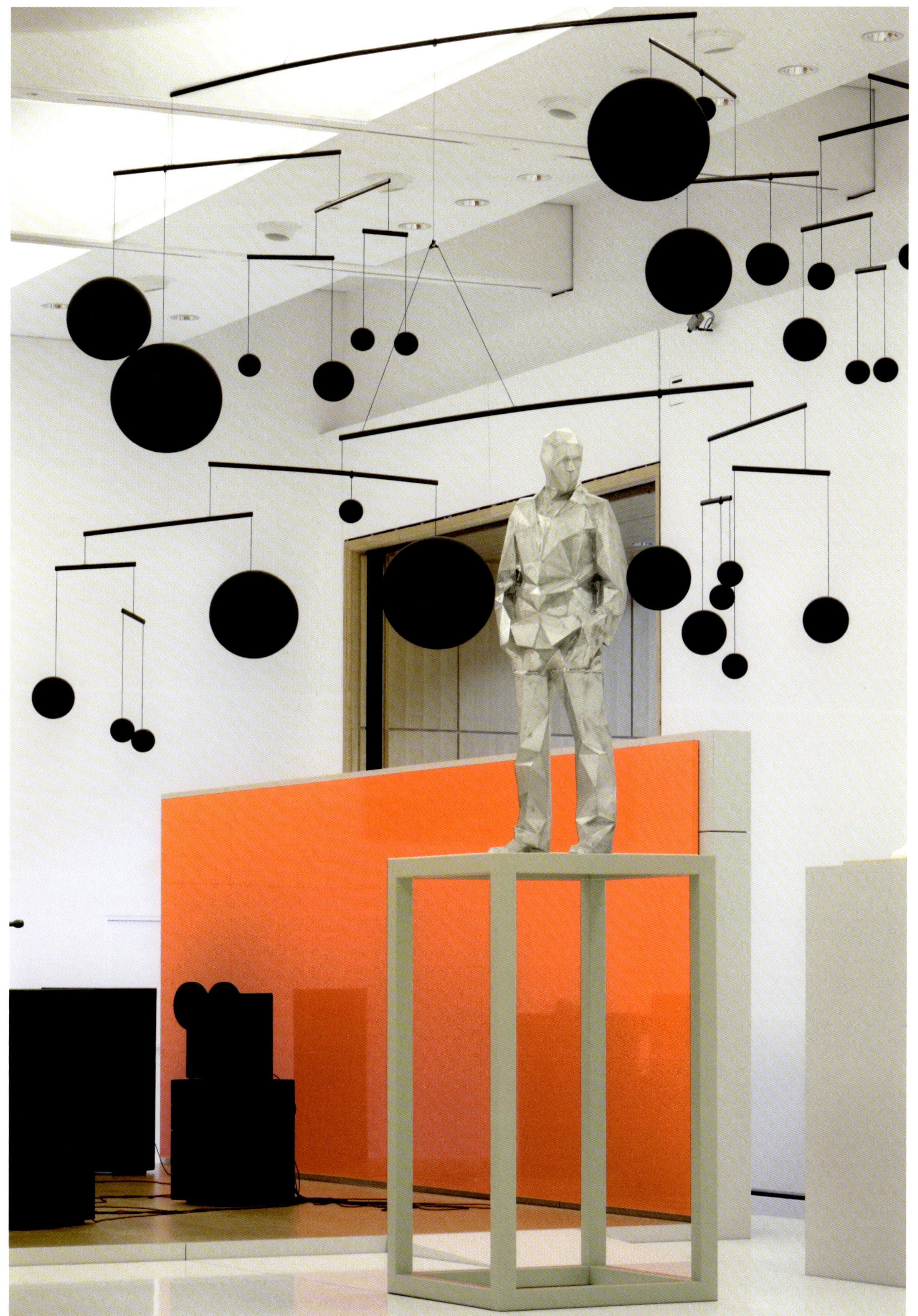

[→ P. 67–83] VIEWS OF THE EXHIBITION *LE PLEIN EMPLOI*, MUSÉE D'ART MODERNE ET CONTEMPORAIN, STRASBOURG, 2005–2006

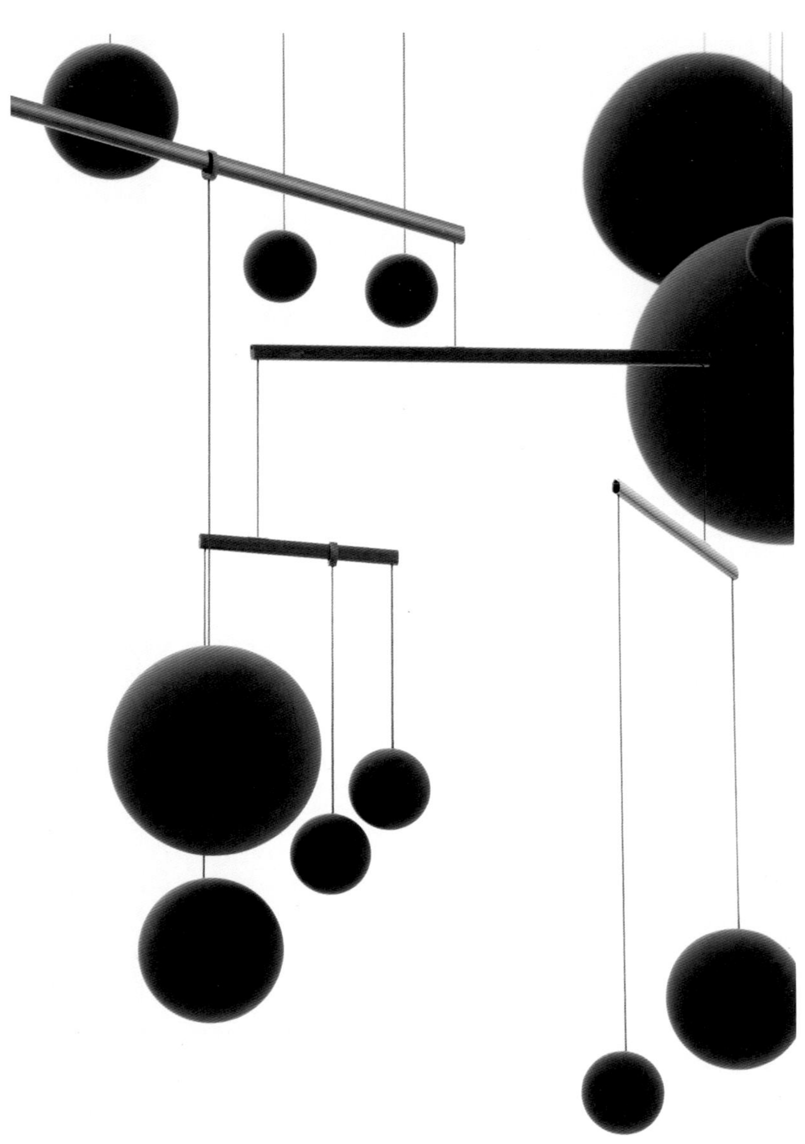

MOBILE, 2005

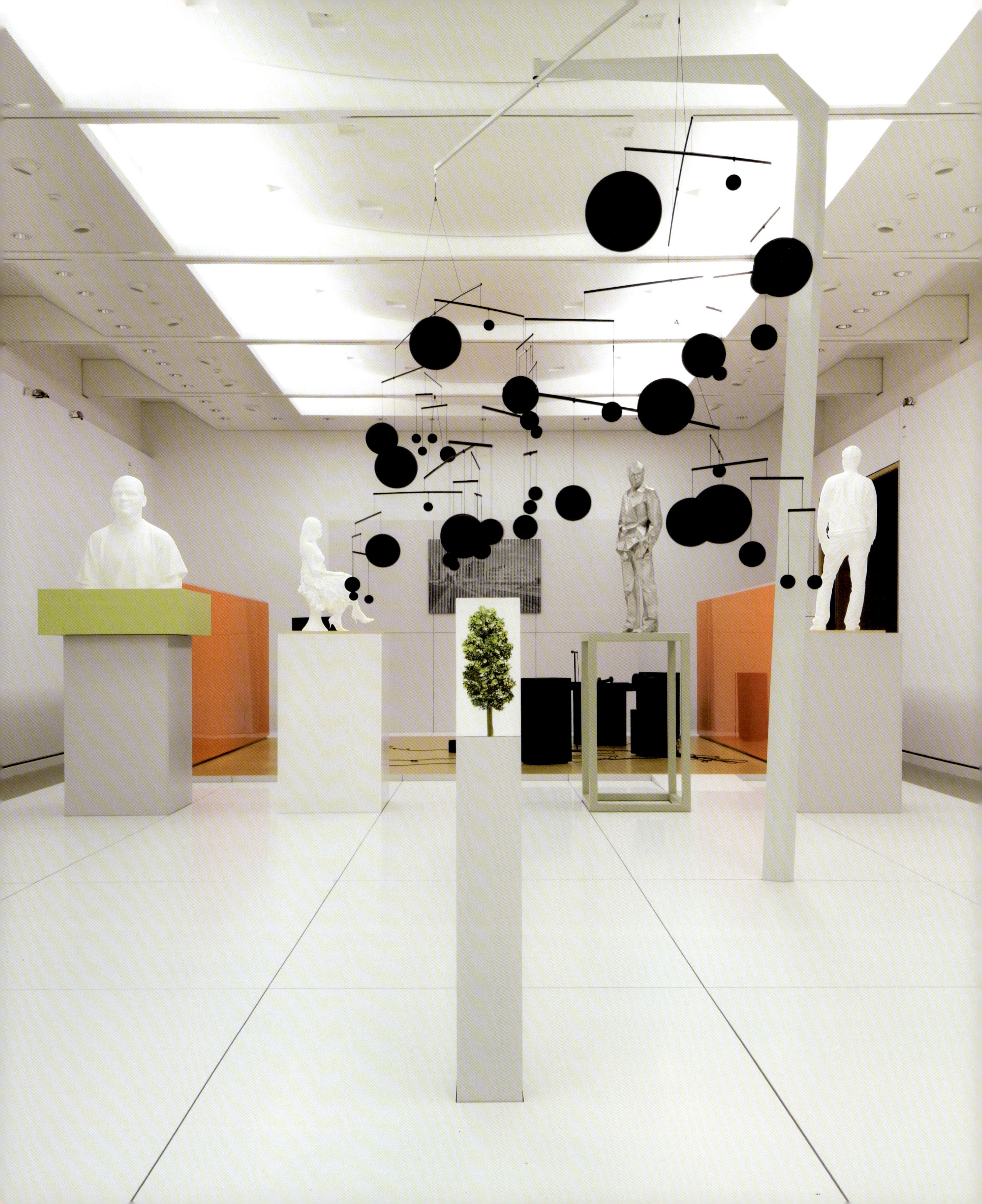

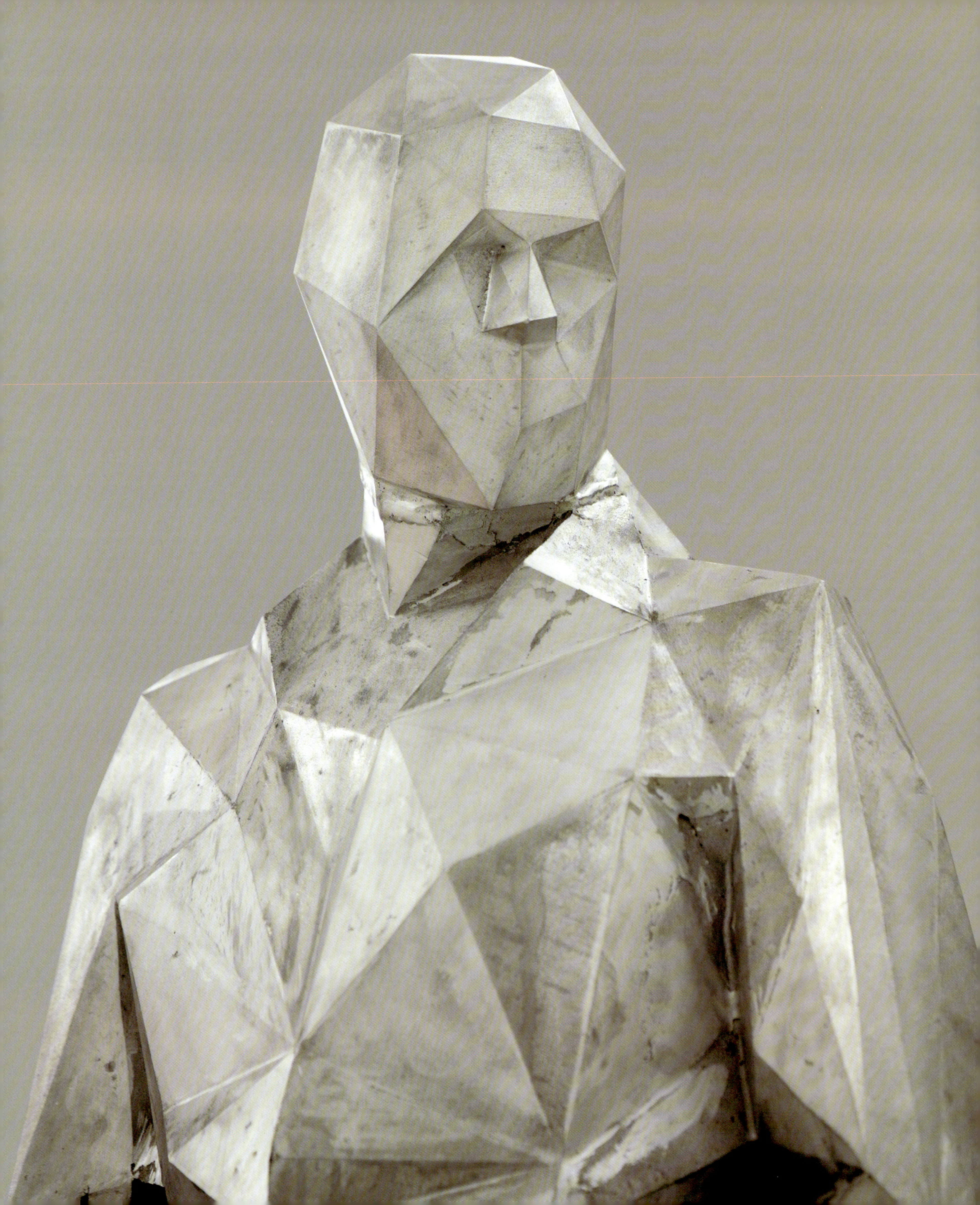

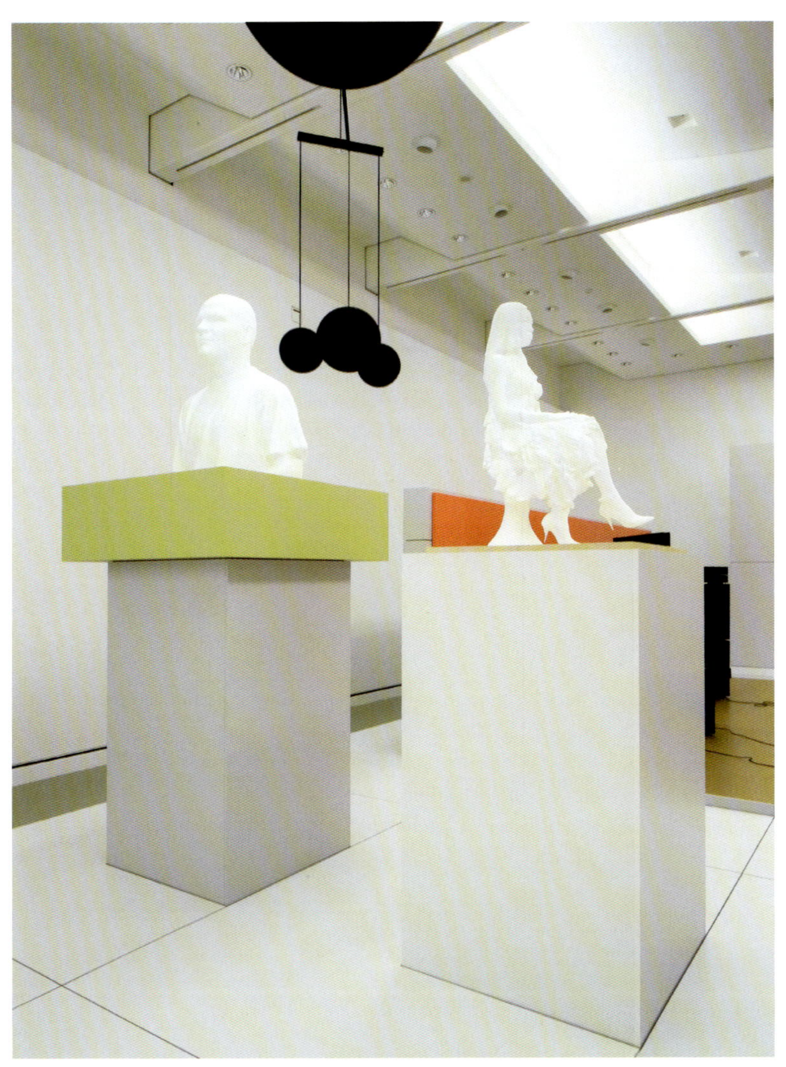 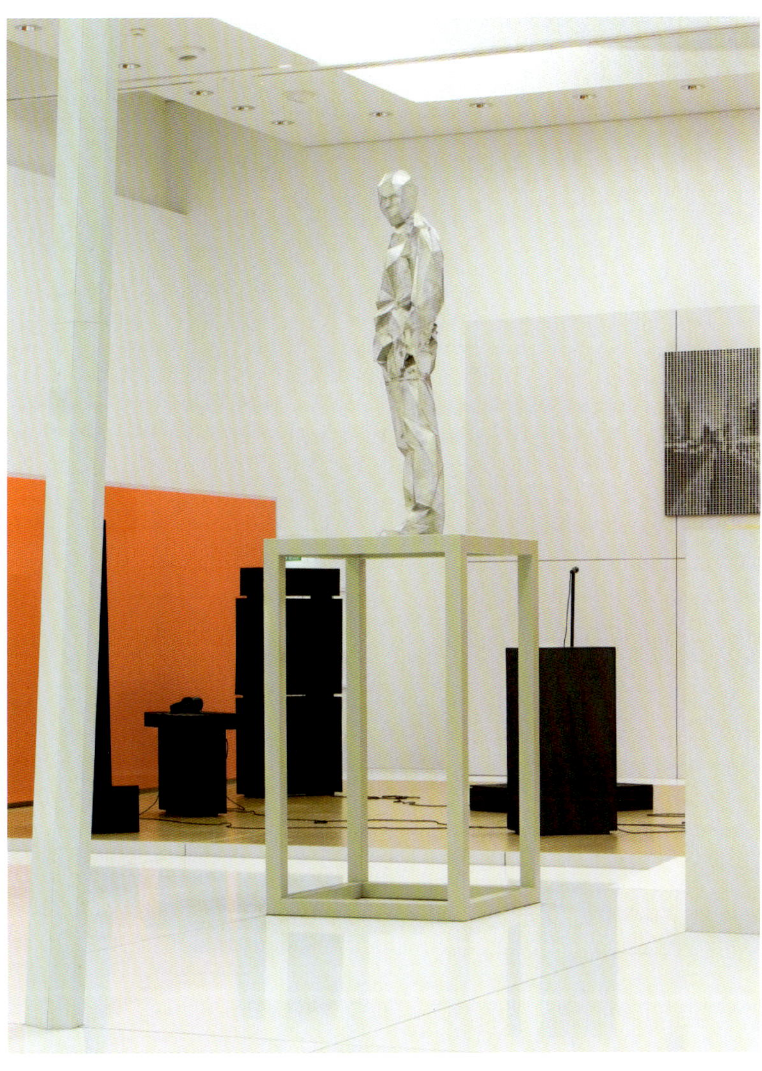

[← P. 70] **LAURENT**, 2005   [ABOVE LEFT] **ERIC**, 2005 AND **YI**, 2005; [ABOVE RIGHT] **LAURENT**, 2005

UNTITLED (THE LITTLE TREE), 2005

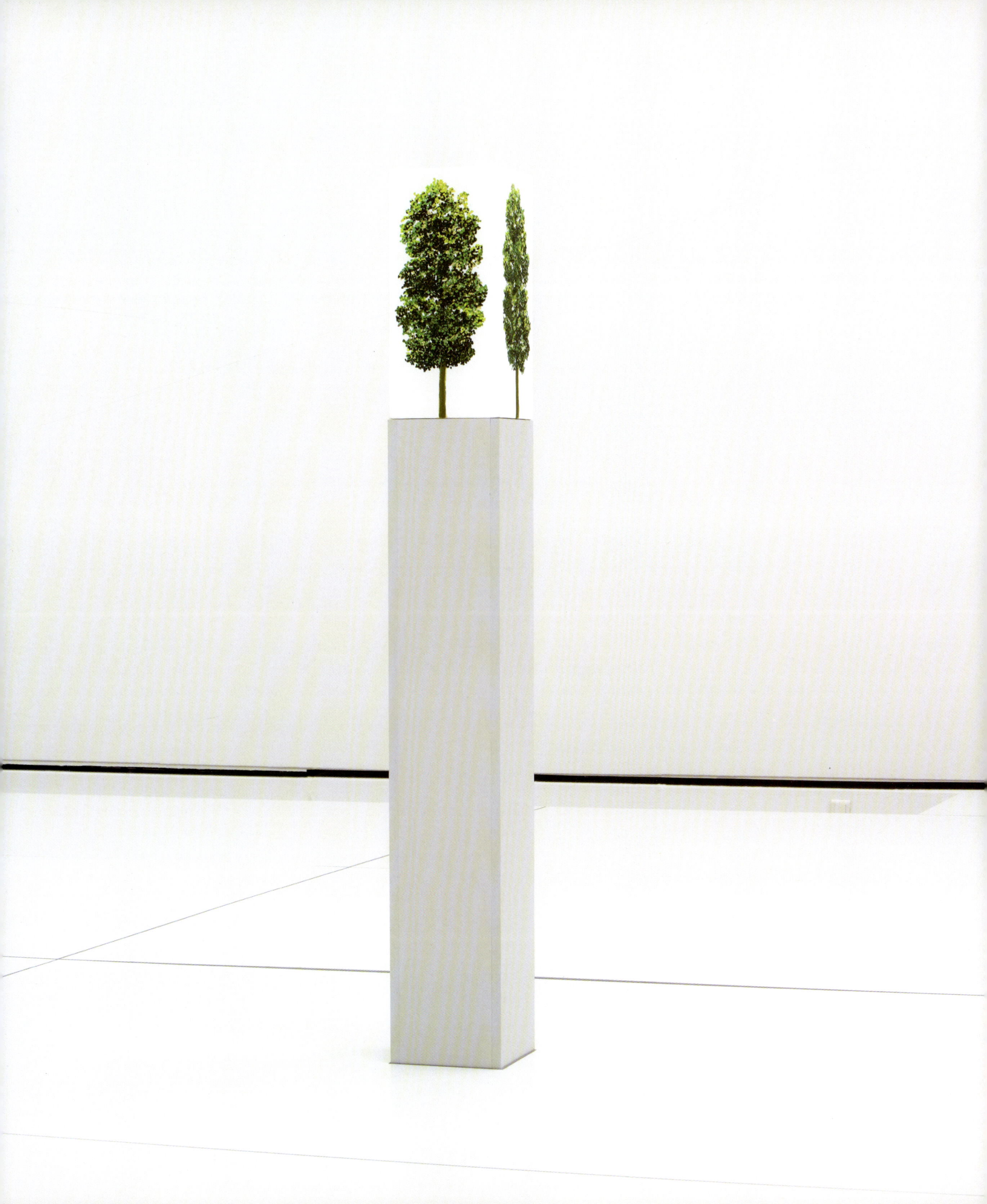

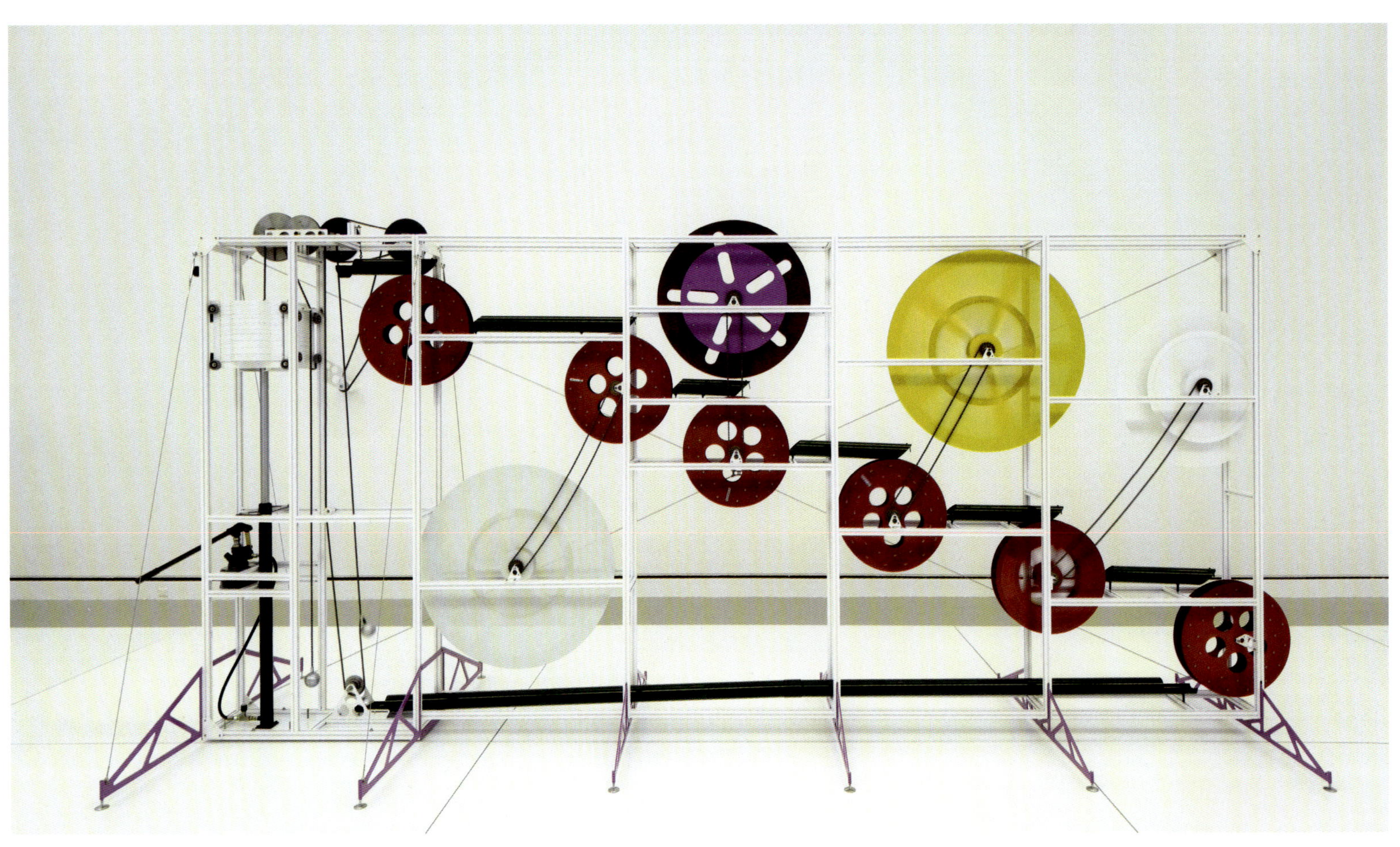

LE COUCOU, 2005   [→ P. 75, FOREGROUND] ORIENTATION TABLE, 2005

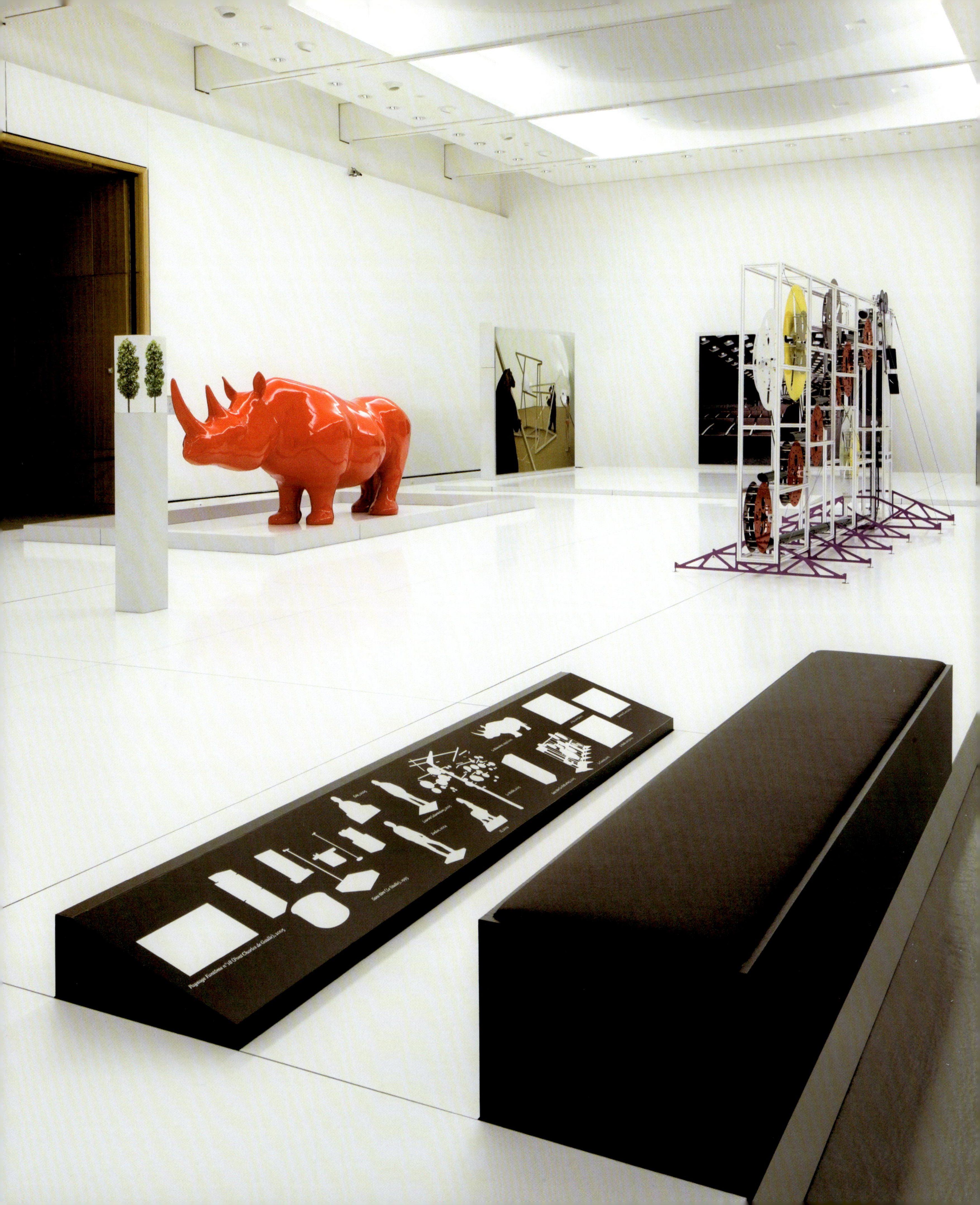

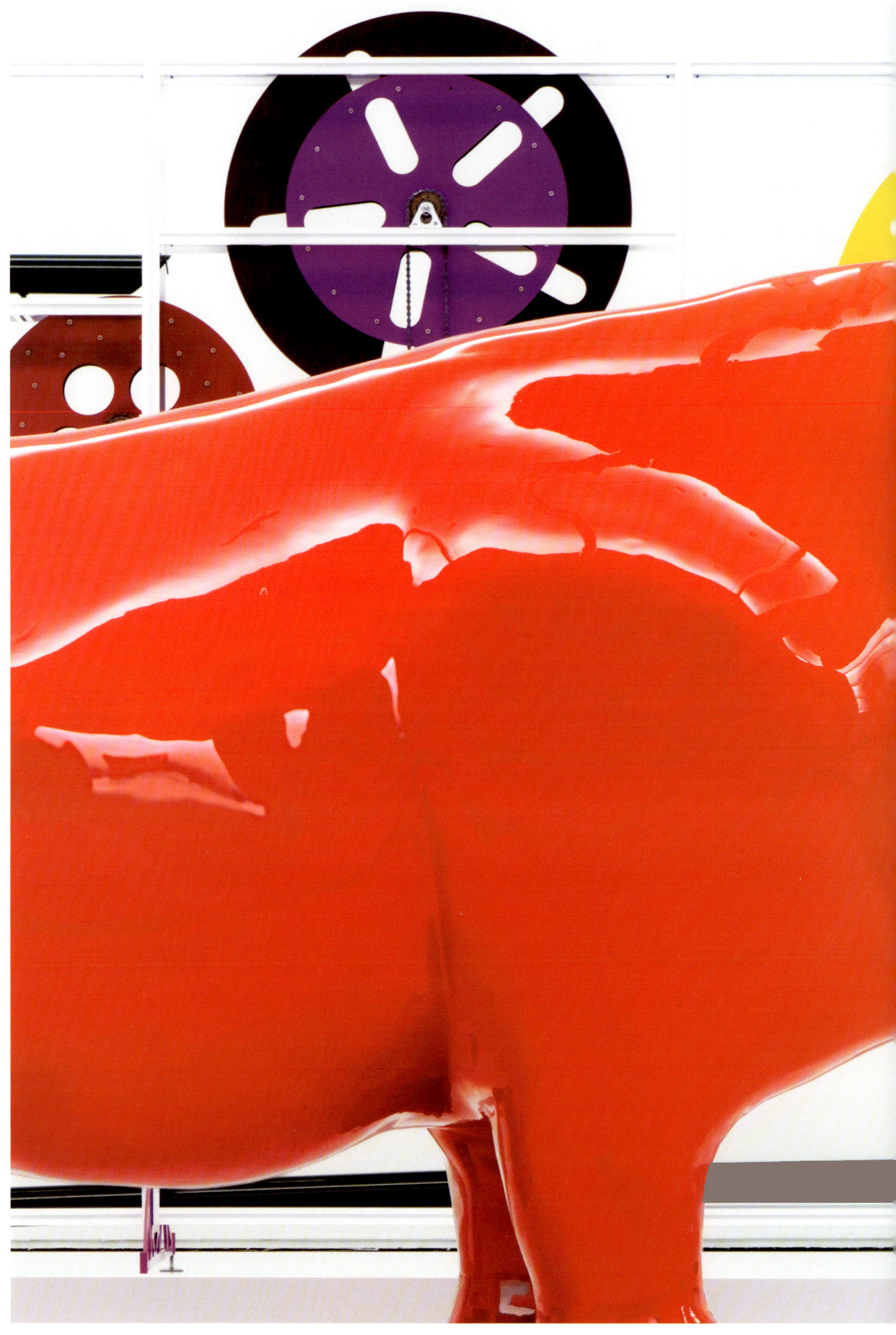

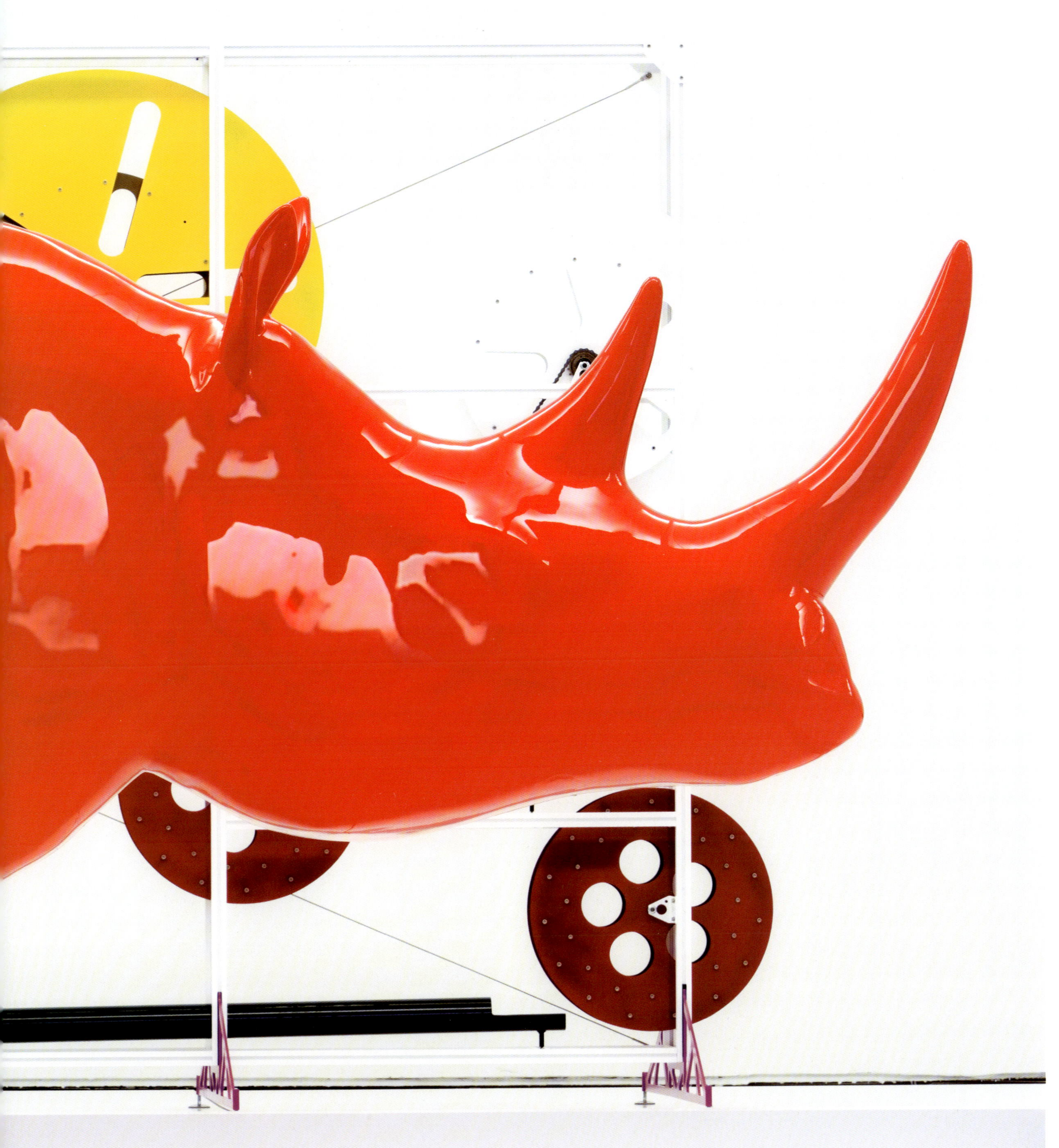

LE RHINOCÉROS (THE RHINOCEROS), 1999

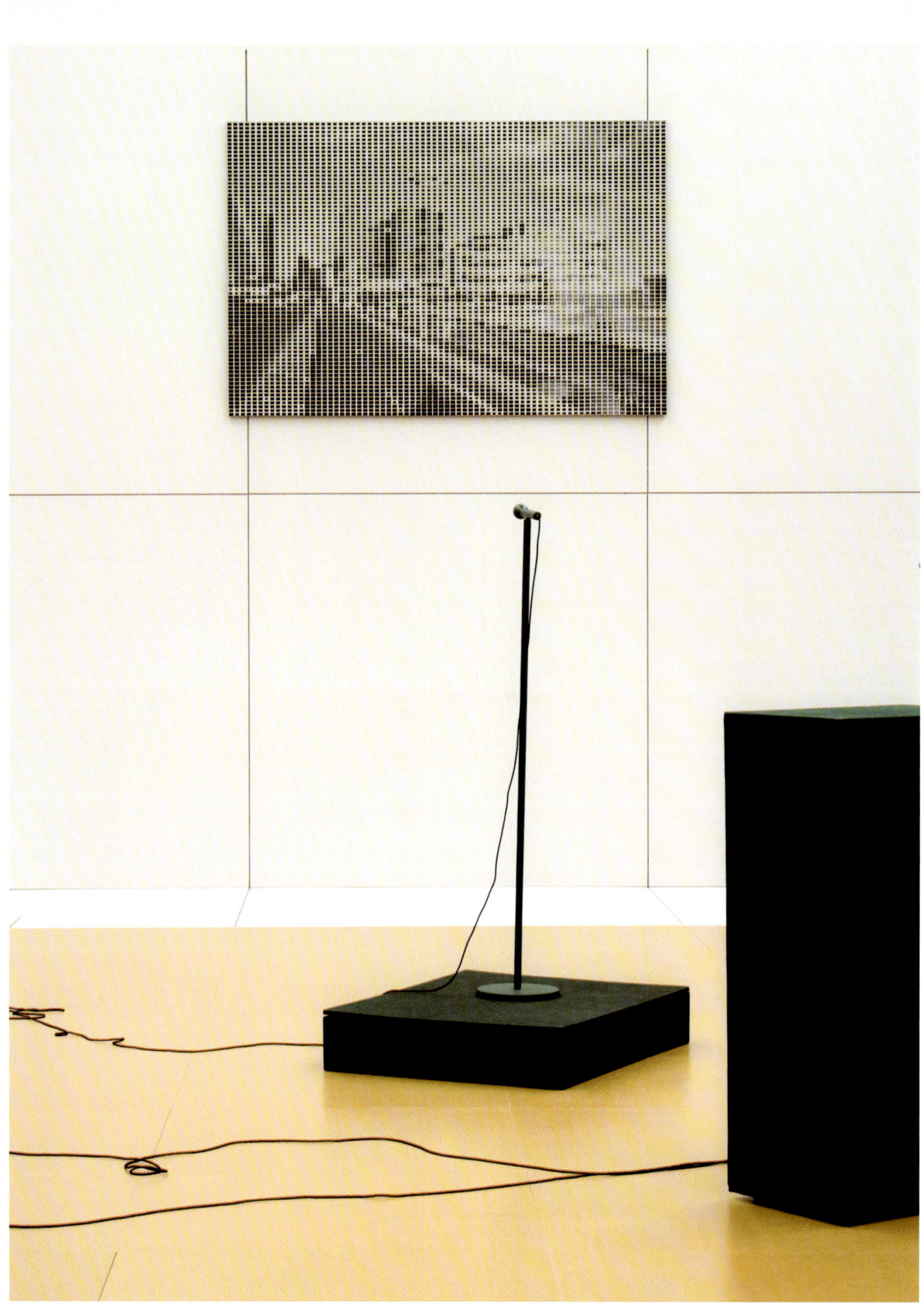

78

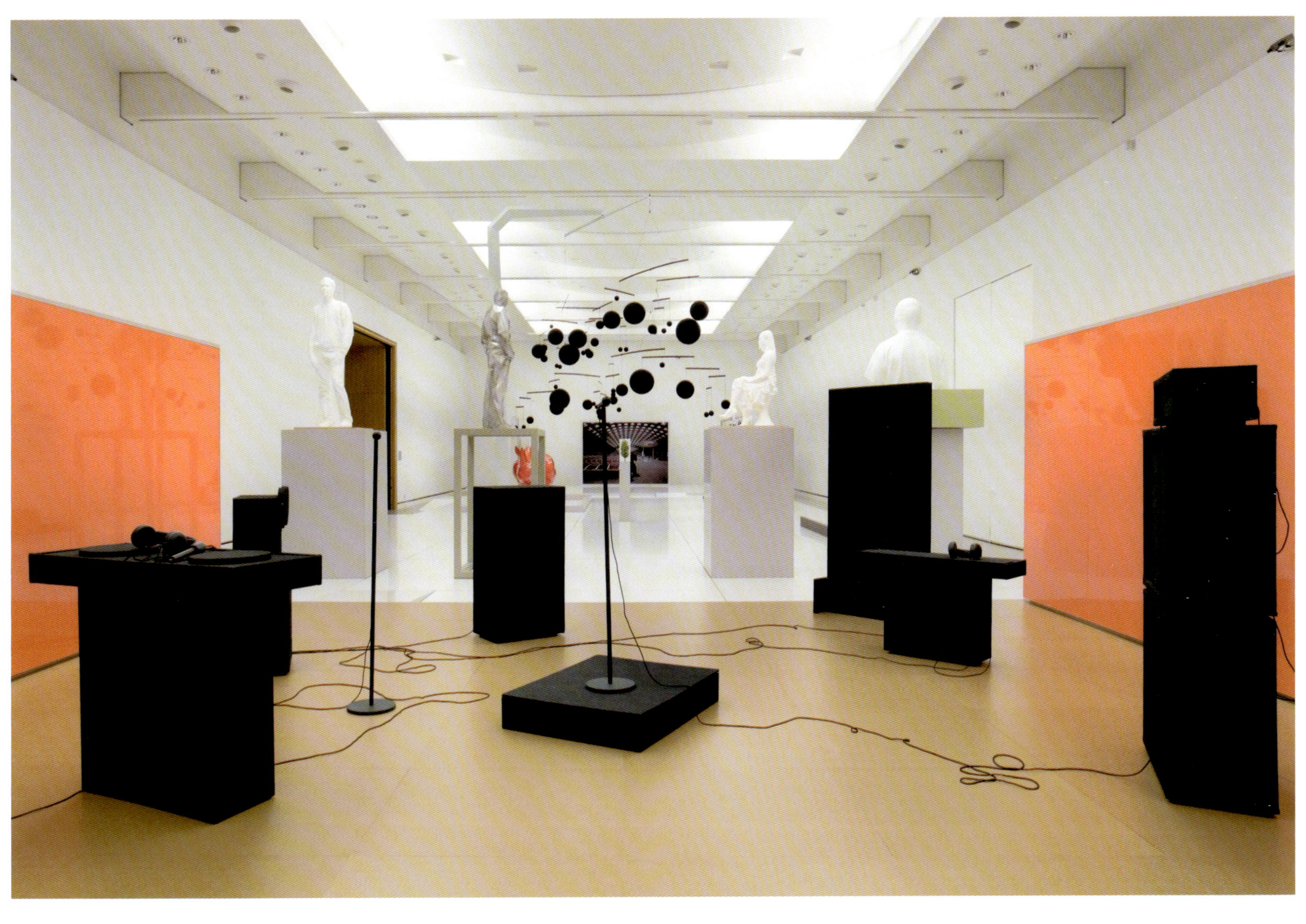

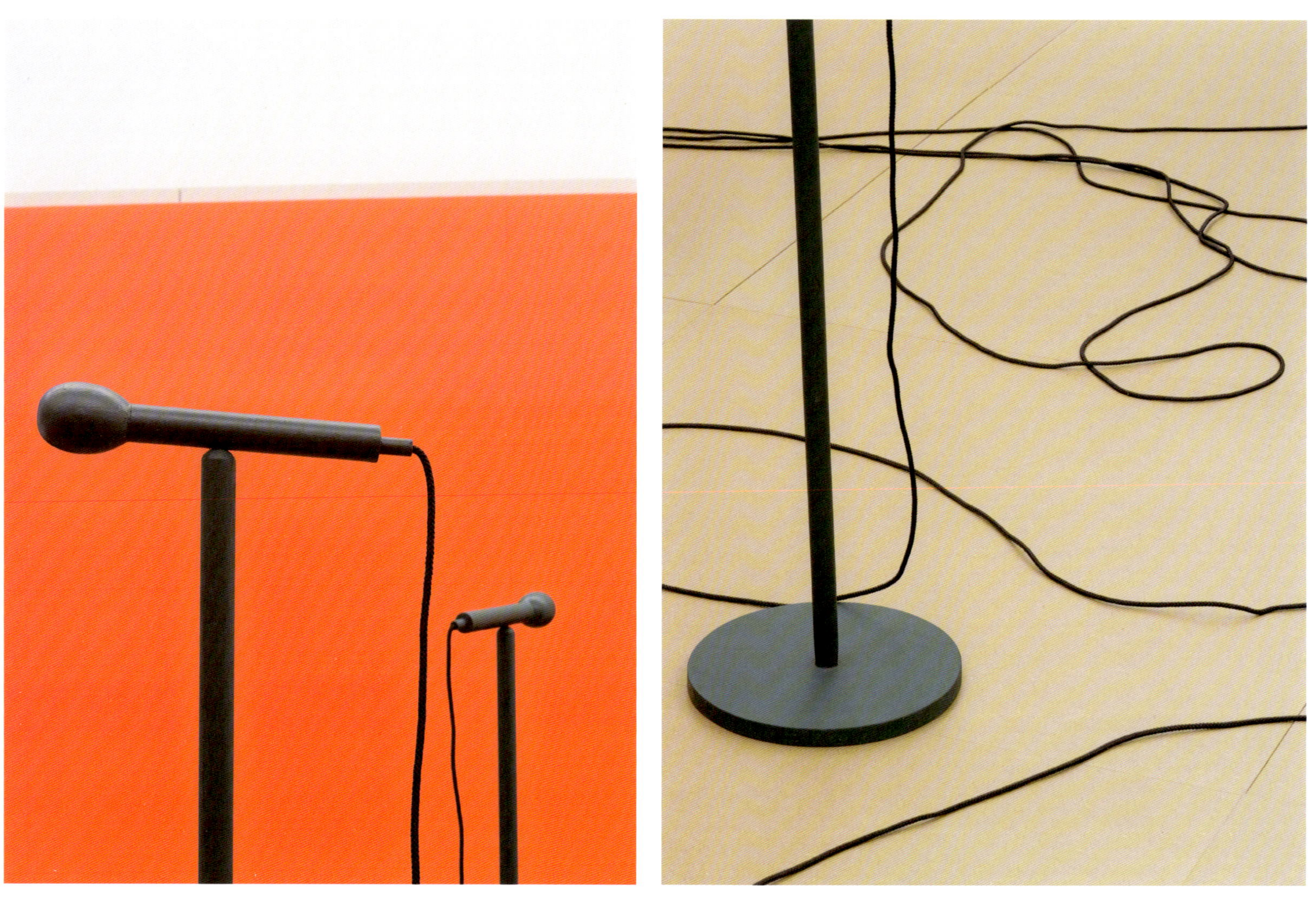

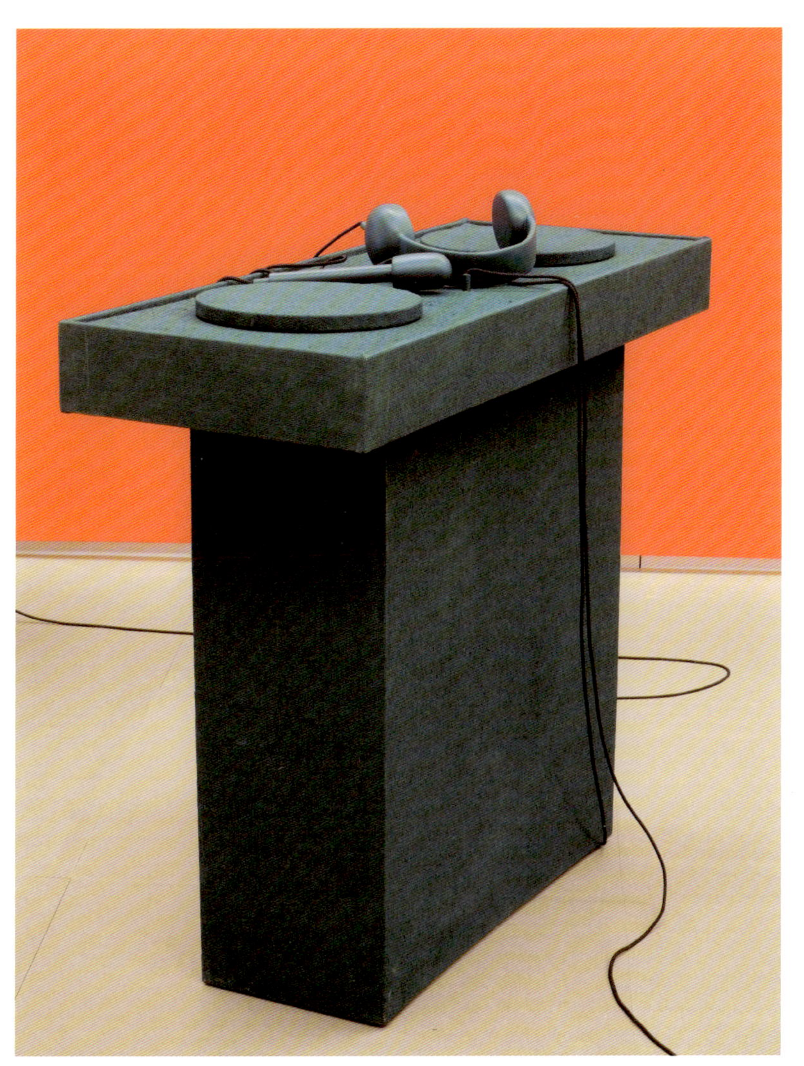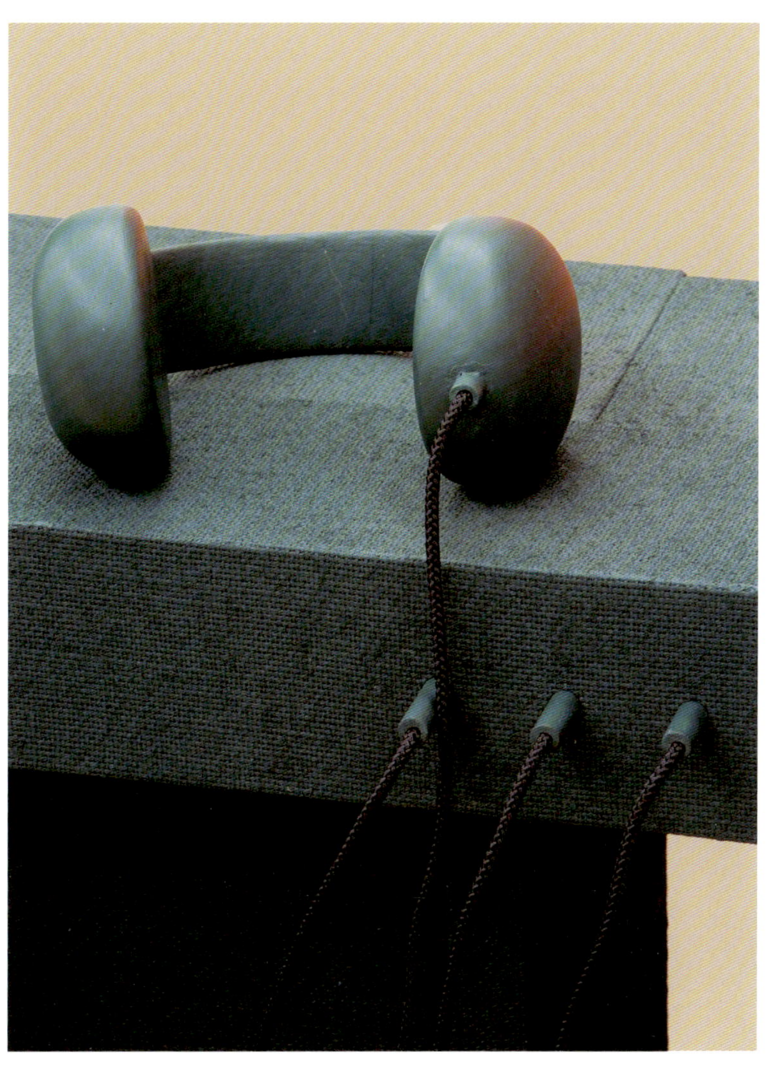

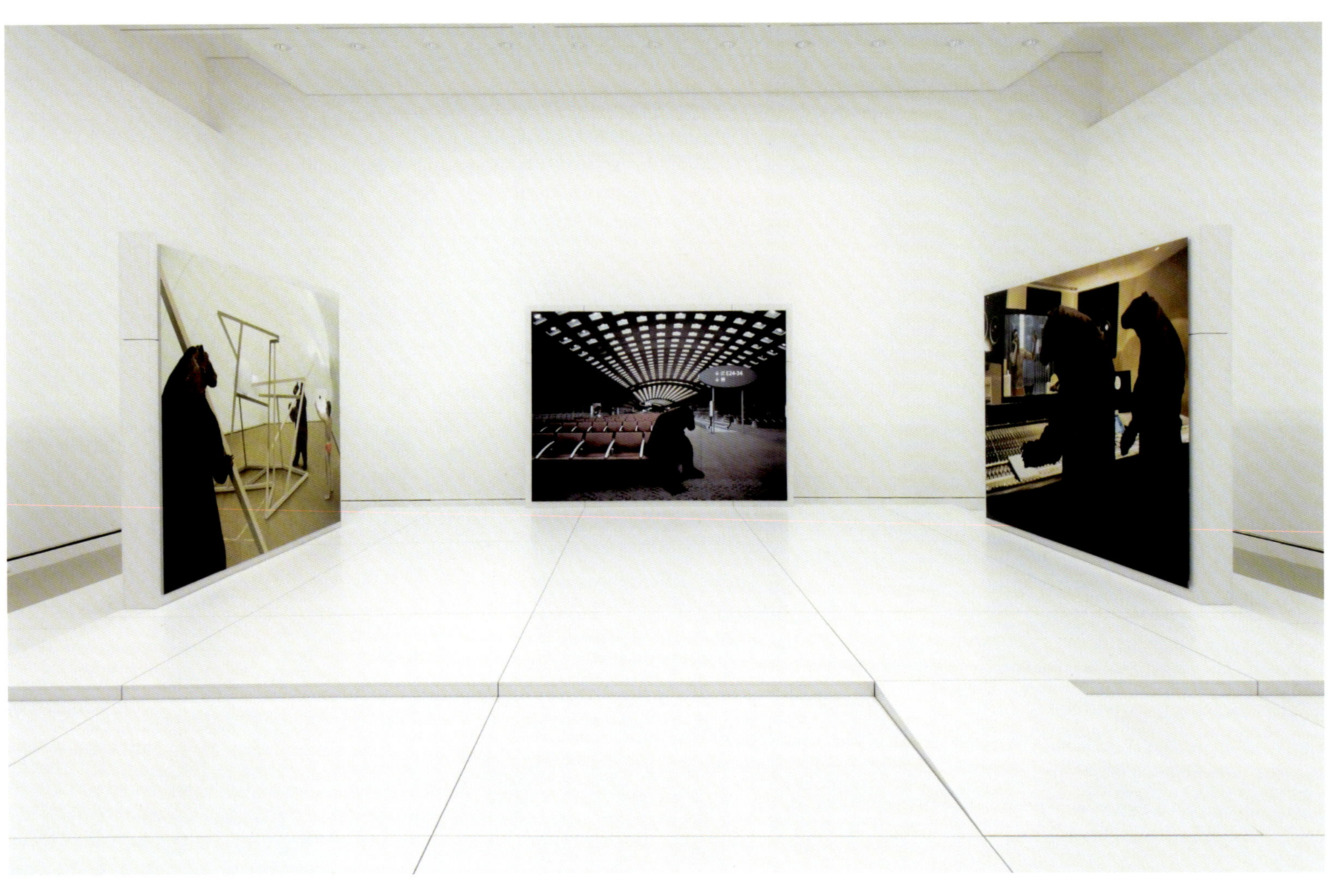

2 BY 4, TERMINAL E, AND THE STUDIO, 2003 / 2004

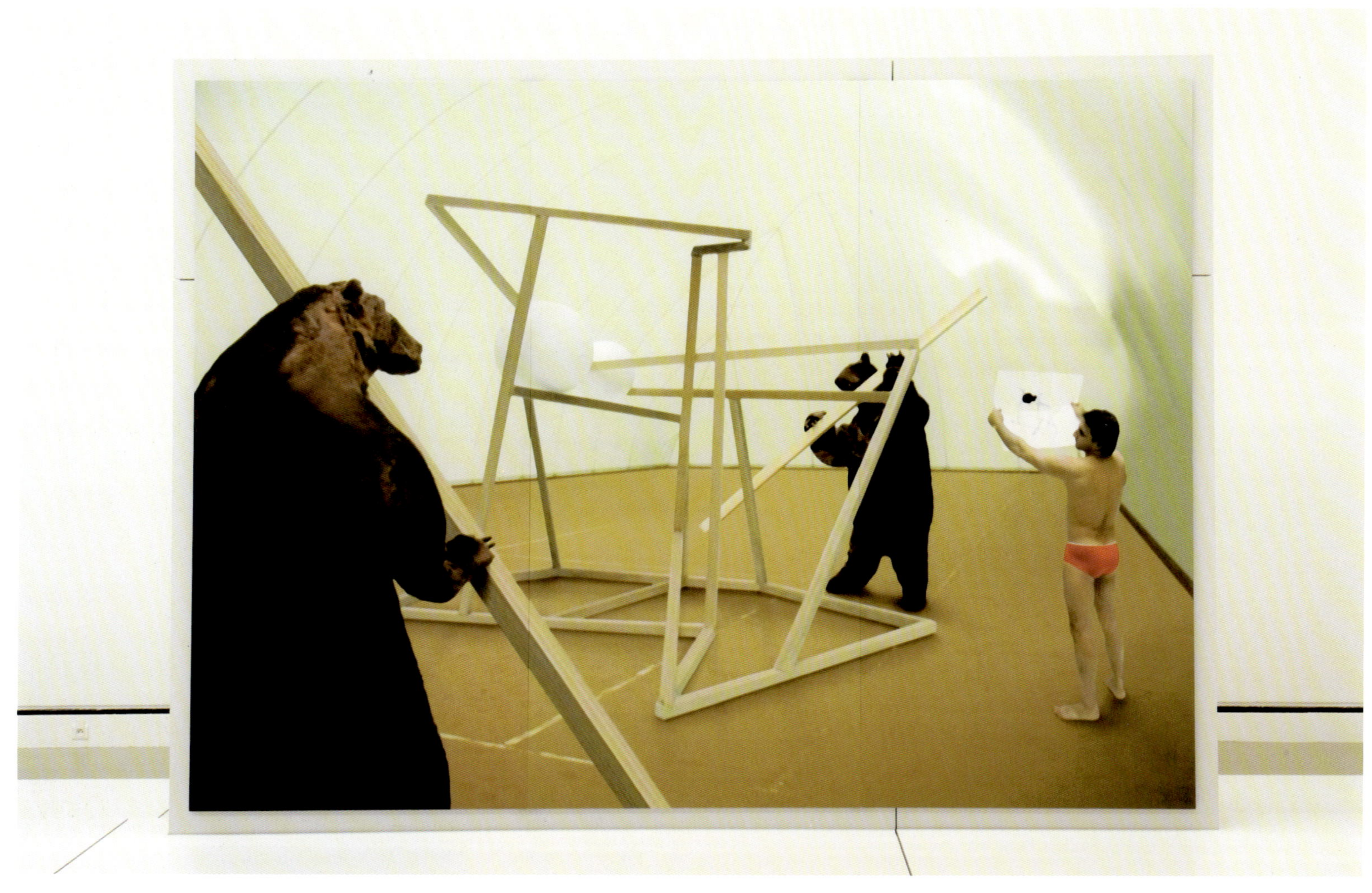

2 BY 4, 2003 / 2004

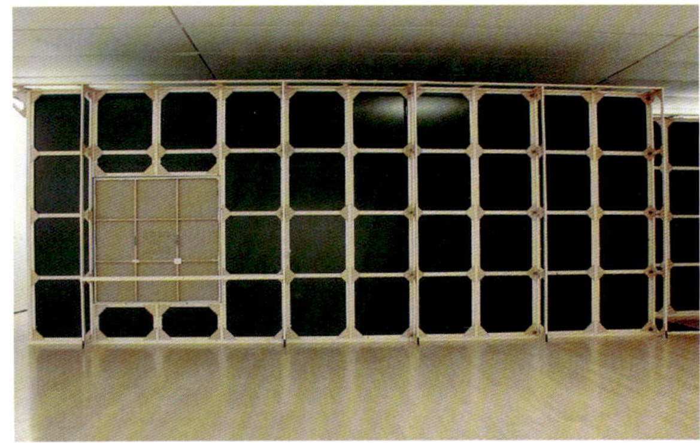

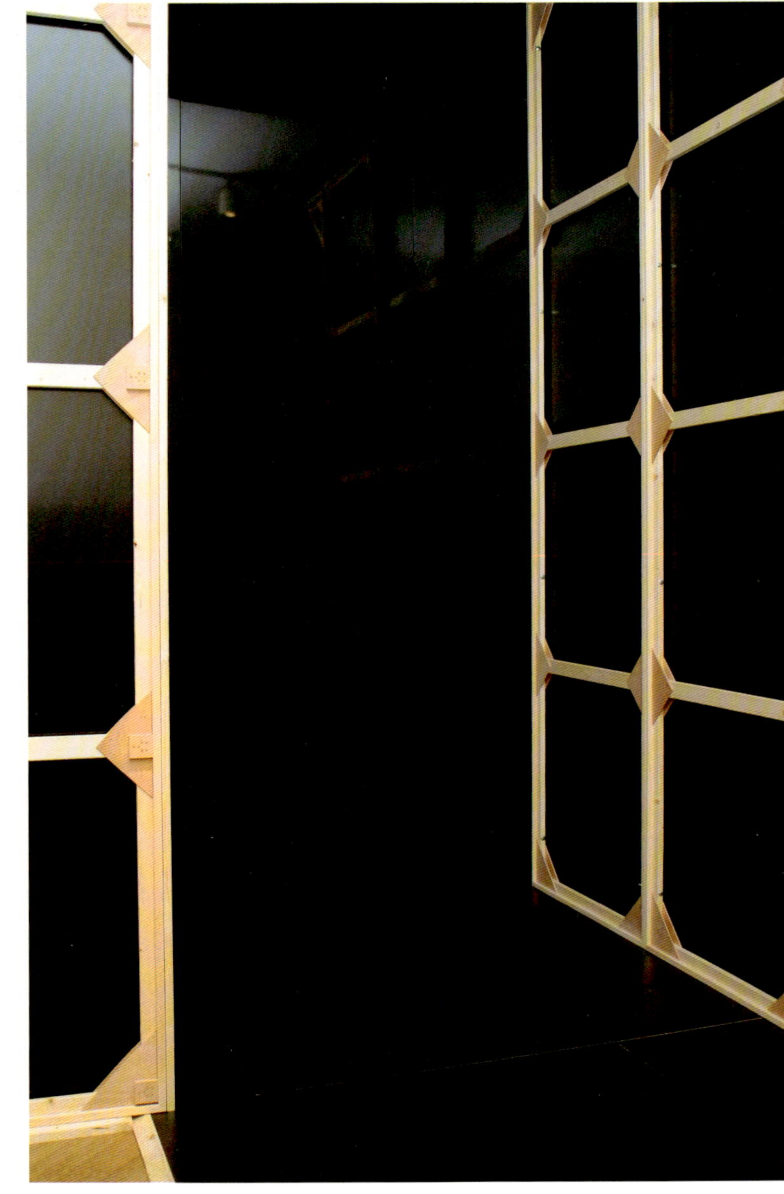

THE PHOTOREALIST PROJECT, 1996 / 2003
INSTALLATION VIEW, *IT HAPPENED TOMORROW,* 7TH BIENNIAL OF CONTEMPORARY
ART, LYON, 2003 , AND NATIONAL ACADEMY MUSEUM, NEW YORK, 2004–2005

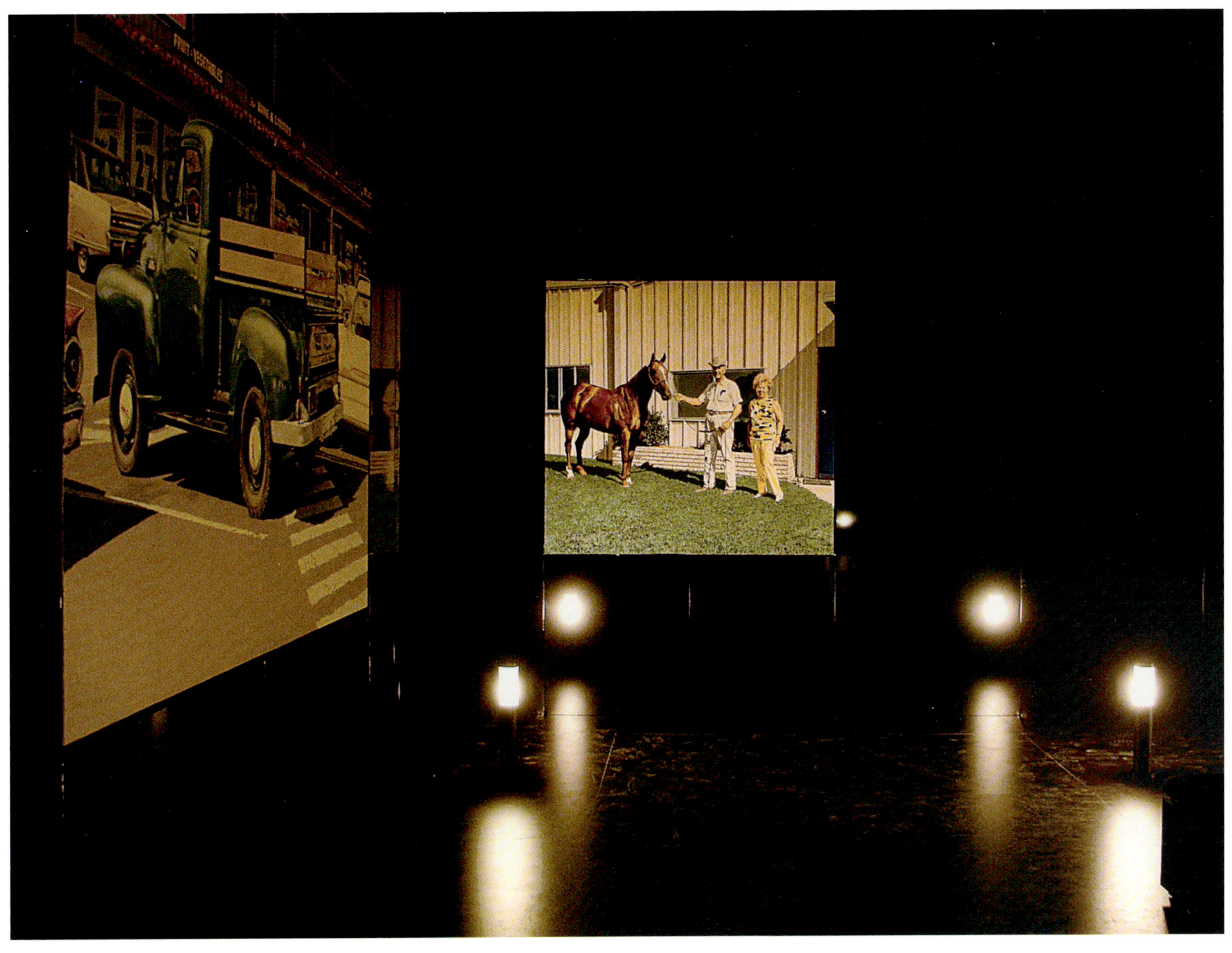

RALPH GOINGS, **BLUE GMC**, 1969
RICHARD MCLEAN, **DIALIZ**, 1971

THE **PHOTOREALIST PROJECT**, 1996 / 2003

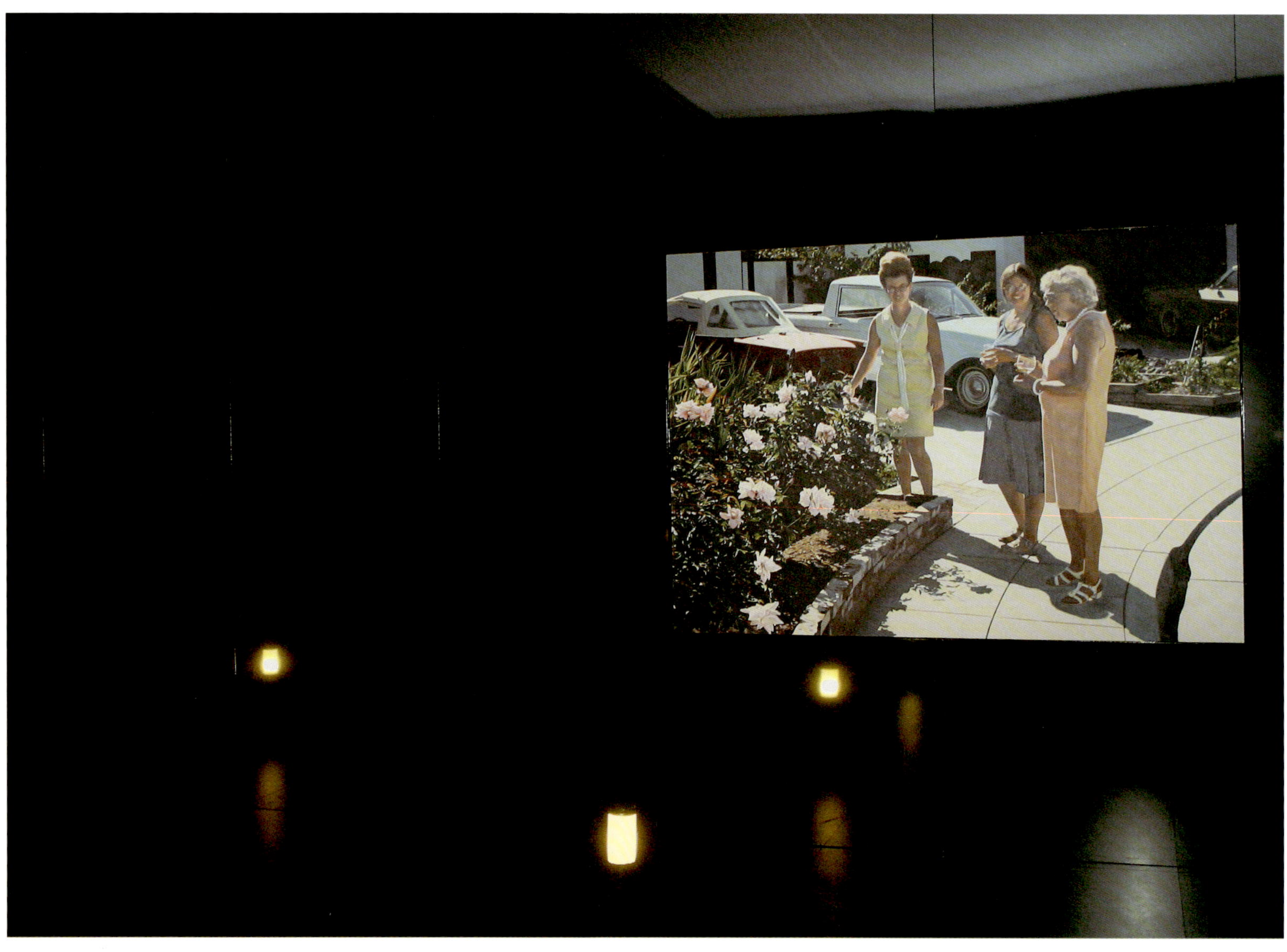

THE PHOTOREALIST PROJECT, *1996 / 2003*   ROBERT BECHTLE, **ROSES**, 1973

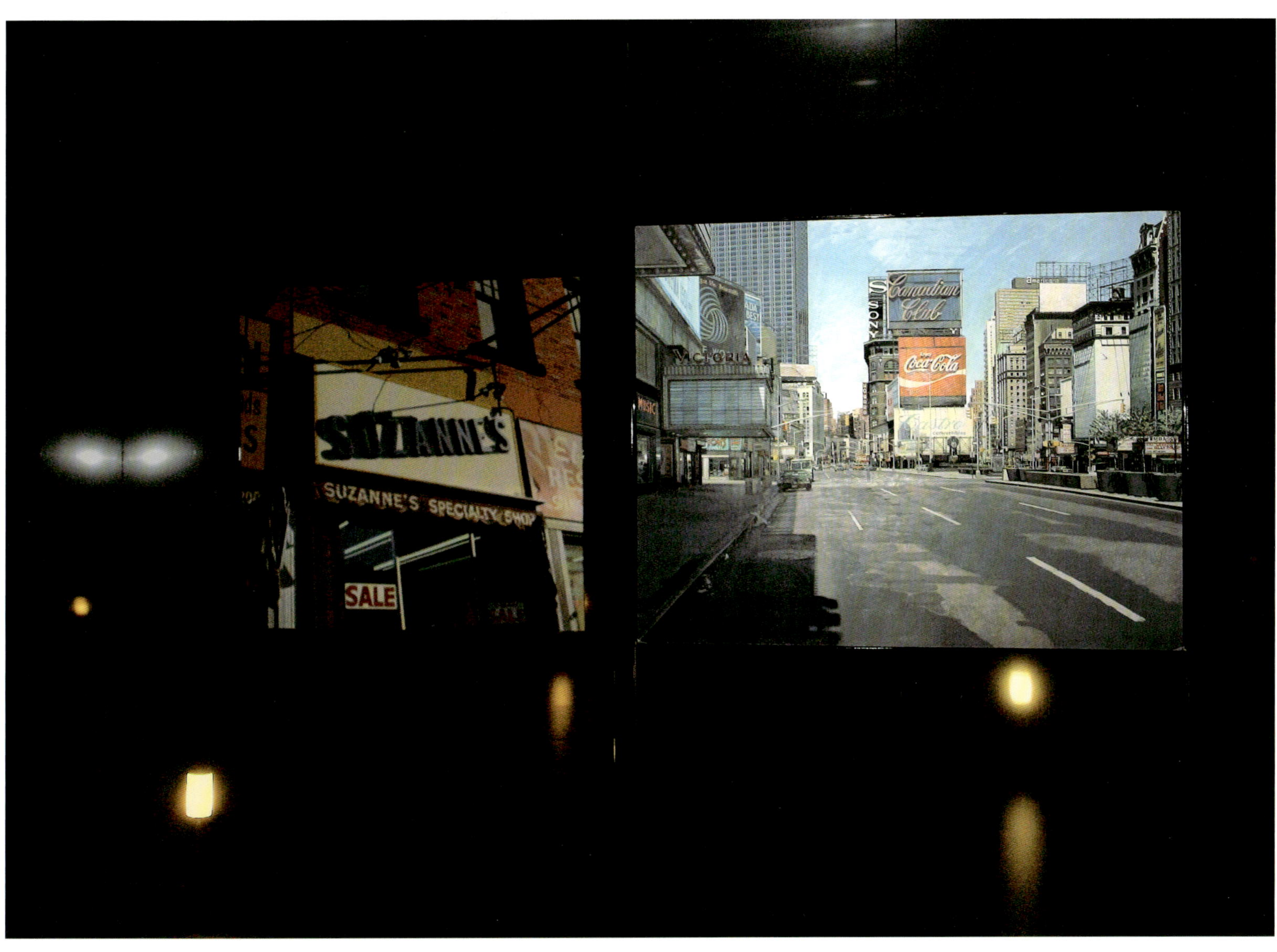

ROBERT COTTINGHAM, **SUZANNE'S**, 1974
RICHARD ESTES, **CANADIAN CLUB**, 1974

THE PHOTOREALIST PROJECT, 1996 / 2003

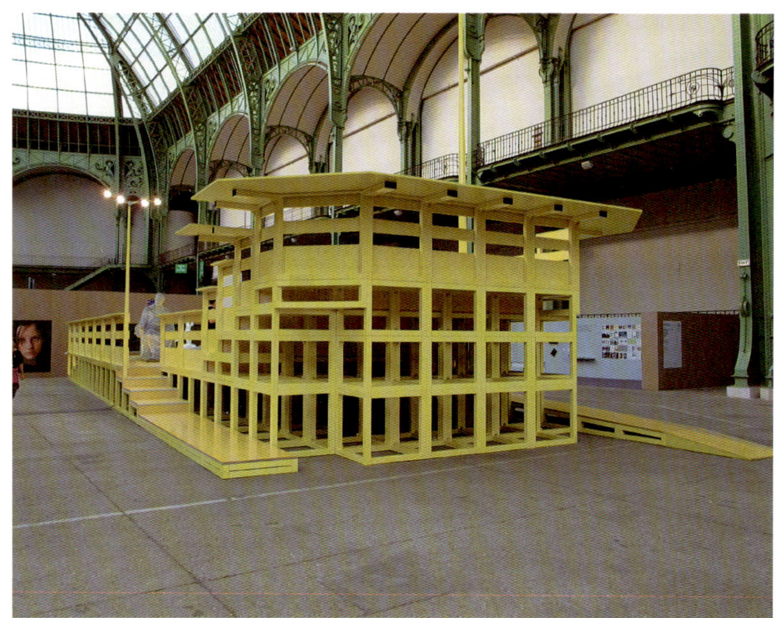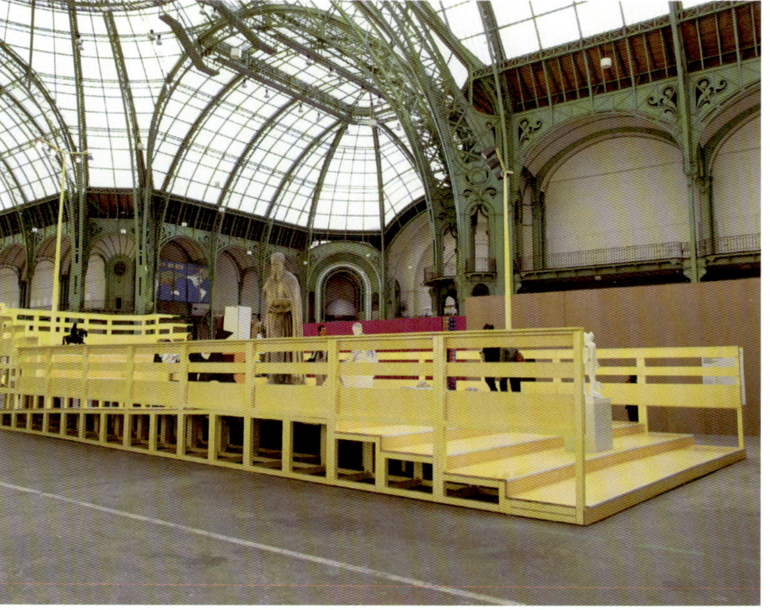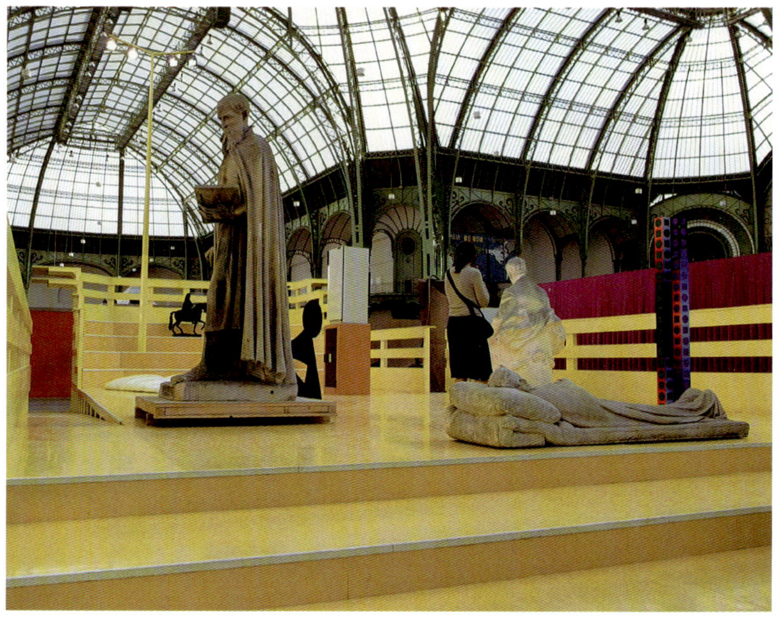

INSTALLATION VIEW, *LA FORCE DE L'ART*, GRAND PALAIS, PARIS, 2006

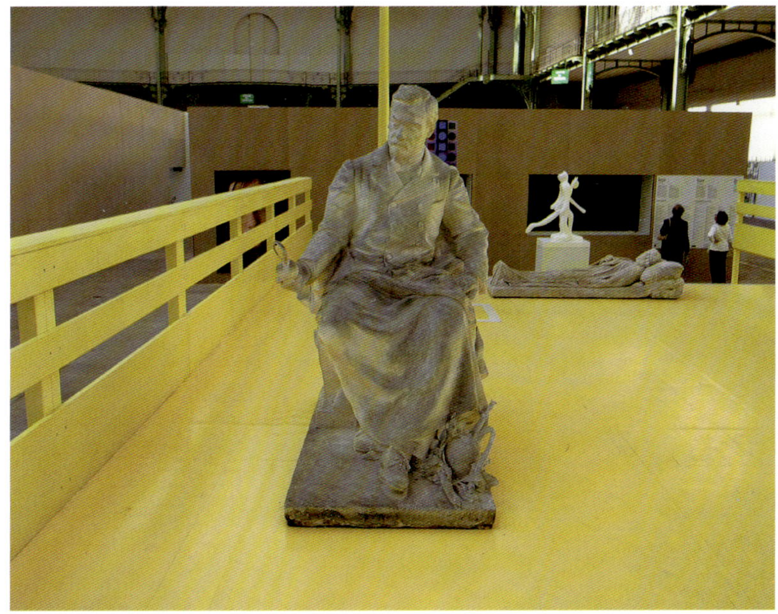
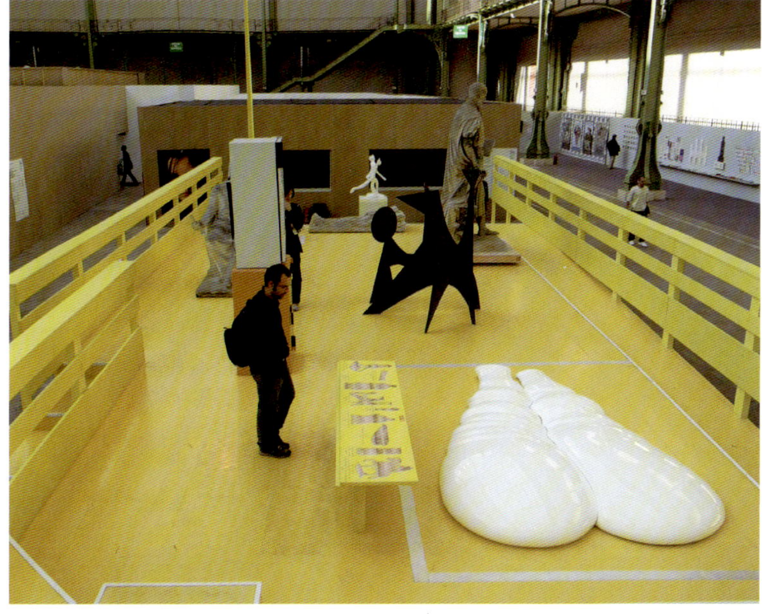
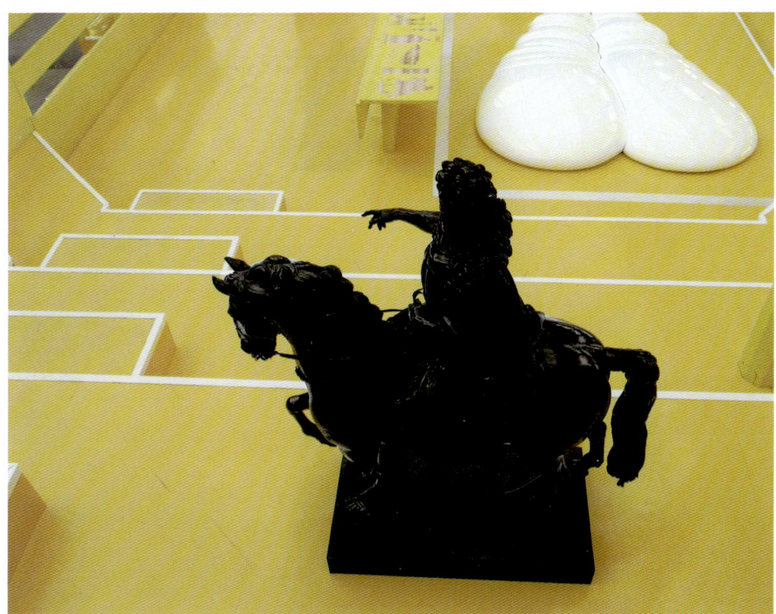
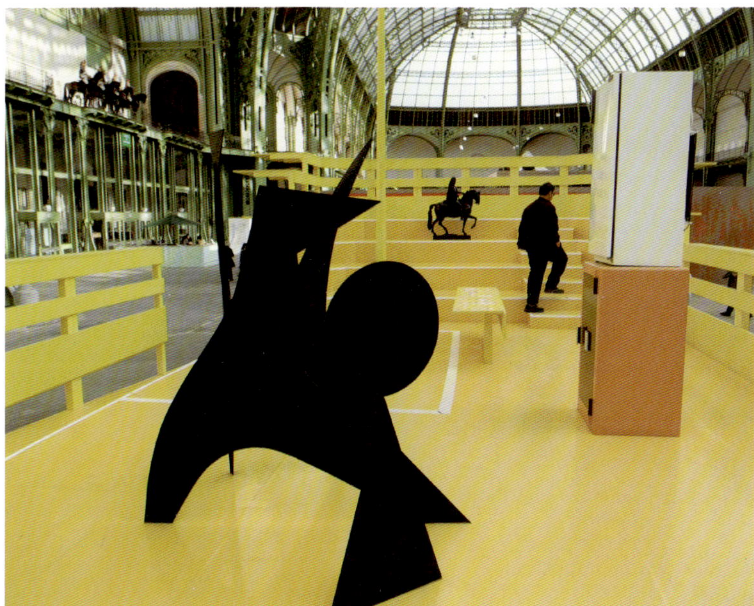

LE BARON DE TRIQUETI, 2006

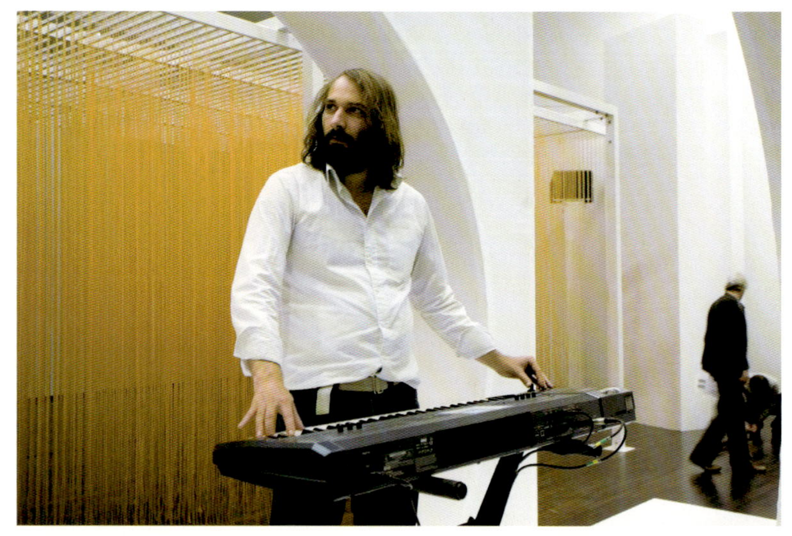

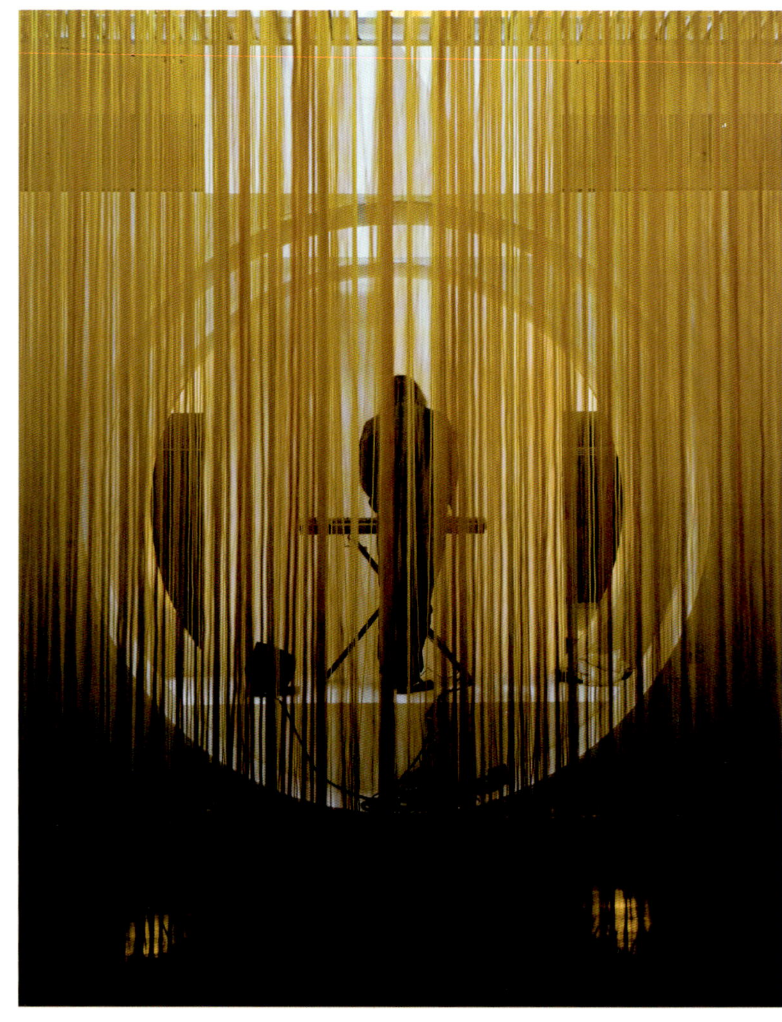

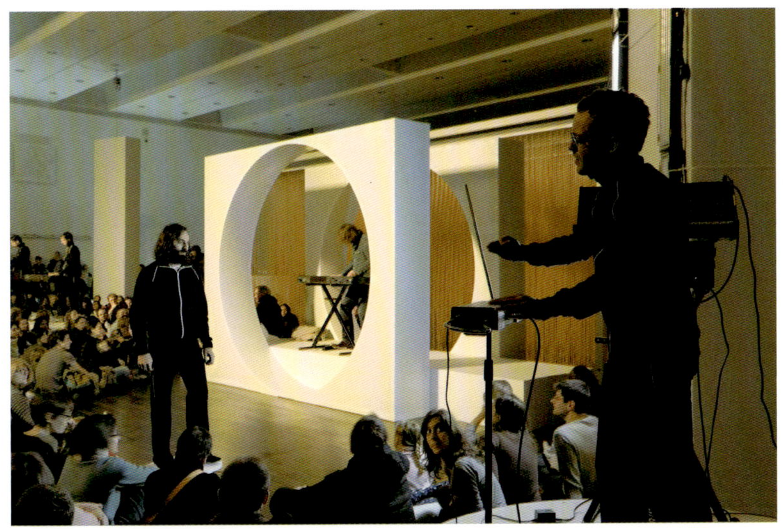 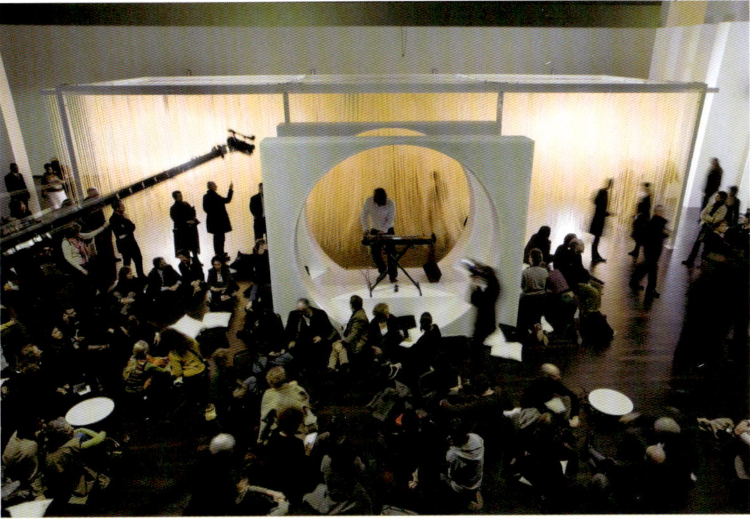

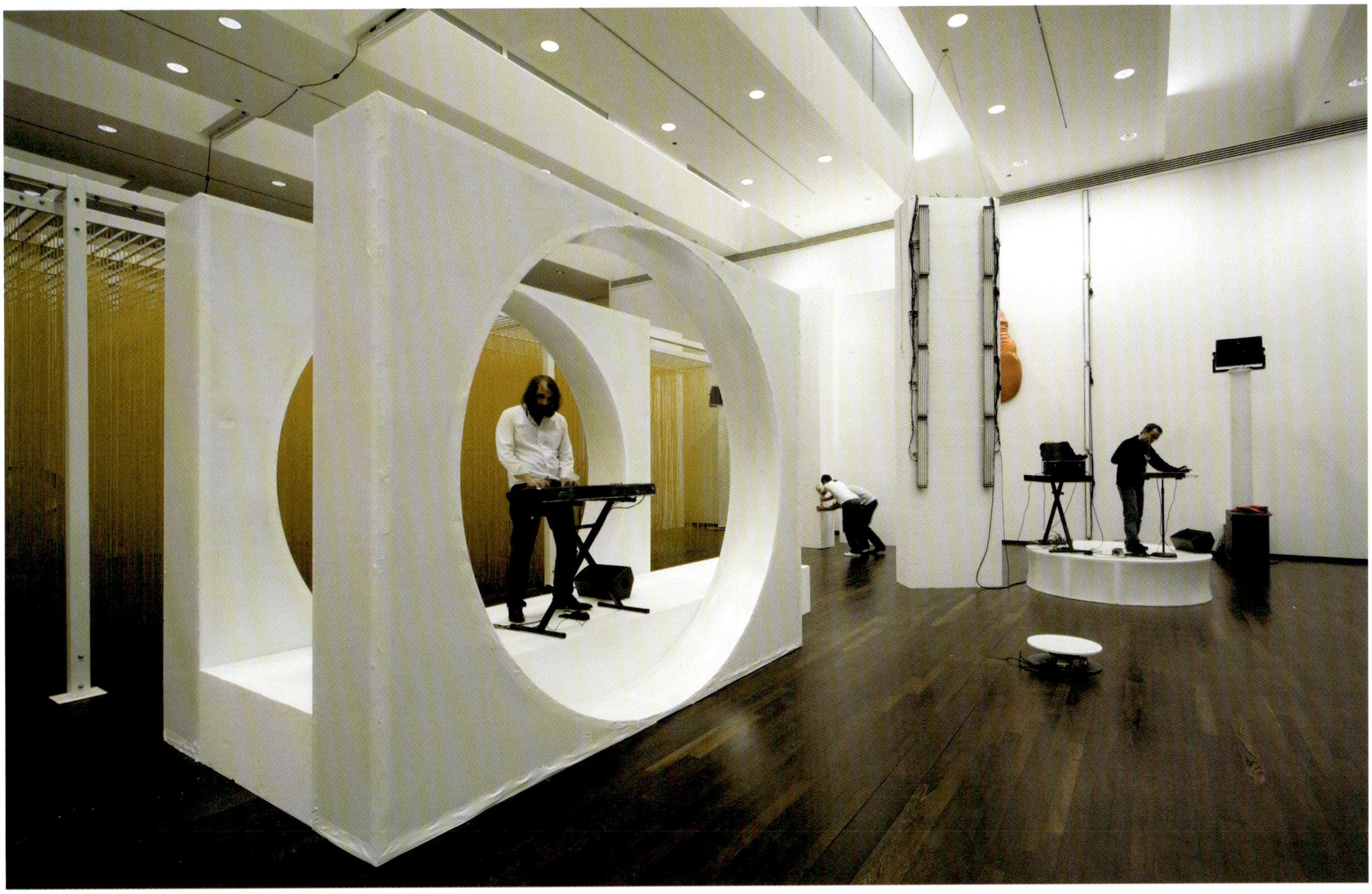

VAL DE MARNE, SHOW, 2006, MAC / VAL, VITRY

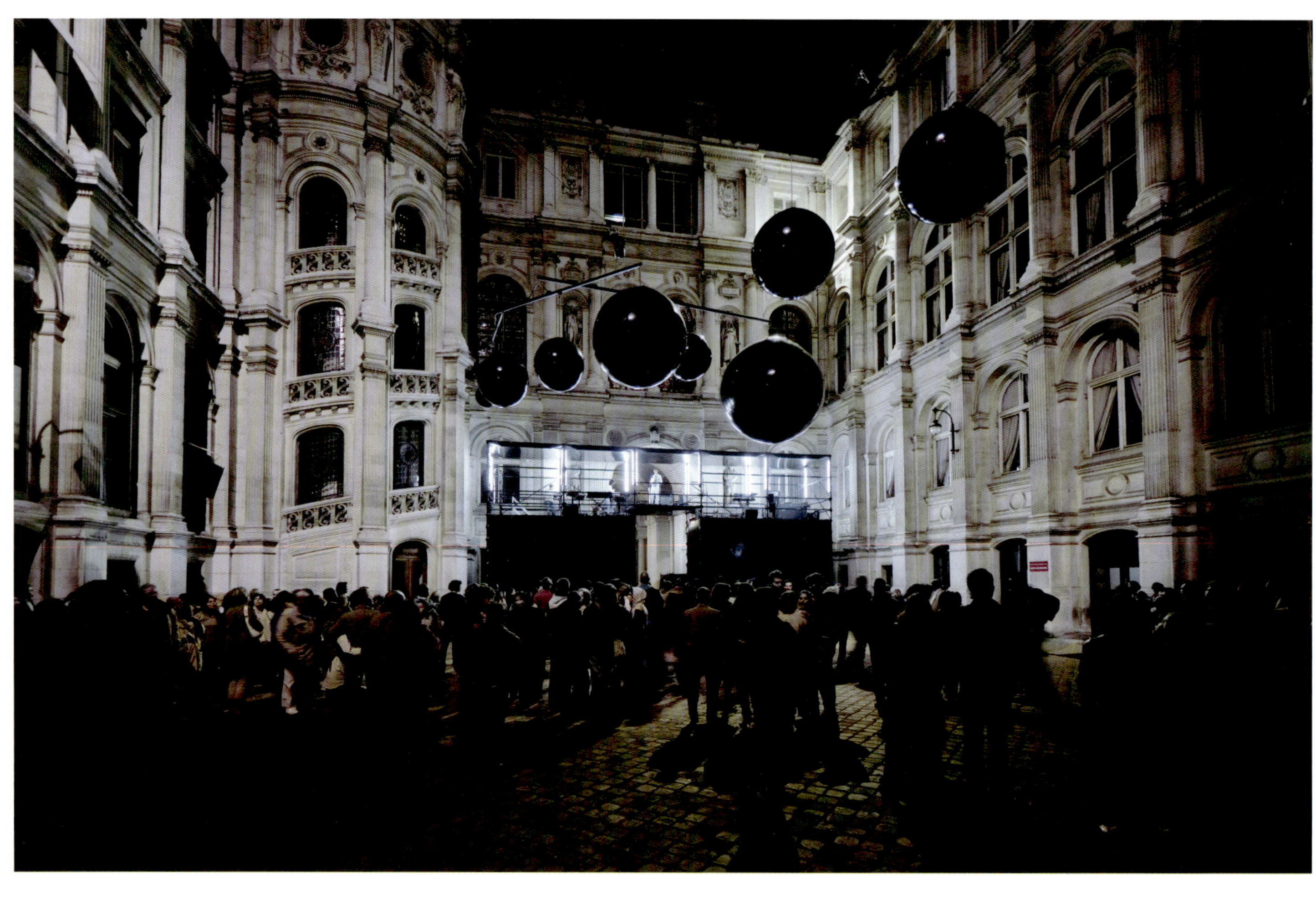

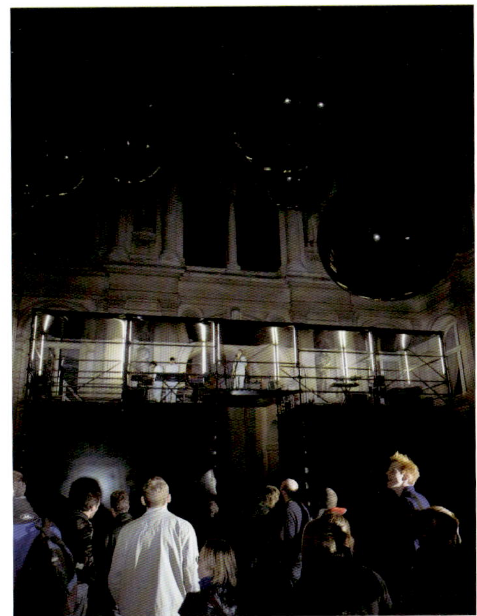

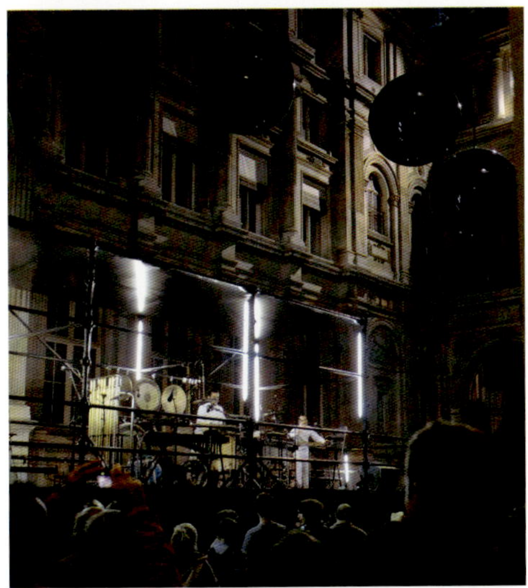

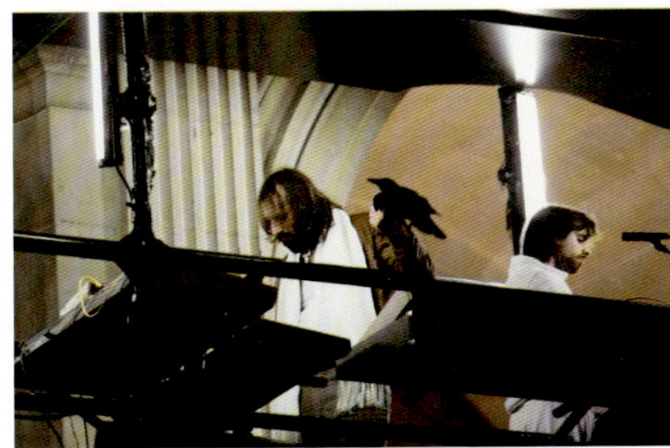

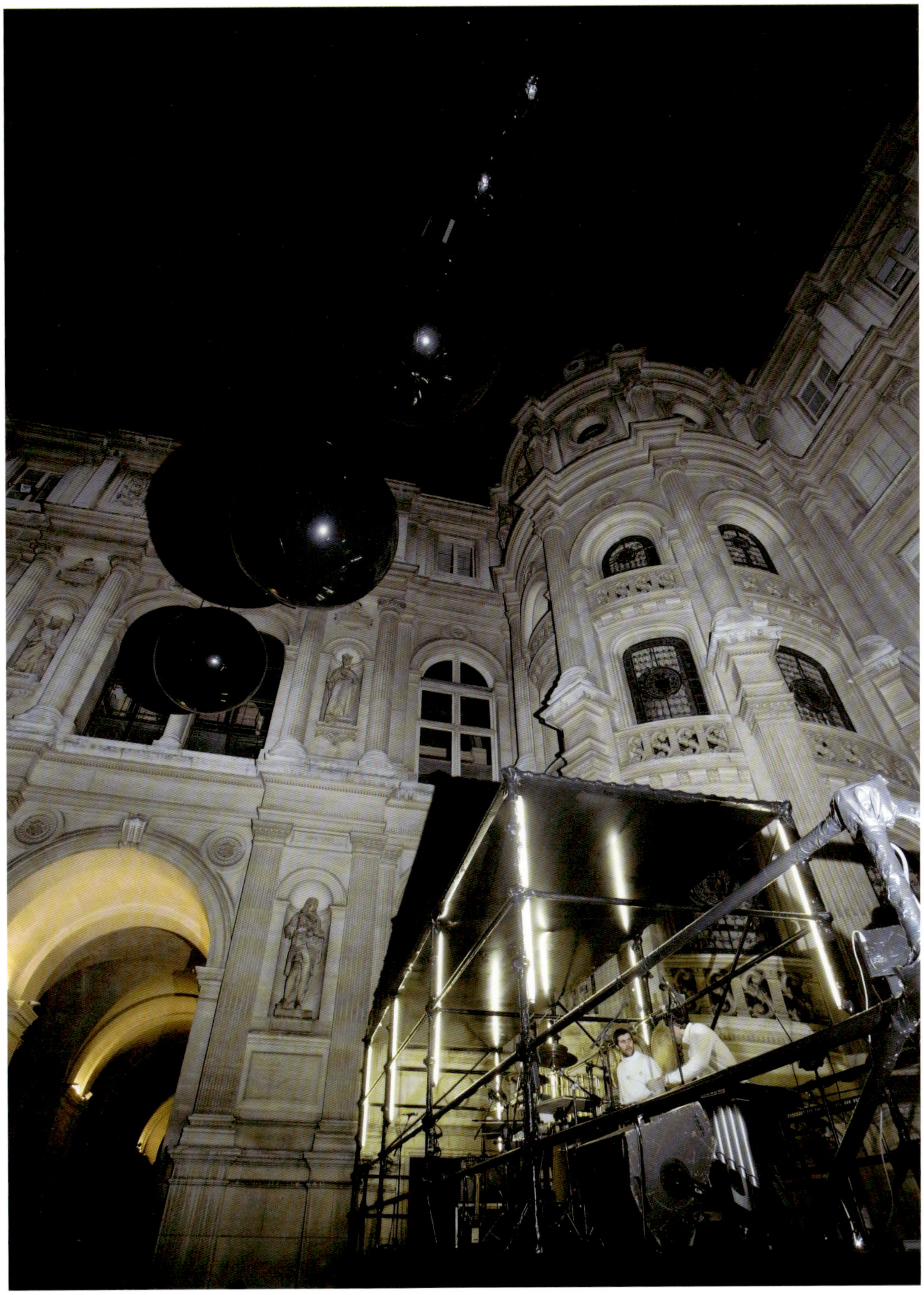

VILLE NOUVELLE, SHOW, 2006, NUIT BLANCHE, HÔTEL DE VILLE, PARIS

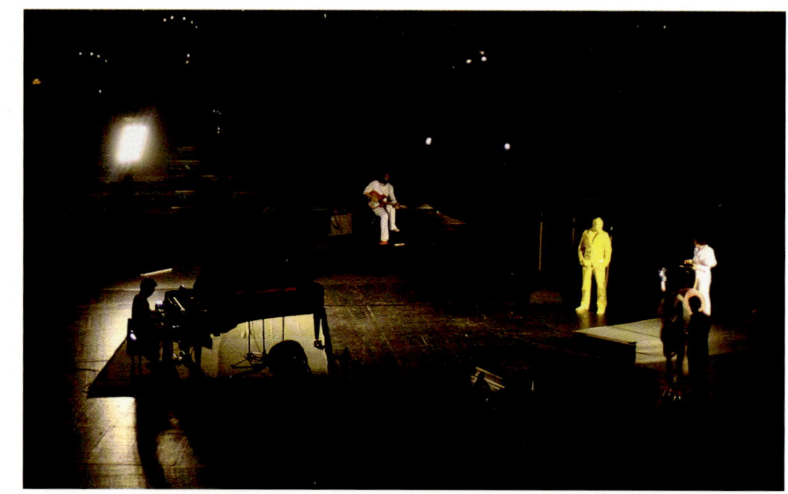

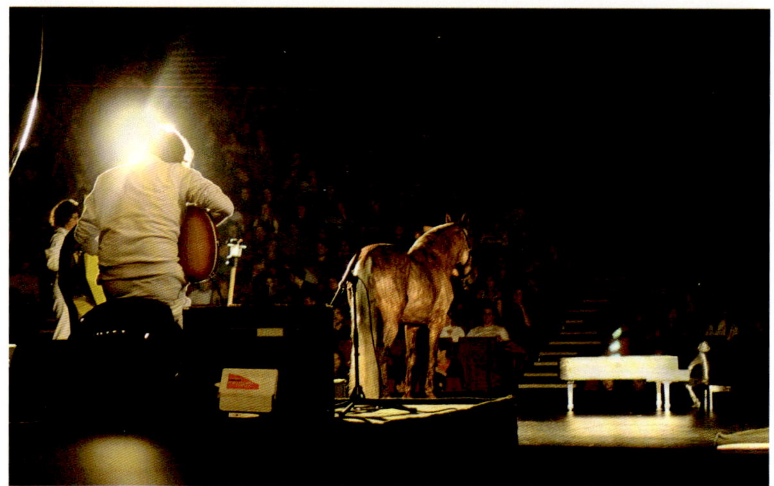

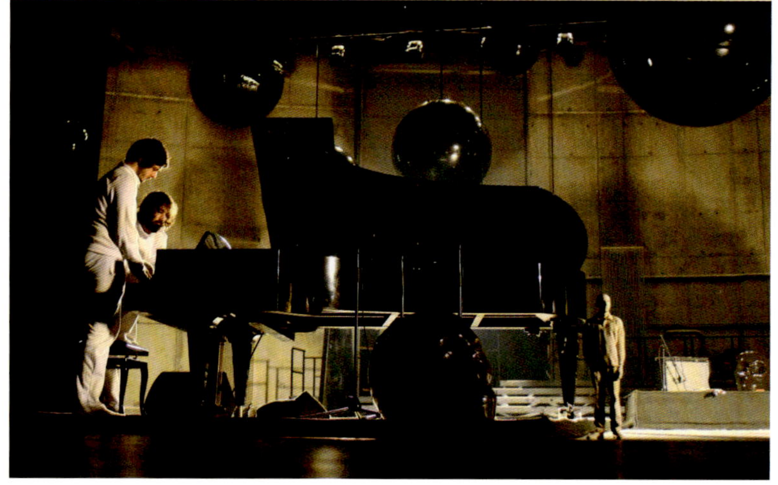

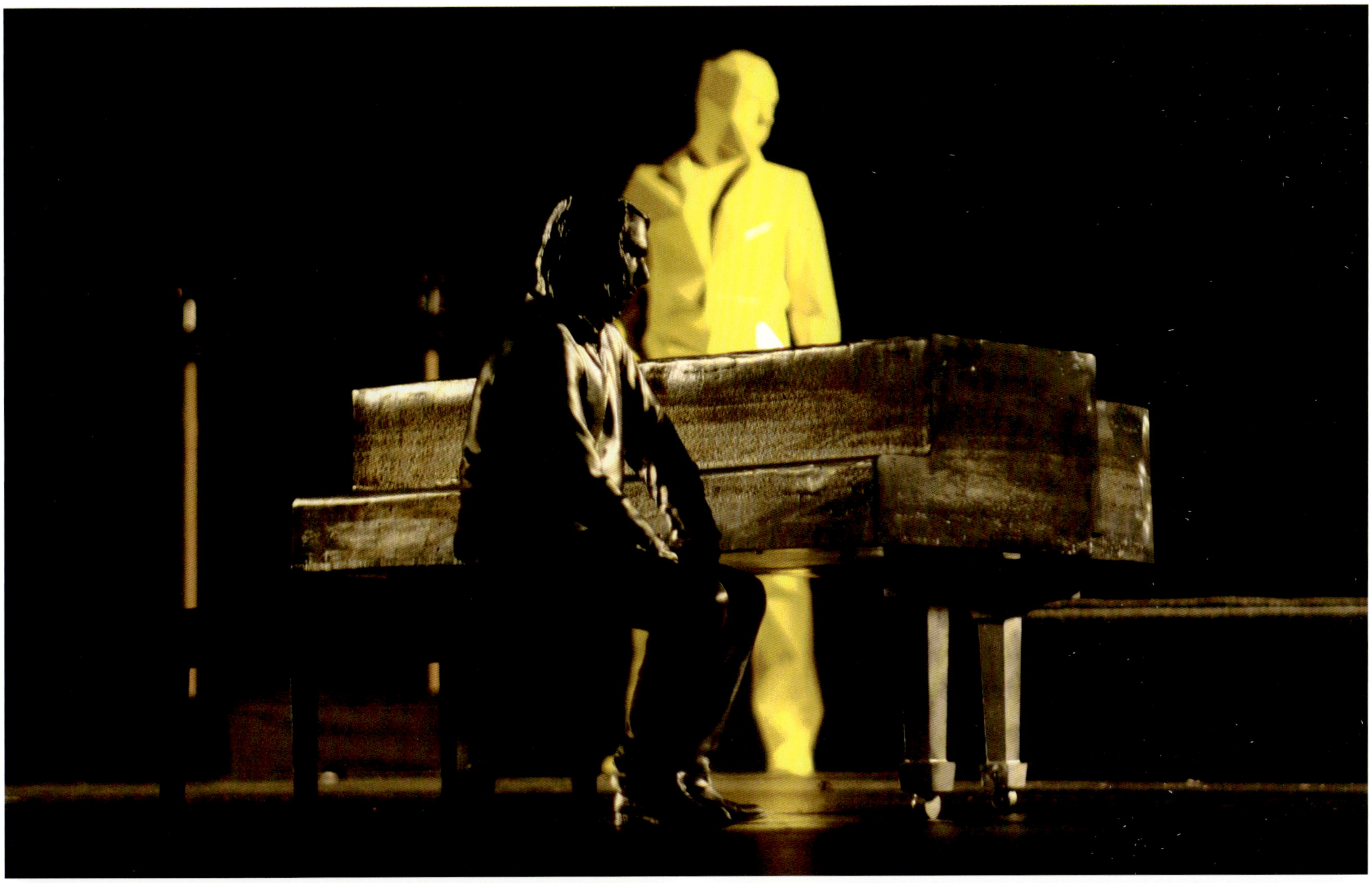

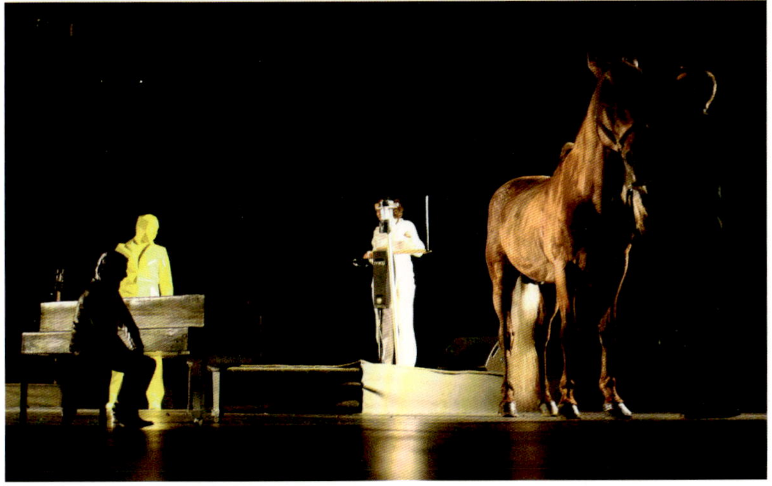

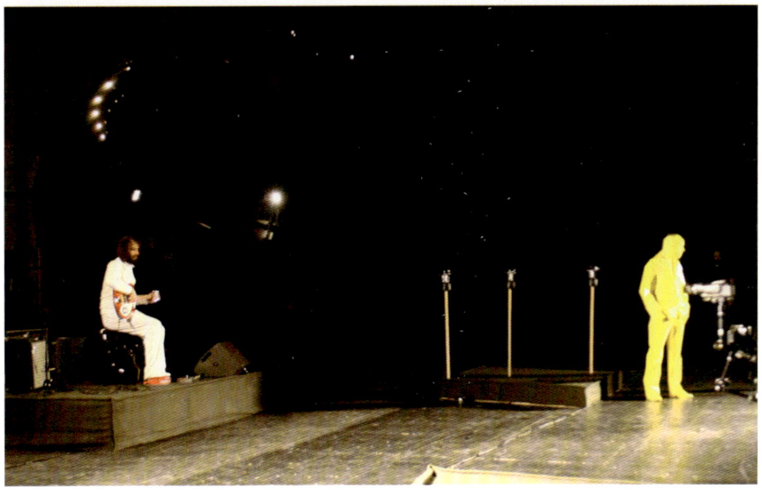

SÉBASTIEN TELLIER RENCONTRE XAVIER VEILHAN, SHOW, EXIT FESTIVAL, MAISON DES ARTS, CRÉTEIL, 2006

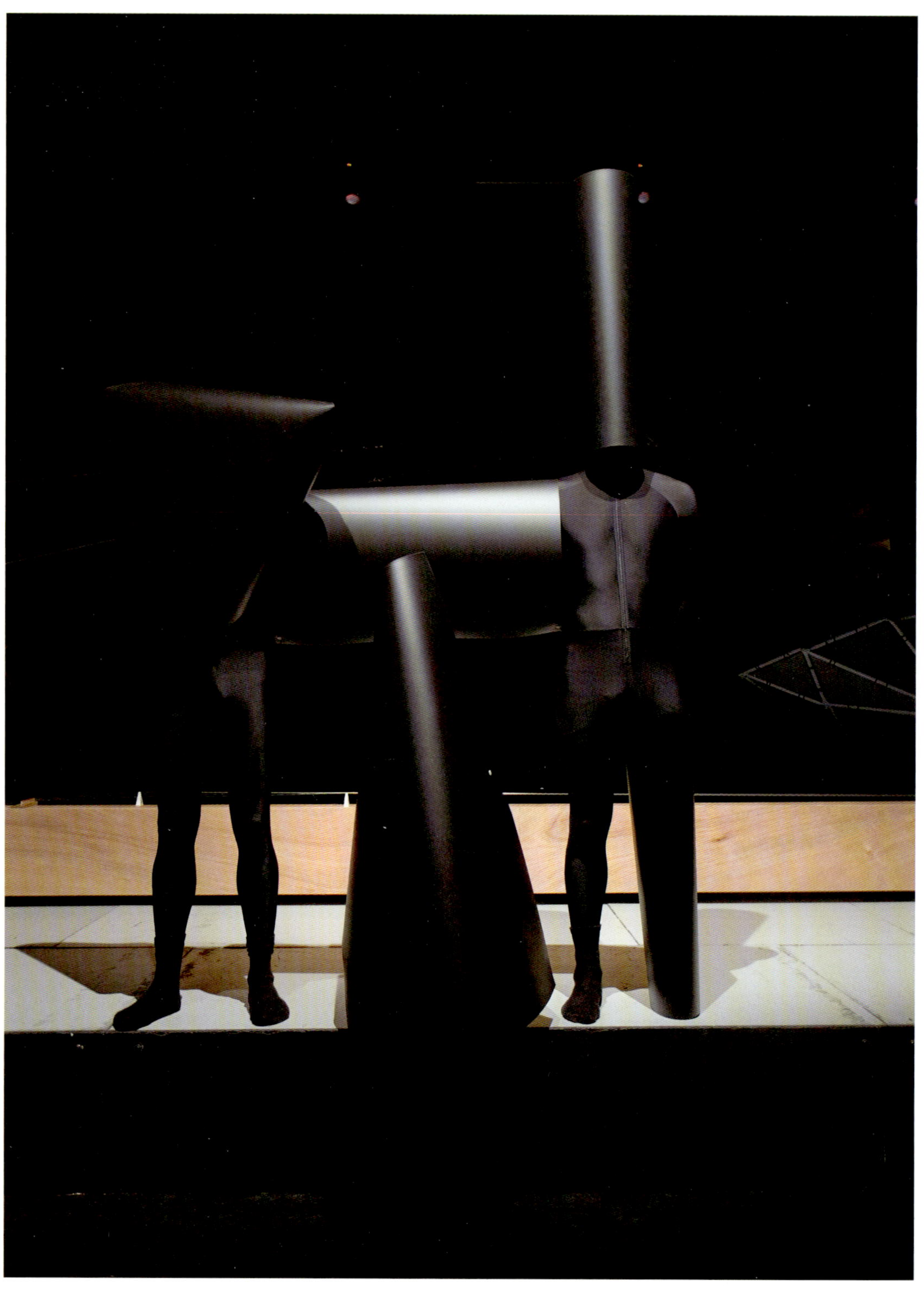

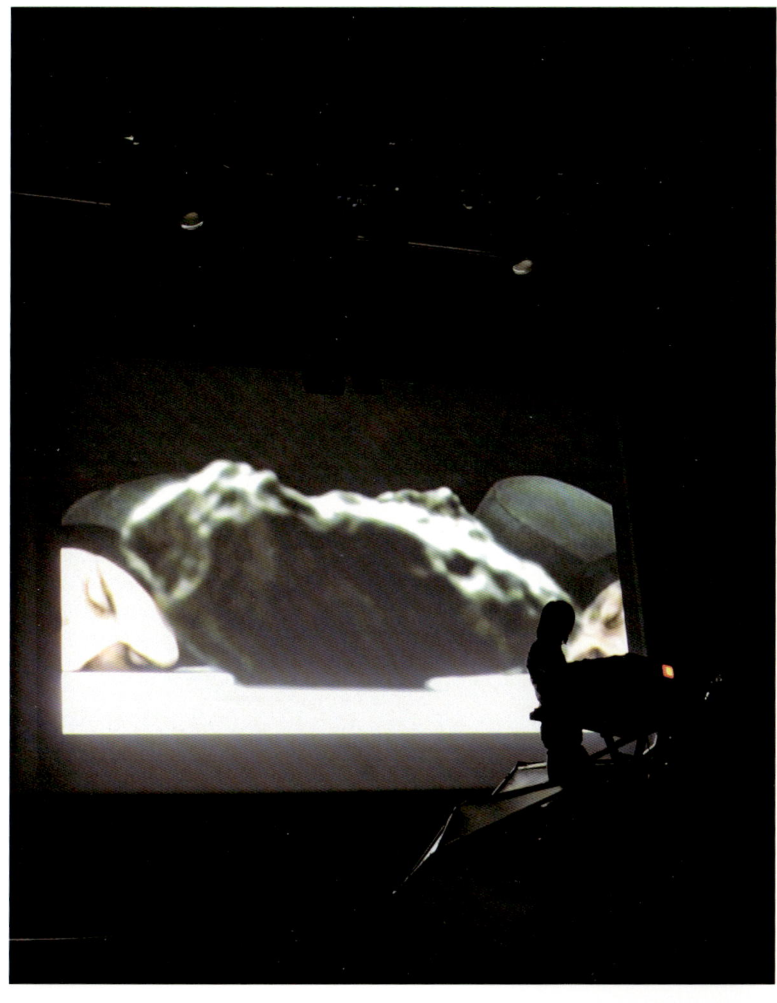
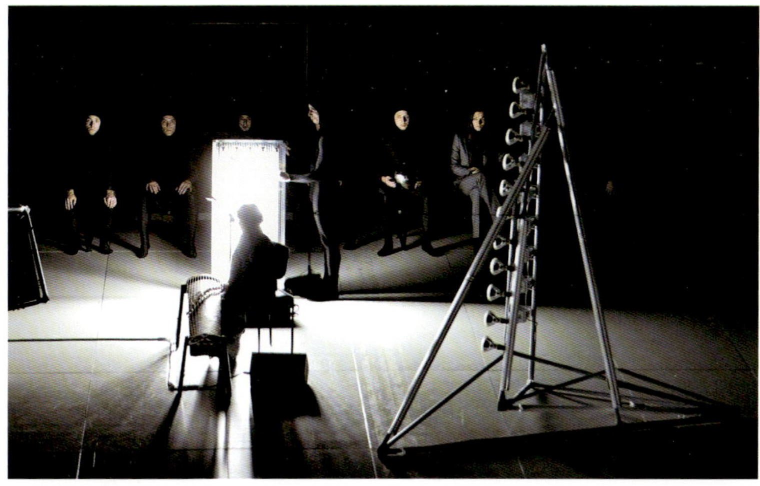
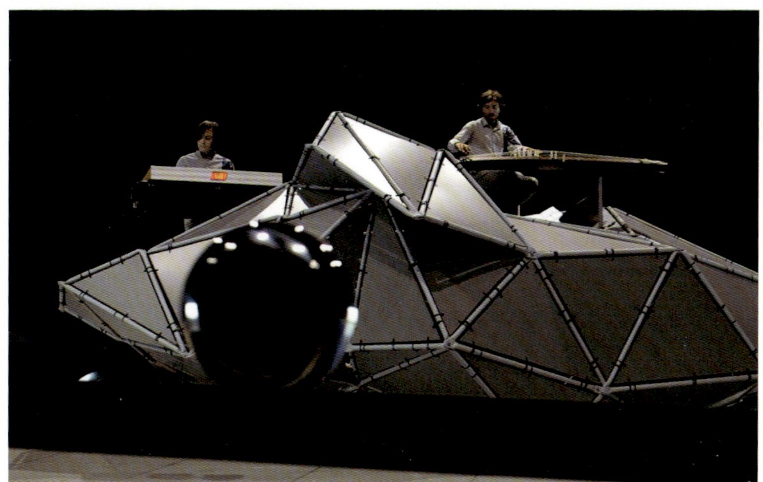
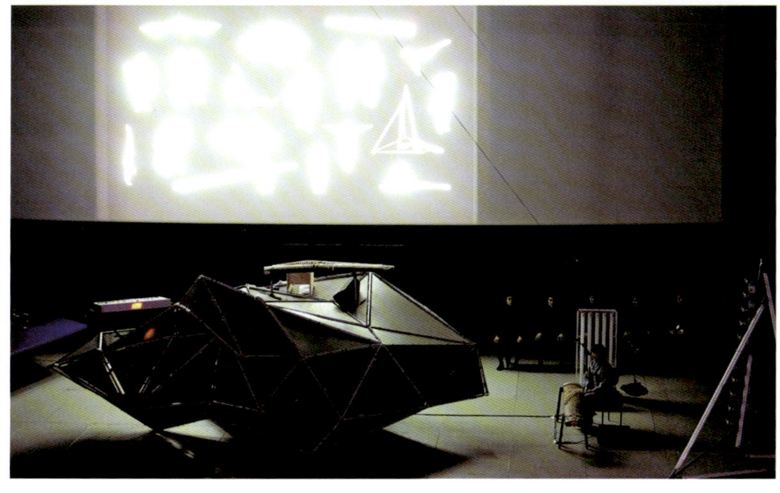
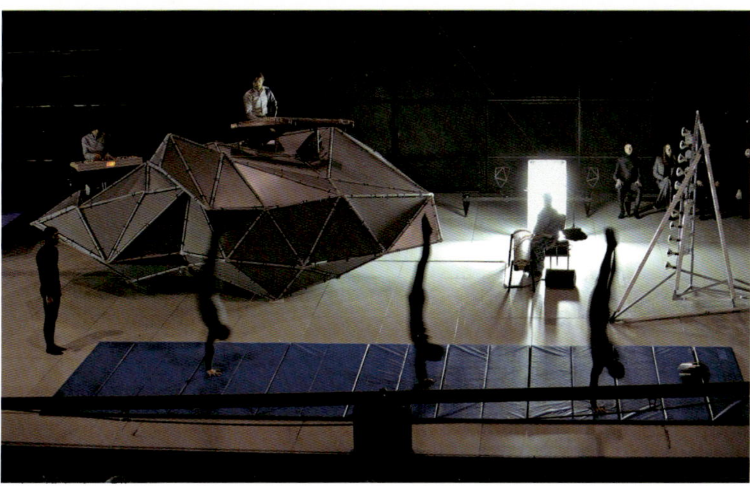

AÉROLITE, SHOW, 2007, CENTRE POMPIDOU, PARIS

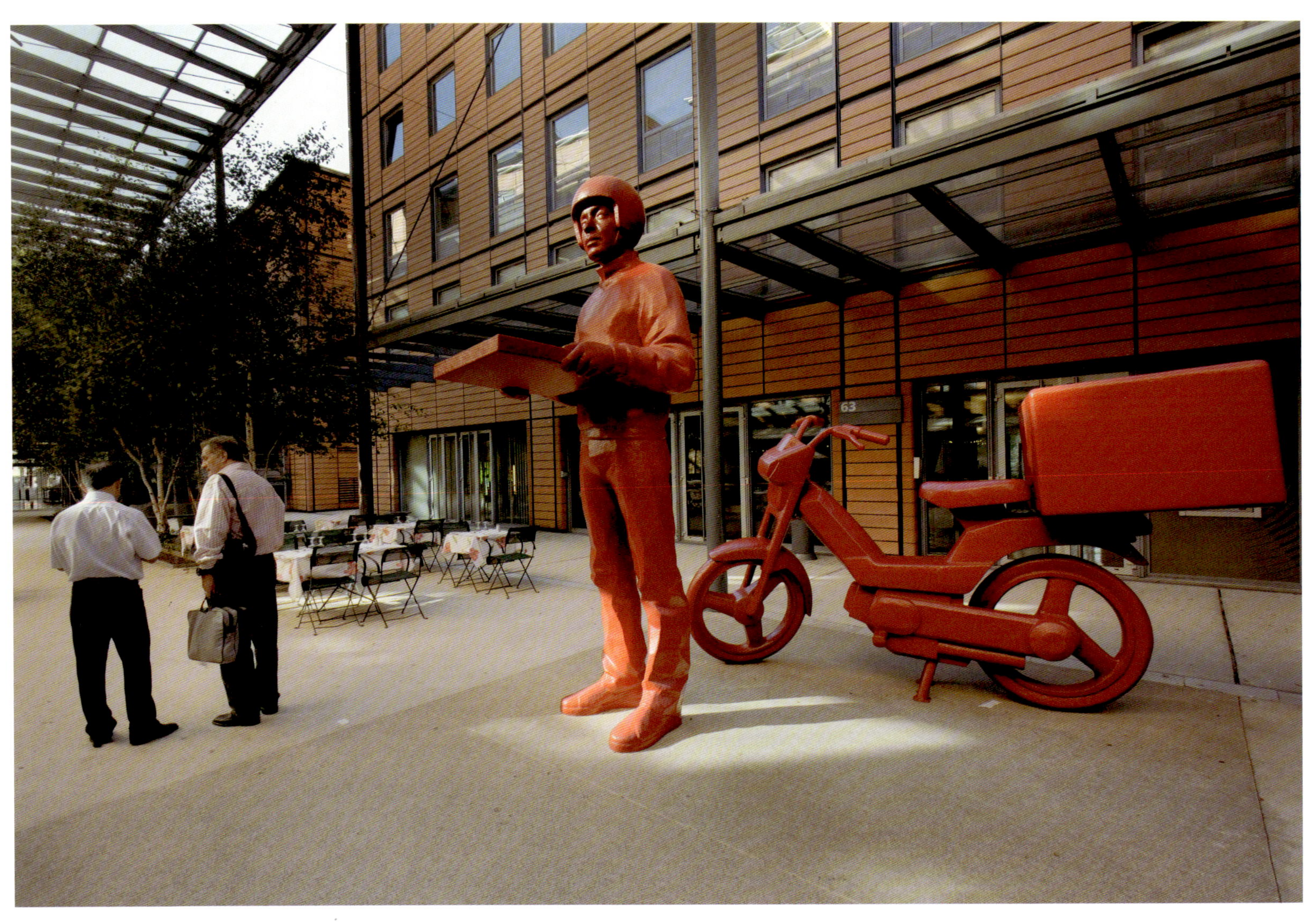

PIZZA DELIVERER (LES HABITANTS), 2006

A VEHICLE IN SIXTEEN STAGES (MEANDERING THROUGH XAVIER VEILHAN'S WORKS)

Pierre Senges

1 The tortoise—Zeno's, I mean, pursued by Achilles: lazy but unpassable, ambling along like all its ilk, adorned with diamond shapes, and seemingly able to carry effortlessly on its shell the lightest riddles concerning space and time: proof that one can evoke notions of speed while progressing from dune to sea at the slow pace of the sand (the rock, slower than the sand). As I speak, the tortoise is probably wandering somewhere near the Gulf of Salerno: indifferent to the indifference of everyone, philosophers, paraphilosophers, logicians, and strollers, not even offended (a tortoise can't be offended), it carries on, as though wishing to expound, as it creeps along, its own version of the paradoxes, and too bad for mathematics. (After careful consideration, in 2,500 years of non-stop walking, it must have covered a good many miles, one way or another, crossing the same borders ten, 12 times, in the rain, right up to this road, right here, where it might represent the contrary of a pothole: and it could be that I drove over it, no more than a minute ago, as if I'd wanted to compare two means of transport.)

2 I'm the vehicle: I eat up the miles as I jolt my way along; I have a vague desire to be a landscape painter, I'd like to catalogue the sidewalks and the stopping places; I am conscious of my being and conscious of my consciousness; I contain and give shelter at the same time, combining transport with play, I could lay bare a much deeper complexity by displaying my mechanisms, valves, and pistons, and it wouldn't take me hours and hours to show the range of my reason—but, to witnesses' eyes, I am but a vehicle: placid, gleaming, heavy, graceless, moiré, and warm, in which, when stationary, wood rubs against wood (or steel against steel); I'm a little (though not much) wheezy, busily throbbing and scurrying around when on the road; however, once under way, e.g. down a slope, I'm endowed with a grace unknown to toads and toadstools, restricted to birds: I'm referring to speed (it eludes but delights me—it would give club armchairs, the big fat ones, trailing along the ground, the look of a javelin).

3 Oh, I could speed along on my own: I know how to convert time into distance—life in front of me? Maybe, we'll see, but the space underneath me, for sure (a vehicle, it must be said, likes to speak about miles). My calling has always been to go from one place to another without ever taking one particular place as my core concern: lying down is not my strong point, occupying, even less; for better or for worse, I leave elegies on the motherland and sonnets on the native home to more settled poets; I know not the meaning of the word "here," derived as it is from an exotic dialect, and will confine myself throughout my life to a discourse on distance, and how I feed on it.

4 I am ignorant of how the snake gets self-knowledge, or at least a vague notion of its being a snake: maybe when coiling round a tree trunk so as to see itself from behind, then sliding on its spine (sustained curiosity is unavoidable, through sensuousness, complacency and nascent reptilian narcissism). Nor do I know how the fly gets by, liable as it is to collide, to take the wrong road, to follow imperfect circles right in the middle of rooms—I for one judge from my shadow, in the evening, in the morning, from the marks of my wheels on the ground, the noise of my prow and stern, the creaking and scraping, and finally, from the headwind (if it skirts me, if it thwarts me), to which must be added, but this is more delicate, the shapes of my passengers: my science of transport is sketchy, empirical; to arrive at it I had to swallow a lot of sand, though something tells me that the container and the contained are somehow related: in terms of proximity, ergonomics, barter, shared interests, intermingling forms, and matching colors.

5 I contain—and having reached my destination (which claims to be my victory, it's the well-being of my passengers: this confounded destination, I got to it by turning my four wheels clockwise, but no one else enjoys it to the full: in it, they wallow, relax, feed and, who knows, plant cabbages there, or place their luggage on it), having reached my destination, doors are opened, I adopt the behavior of a beetle: along both my flanks there's a running board that can be pressed into service. Thus I remain, empty of my contents, cooling down, out of place, with my face screwed up to resist the head wind—my contents, two or three of those people, maybe my owners, maybe just coach travelers, don't show me much gratitude: I'm fobbed off with a flick of a rag on the mudguard and a kick on the tires (if they're rubber). (Believe me, or believe me not: I have contained royal blood—how can I say this? I have jolted crowned heads, and not just princely ones, possibly in ceremonial dress, going through the town gates to visit their people: a monarch on the back seat, periwig shaken at each bend in the road, enjoying the suspension as if it were his childhood cradle or, who knows, a symbol of consideration due to his rank: my springs and cushions and foam rubber are what need to be interposed between the bumpiness of our ground and the munificent bum of a king, equipollent with azure and gules.)

6 I am not unaware of the landscape: nose to the grindstone, or even to the handlebars, with a narrow field aperture—this has never prevented me from enjoying the view at either side of my journey, such as red carpet, guards of honor, verges and sides, splashes on the way and long parvis at my journey's end. The fact is that for such a vehicle as me, the landscape exists, comes into existence; it's the world itself, barely flattened out, that my eager speed tends to elbow aside without ever preventing me from saluting it in passing, showing it marks of my respect according to its merits, the respect owed by the transient to the permanent—in any case, I'd be well advised to raise my hat to it, to the landscape: the tiniest lapse in concentration and I'd be part of it once and for all, me and my content; now a remarkable ruin, flat on my back.

7 And I have a feeling for perspective: the number of artists I've carried and shaken, some wiping their rags en route, others stirring turpentine, sharpening charcoal, cutting things with knives. In just a few seasons, I've known Impressionists, Tachists, amusing surveyors, poets using blue for lack of red, engineers, masters of chiaroscuro, fuzziness and smokiness, master of absent contour, as one says of demi-figures, others who sprayed their oil onto the canvas, "on the motif." There's no one now who can tell me what to do: skyline, vanishing point, geometry, shrinkage, the pure square gone trapezoid—I know all that; I know how to tell the real from the fake, I have seen black and white checkered pavements, I have seen straight lines drawing close together, but I know also how to accept invitations to those magic places where parallel lines end up meeting: with a mixture of composure and incredulity, and the laugh reserved for jokes too often heard.

8 If it's not already the case: one of these days, I'll be a magnificent wreck: people will descend to the depths of the water to admire my shells; lovers of the beautiful, and collectors in their bathyscaphs, will come to see how the moray eel haunts me, how I gorge, bloat myself on sponges, store up treasures that got lost the same time I got lost, in the same shipwreck. I'll be pitiful as well as wonderful, and delightful commentaries will be drawn out of me, snippets of history will be deduced, and human lives conjured up at the sight of my rims—once engulfed, I'll accept pity and envy. Means will have to be found to set me afloat again with the hope of opening my coffers and seeing precious stones pour out of them, green glints, blue glints, contradictory, or silverware—if not, I'll refloat myself: it'll be a natural movement, restoring the balance with the help of Archimedes: from below the surface of a lake, unexpectedly, right in the middle of the afternoon, under a pale grey sky, I'll rise from the water and appear to fishermen: it'll be as blunt as the cork bursting out of a champagne bottle, with bubbles, drums, and splashes, I'll appear without warning, like an archaism brought back to light, or rather a miracle: the ship of the future, impatient to reveal itself to humans.

9 Or I'll be the wreck on the verge, lacking the majesty of the ocean's depths, and the mock lightness, the mock imponderability (and the background of dancing seaweed) suggested by water: a strip of earth, nothing else, two stones, mushrooms, bits of wrapping also washed up, balloons, and inner tubes—and I'll be doomed to dry out, gradually to lose the thickness of my flesh, or at least what served as flesh, filigreed by winds and oxidation, soon to show the setting sun a kind of framework I'd never previously known; from afar, against the light, one will be able to make out various carcasses: camel, iguanodon, beluga, immense sardine, or tapir, or odd-toed ungulates (rhinoceros unicornis). Through this carcass of hoops and spokes, as through a willow dummy, air will enter, also a few gazes, dawn and dusk, rain, dead leaves, and entire families of field mice—some witnesses will try to guess at what I'd been from what I've become.

10 A vehicle shelters, carries, dashes, makes up for lost time, but sometimes also hinges and links and flashes; it braves the rain head-on, the forks and humpback bridges, the three-way junctions which, on the world scale, are the mark of the devil on the landscape. The vehicle has various other tasks, it also knows about accidents, the way a warm-blooded creature knows, let's say, about love and setbacks: it may then lose some of its control, roar when it should be silent, open its big mouth when it should keep quiet—besides hurtling down, it rushes at an obstacle without knowing whether it's a wall or a dog, a hairpin or (for example) a clergyman from the time when they still wore cassocks and wended their way like gas-lamp extinguishers with their noses wedged between the Old and New Testaments. It may happen (I suppose) that I lose my way for a second and immediately knock down a figure so neatly outlined in the night, in the rain, that it looks like a diver in a tight-fitting rubber suit, lifting high his flippers at each step, indifferent to the world in his mask and snorkel. The accident needn't be painful, wetsuits can mitigate friction; or my victim might be lithe, might move like a ballet dancer, and the wetsuit might be a leotard—instead of a crisis, impact, and mishap, in any case, the accident could give rise to a very harmonious series of caresses, conflagrations, entrechats, muffled silences, and beautiful exchanges: maybe even some comprehension. I would have knocked down a human being, one who might refuse to leave me afterward, who might settle in as a spectator, lodger, companion, or guard on one or other part of my chassis, in my boot, somewhere, enmeshed like a bird in a cage or ensconced like a sleeper in a rocking chair. It would only take a thrust of the body, and the person, though free to leave, would apparently have chosen to take up residence there; I might at times feel like a whale that had Jonas behind its baleens; but instead of a prisoner, I could thus have a guide.

11 (Not always convinced of being a vehicle—why not a typewriter, after all? I click, cough, feel the quiver of small hammers and the roll of cylinders—or a sewing-machine? The old ones needed a pedal and gear, a wheel, a belt, a transmission system, might have pretended they were traveling, might pass for a handcar, were it not for the absence of rails. What do I need to warrant the title of vehicle? Waking up far from where I fell asleep? Or a sturdy back to carry passengers, though not the kind a bridge has, i.e. without the dogged, impassive, arched, or hunched posture of a dead dragon stiffened above a chasm? I need to be changeable without being a weather vane, to be burning without being a stove, to blow without being a balloon, to rotate without being a windmill, to go back and forth without being a weaving loom, to beat the bushes without being a beater at a hunt, and to move languorously at each hillock, but not to content myself with being a child's swing.)

12 I palpate myself: if I were a submarine, my body would be tense, I'd have no eyes or ears, and I would move forward blindly; if I were a locomotive, I'd feel the dizziness of rushing while hemmed in by two rails, and a nostalgia for coal. According to what little information I have about myself, to whatever I've picked up over the years, I have the feeling I'm a combination of cold mechanism and animal fire—this flatters me if it means I'm like one of those ancient Greek monsters, half this and half that, bull's head and horse's body; among my cousins I'd have the centaurs, along with unsettling congeries of eagle, goat, tiger, and serpent. I sometimes imagine having sprung from the union of a stallion and a cart: I am not their offspring, certainly not, no question here of descent, but of the mating itself, latent, going on from the first day, as if horse and cart had become inseparable and had resigned themselves to be living this way—a slightly grotesque way, maybe, but not so unpleasant at that, given their passionate love.

13 A vehicle doesn't settle for going from point a to point ξ by following the most practical line: it can also be a shelter, it can be used as a refuge, an inn at a pinch, and, for extended visits, a villa, with main entrance, hall, rooms, and lean-to. One owes one's passengers a minimum of comfort, scale, lighting, warmth, transparency of windows, the hospitality of a country fireplace in the winter, armrests, footrests, reasonable ceiling height. The laws of hospitality, however, are not compatible with those of transport, if transport means performance, efficiency, combustion, miles swallowed and immediately spat out again: the rules of comfort are at odds with a desire for speed, which longs for smallness—all of us cheat, more or less, so what? By trickery and optical illusions, miracles of interlocking, phony scale invariants, and misleading homothecy, insides that are wider than the outside, like a lining twice as big as a coat. Does it work? God only knows, as well as a few engineers, to whom we owe our life—personally, I'd like to be lived in and driven by one of Velázquez's dwarves, in attractive costume, as seen in most of his paintings: they don't always look too friendly, but they don't get in the way, this is the main thing—and they have a very highly developed sense of courtesy, I know of nothing so salutary in confined spaces.

14 The breakdown: a chance to laugh at my own expense, a chance given to pedestrians, those creatures trailing along at anteater speed, conscious of being slow and clumsy creatures, with dangling arms, for whom wandering around means losing balance and regaining it just in time, then losing it, then regaining it anew—so happy to see me, the vehicle, the impressive steed, resting by the roadside, in a bad way. At such times, they may well feel, let's say, as free as a draught, certainly not as a bird; they rest their superb human autonomy on the arch of their feet—while I, then, remain, to experience immobility, with cover open, entrails exposed, definitely out of it. This is the breakdown, I creak, though less and less, and above all I grow duller: to get me going would need a landslide; meanwhile I'm pitiable, and I know it: meanwhile, auscultation, feeling my edges, my angles, my surfaces, my abscissae, my ordinates, my lumbar vertebrae, my hubs, my diameters, my diagonals, and, much deeper inside, the hidden backroom from which, miraculously (ingeniously), movement is transmitted. I'm also being decorticated: as if removing the bare essential might make me overflow with energy—under the gaze, still, of passersby (poking fun), I let myself be hollowed out, with no fear of appearances—no fear of death, I mean—persuaded as I am that breakdowns are the best way to reach a higher level of efficiency: progress, in a word, refinement, and from one breakdown to the next, from one accident to the next, the perfection of my being. I'm not being repaired, I'm being clarified and, as the wounds accumulate, I'll end up turning into the flying fish I've always sworn I'd become: speeding along as a conqueror under the very noses of the witnesses, above the milestones.

15 Who knows what keeps me alive (no one, is the answer, least of all myself): a gentle slope might suffice as an illusion or subterfuge to drive me forward and provide a reason for my existence, slowly at first, then faster and faster. If I'm a dirigible, recognizable by my hospitable sausage profile, then air and wind are what keep me alive, as well as the chubbiness of my flanks—if I'm a flatboat, I'm given life by the lapping water, for which I have the utmost respect—if I happened to have the harsher, heavier shapes of an automobile, it's petrol vapors: ill-contained, cramped, compressed in a jar that cannot but tremble, they do their level best to escape, shaking me as they do—if I'm a velocipede, my soul (my life) is a thing of balance, with a center radiating out to its periphery—if I'm an old plough, I move like a wardrobe, tilting—if I'm a wheelbarrow, a single wheel will be insufficient for my claim to vehicle-hood, and I'll have to settle for membership of the kneading trough family. (As a penny-farthing, I draw my raison d'être from the contrast between two wheels: one grandiose, circadian, the true wheel of fate and fortune, the other tiny, on the scale of a toy bell chiming at the end of a tail and giving gentlemen their arched-back posture: dignity personified.)

16 There are various ways to die—the worse (probably) is to rust in a field and agonize for a hundred years, black lace, then red, then grey (so many centuries needed for a return to the earth; this is not so much immortality as inertia, or what might be called the doggedness of the vehicle). Or to sink and catch fire, to leave this desolate land in flames, dragon or devil's glory, instability of fuels—or again, the accident: to die and be swept to the side by a street cleaner, to litter the ground for six months, if not 12, and be cannibalized, part by part, until all that remains of myself is a pool of oil or a chewed-up leather harness. Otherwise, a return to where I probably came from: workshop or barn, where I was valiantly constructed, fitting this into that, adjusting verticals onto horizontals, which, after all, is the beginning of all works—I'll be dragged there, I suppose, the day after the day I can no longer manage another turn of the wheel: they'll remove the nails from the planks and loosen the bolts, they'll relieve me, they'll remove everything that pins me to the ground and weighs on my shoulders; I'll feel as though liberated from my armor, I'll wait for the moment when I'm naked, without sheet metal or battens; I'll hope to live the minute when I'm once more just a soul torn from a body, sublime, luminous in the light—the miracle of evading the fate of matter by evaporating into the sky: it's my due. Except it won't happen exactly like that: there'll be neither nakedness nor a soul, luminous in the light; I'll disappear entirely, I'll be mute once the last nail is gone; I will be neither in my entirety nor in any of my parts, there'll be nothing left of myself other than the idea of a journey, and some vague reminiscence of Zeno's tortoise, lazy, almost at a standstill, and yet unpassable.

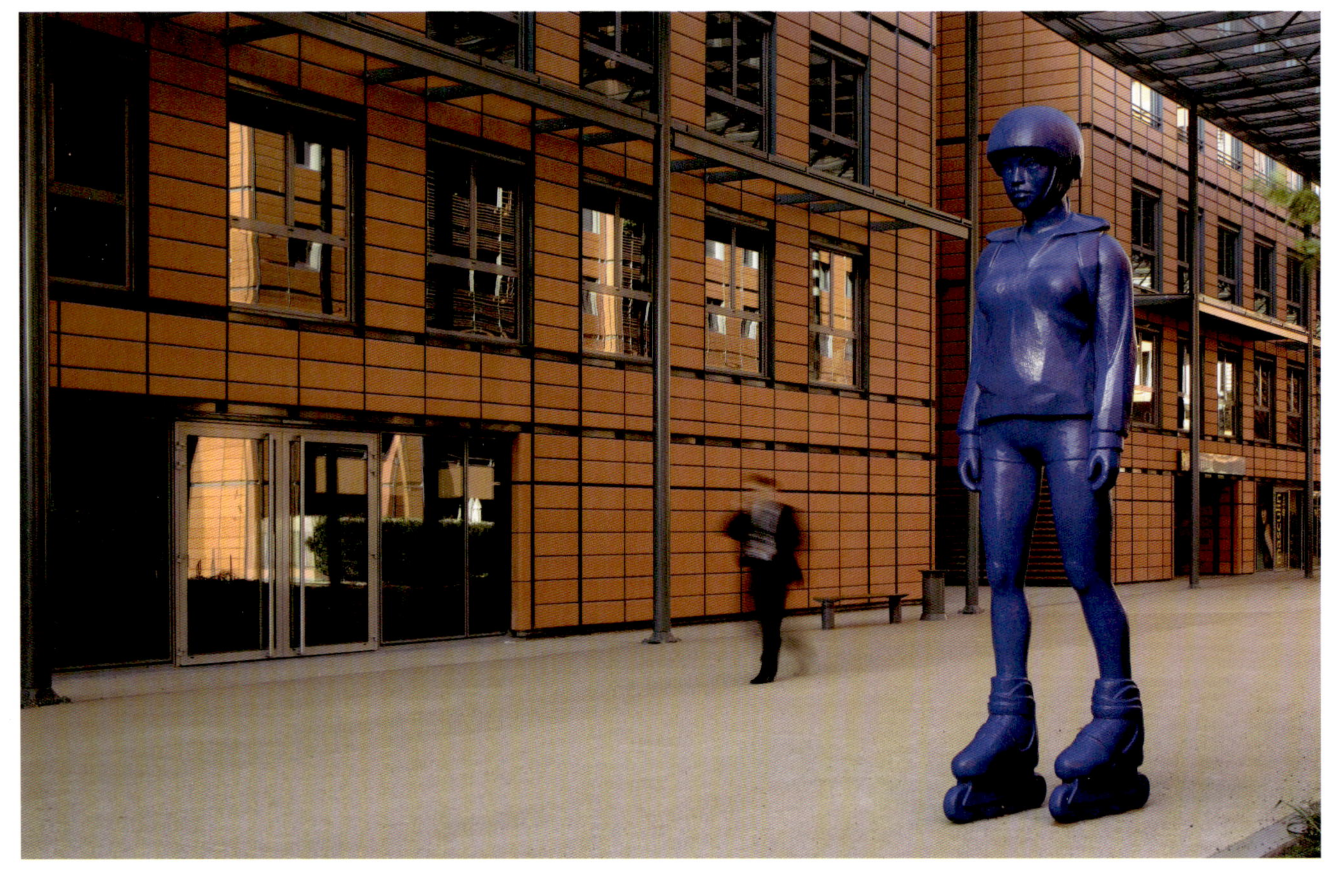

THE ROLLER GIRL (LES HABITANTS), 2006. PERMANENT INSTALLATION, CITÉ INTERNATIONALE, LYON

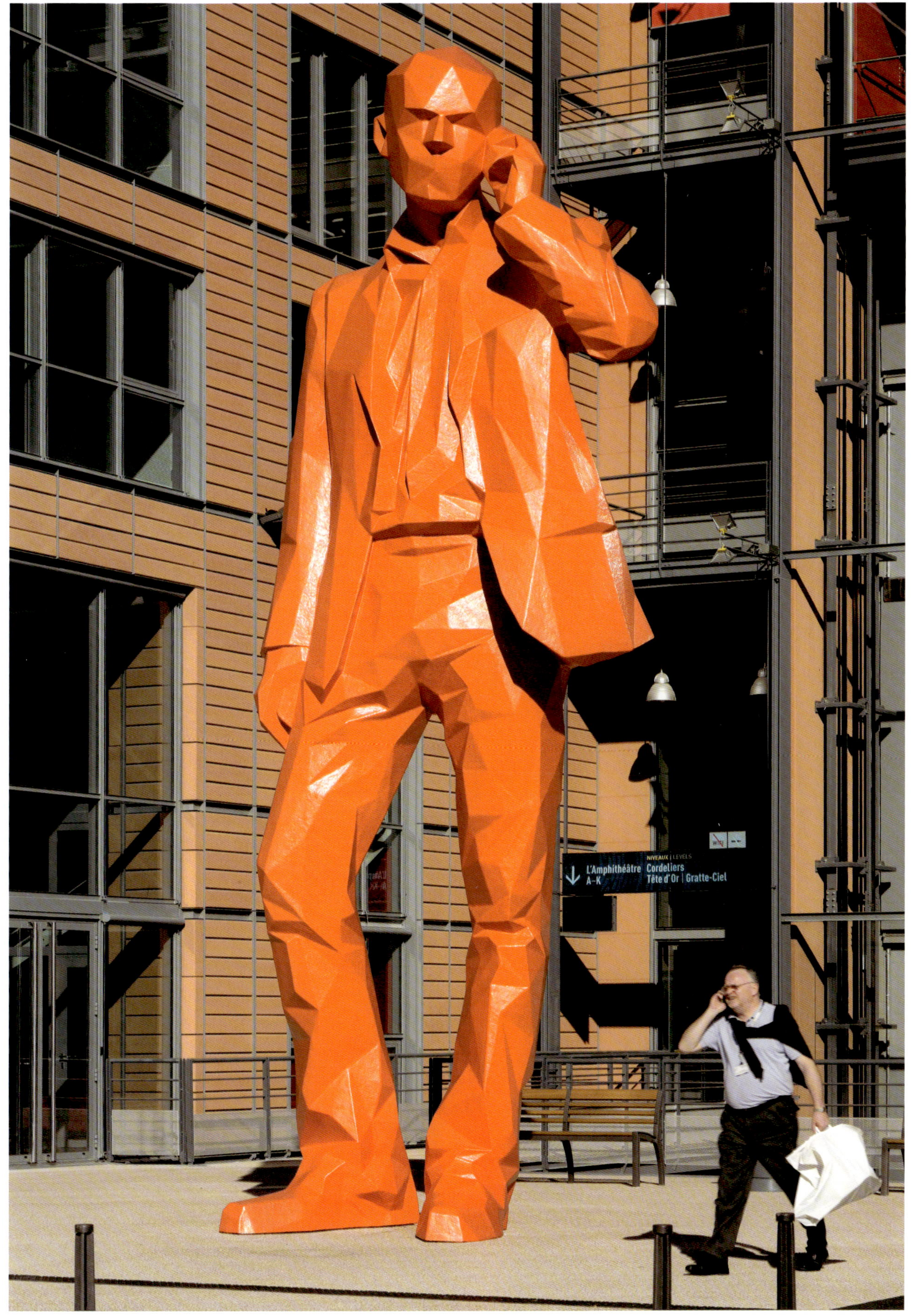

MAN ON THE PHONE (LES HABITANTS), 2006. PERMANENT INSTALLATION, CITÉ INTERNATIONALE, LYON

[→ P. 109] **PENGUINS (LES HABITANTS)**, 2006. PERMANENT INSTALLATION, CITÉ INTERNATIONALE, LYON
[→ P. 110–111] **THE LION**, 2004. PERMANENT INSTALLATION, PLACE STALINGRAD, BORDEAUX

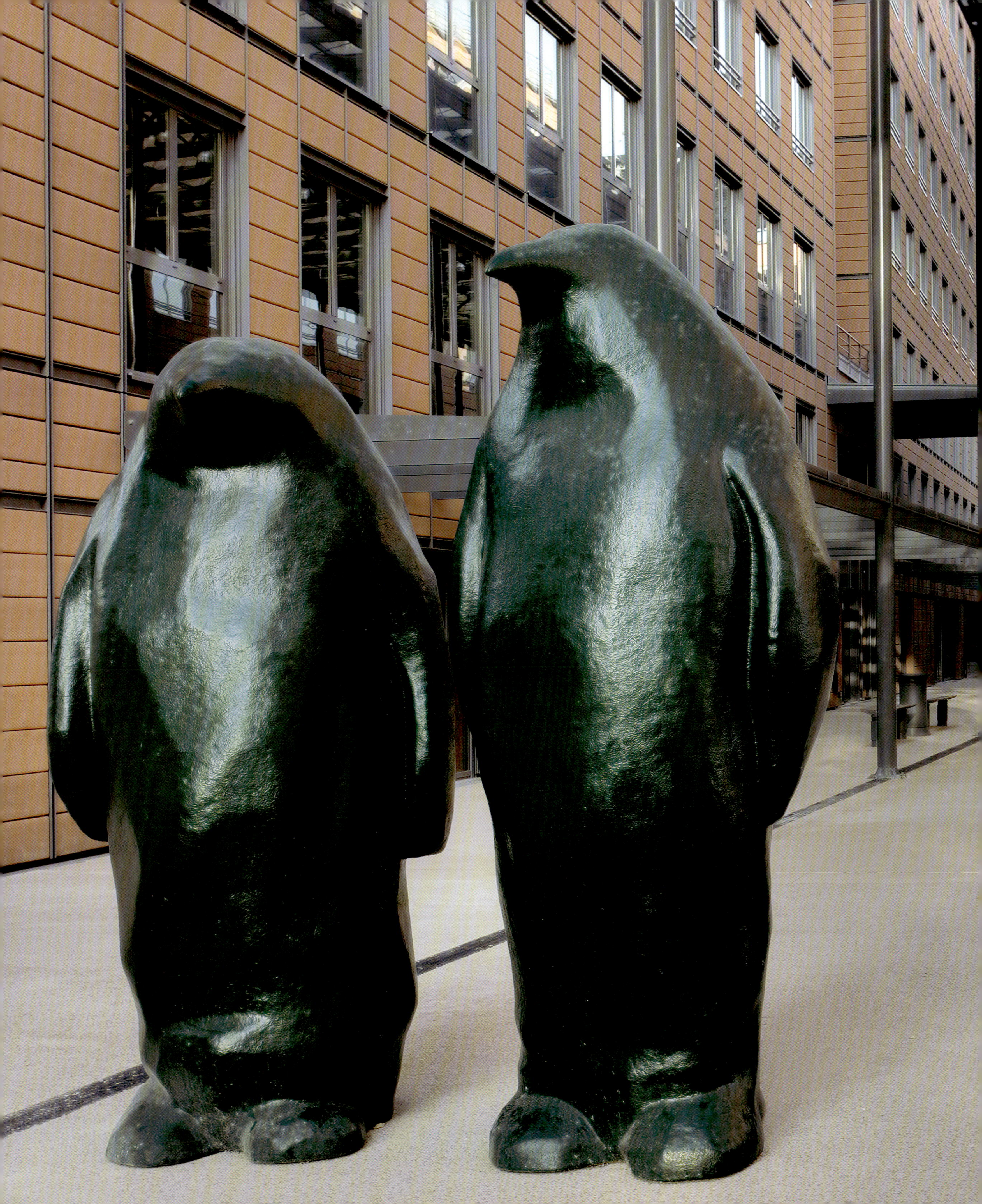

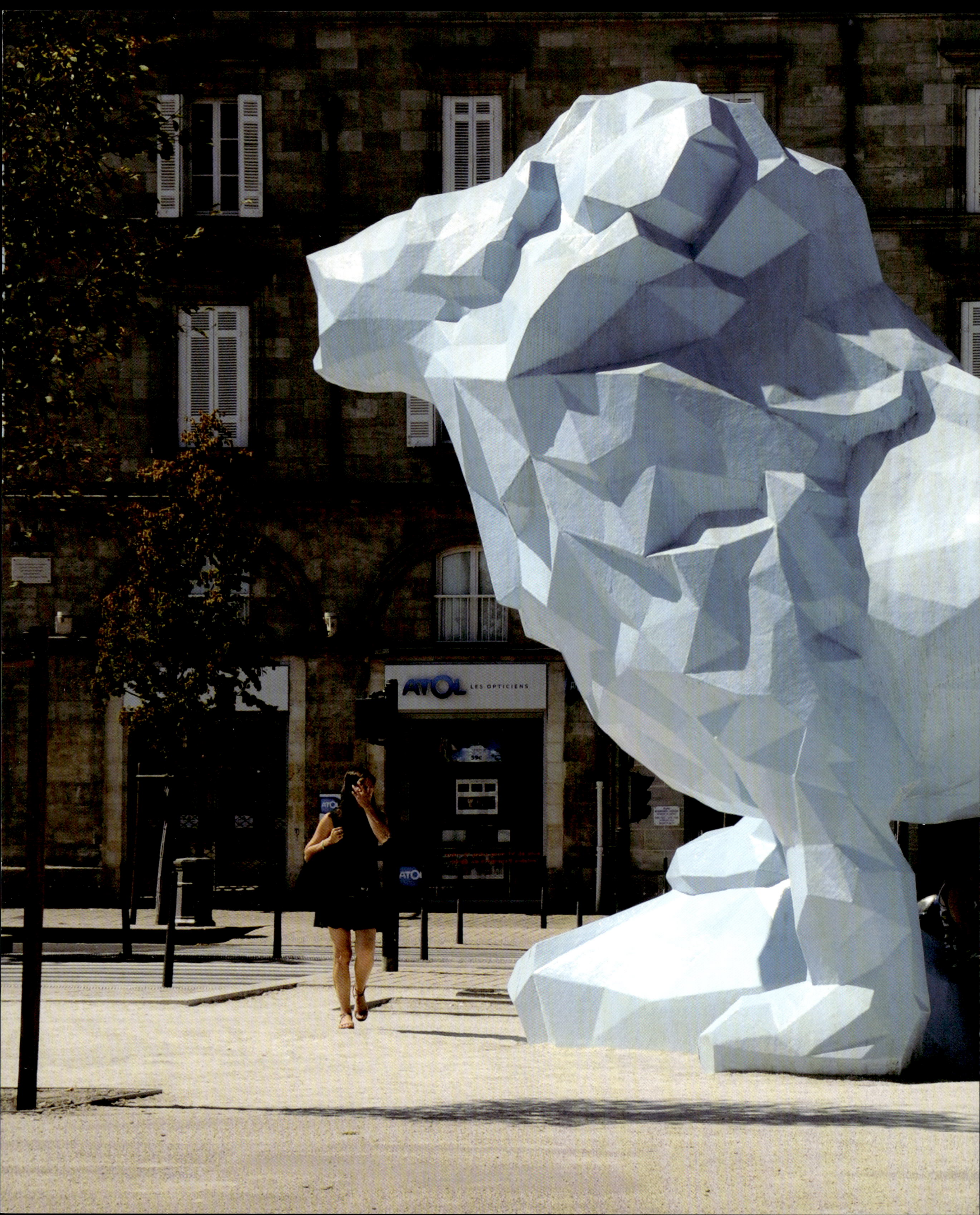

ATOL LES OPTICIENS

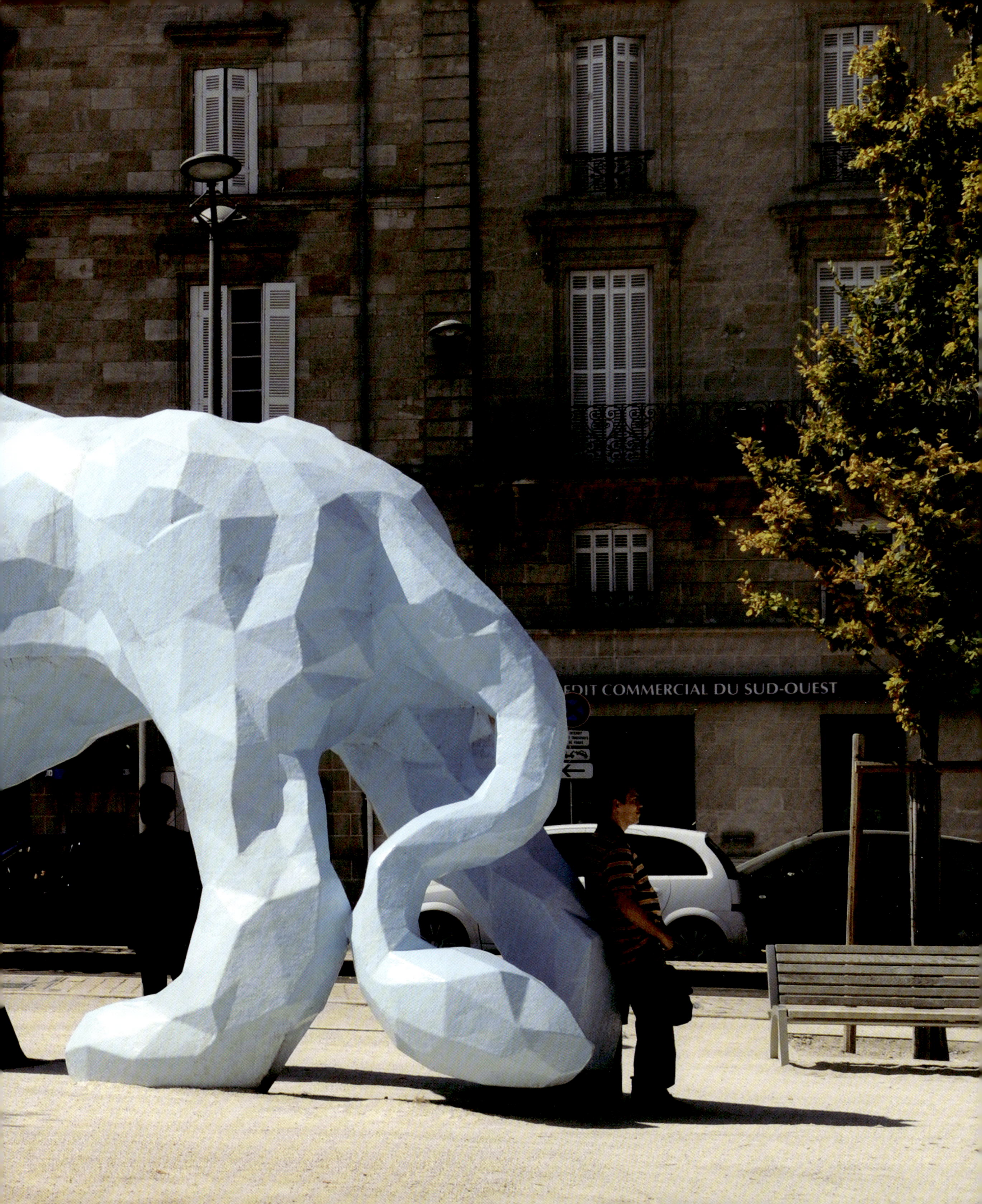

EDIT COMMERCIAL DU SUD-OUEST

VEILHAN VERSAILLES

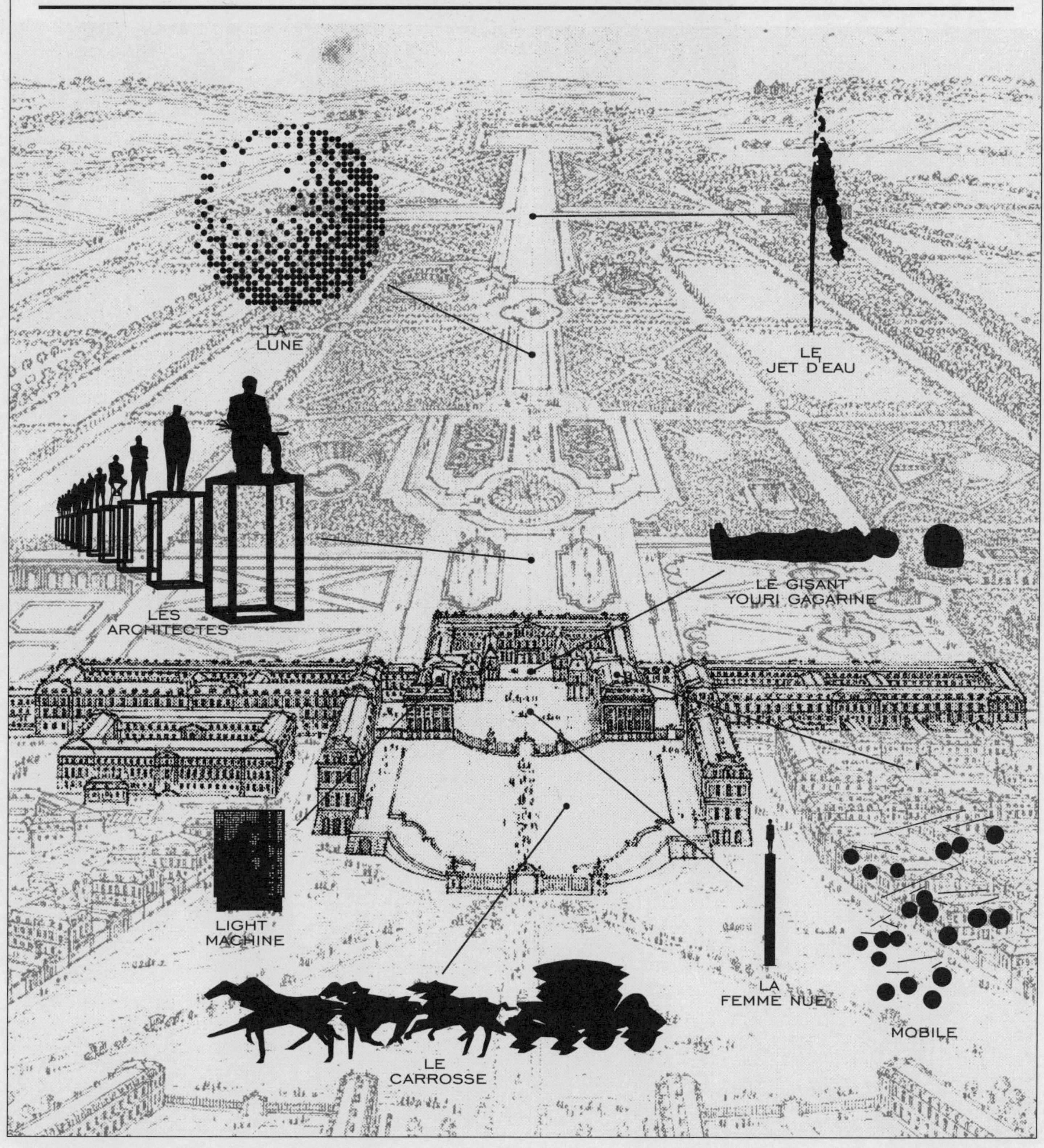

THE MAP, 2009

114

CLAUDE PARENT, DETAIL FROM **LES ARCHITECTES (THE ARCHITECTS)**, FONDERIE LANDOWSKI, BAGNOLET, 2009

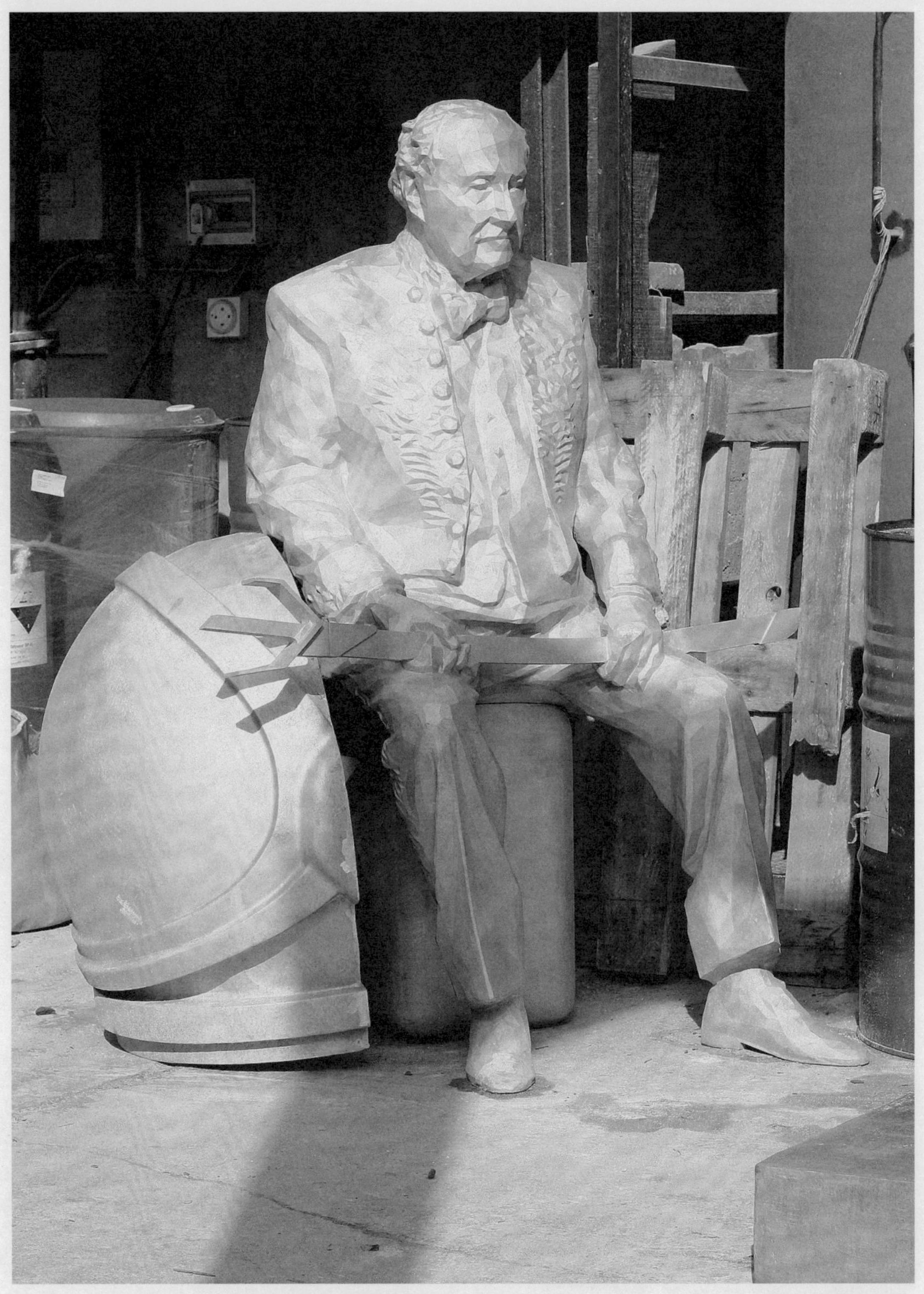

A JOURNEY THROUGH SPACE
INTERVIEW WITH XAVIER VEILHAN

Michel Gauthier

MICHEL GAUTHIER — The first work visitors see on entering the Cour d'Honneur at the Château de Versailles is *Le Carrosse*, a monochrome sculpture of a 17th-century coach and horses. But the representation is unusual, because it is shot through by a wave that makes it appear to vibrate …

XAVIER VEILHAN — It's the effect of galloping and speed, the surging of form and shapes.

MICHEL GAUTHIER — The work confirms your rather neo-Futurist interest in means of transport. Your earlier work featured motorcycles, cars, dirigibles, bicycles, boats, and horses. The journey through space is sometimes accompanied by a journey through time—for example the Model T Ford, which took us back to the early days of mass-produced automobiles, and now there is this *Grand Siècle* coach. What do these vehicles mean for you?

XAVIER VEILHAN — I think of all these vehicles as extensions of our bodies and our senses. The world seems more and more like an anthropomorphic construction to me: objects, from the smallest to the largest, are built in terms of our bodies and their functions. The images and objects that I construct likewise meet this criterion, to which should be added the notions of time and space and technological and financial means. If the subject, context (in terms of time, money, and desire, among others) and result all come together, then success is guaranteed. I'm interested in anything that allows me to multiply the gaze. The development of means of transport is one such thing. I love cars, boats, skis, bicycles, airplanes, and the like, as tools enabling a different, dynamic vision and associating the gaze with a physical sensation.

MICHEL GAUTHIER — The same goes for horses, which feature in several of your works.

XAVIER VEILHAN — Yes, but with horses, another dimension comes into play. I'm interested in the relationship between mankind and animals in general. Animals have the paradoxical capacity to define man. The way that animals have been instrumentalized for our benefit is not simply due to formal characteristics—the fact that you can sit on the back of a horse—but also to a relationship based on an exchange between man and animal (service for food), which prefigures the complex economy in which we are afloat.

MICHEL GAUTHIER — *Le Carrosse* seems to me to be at the juncture of two issues that recur throughout your work. On the one hand are images that the viewer grasps at first sight. You just have to catch a glimpse of your rhinoceros to know what it is. The animal is recognized in a flash. On the other hand are images that are only visible in certain conditions—the works in the *Light Machines* and *Ghost Landscapes* series. In *Le Carrosse*, the image is both crisp and blurred …

XAVIER VEILHAN — Art is at the juncture between a world of images and its three-dimensional setting. When people talk about degrees of perception, I think metaphorically about the understanding of reality in general: we often grasp reality as a set of discrete elements. I am interested in the mental formalization that we all have of the objects

I represent: it is distorted by time, subjectivity, and the approximations of memory. The work is a success when that which is represented remains identifiable while still taking this subjectivity into account. The synthetic dimension of my work is rooted in this research. The work becomes a word, delineating the space of a word such as "rhinoceros," while containing evocations and indications that the word itself cannot transcribe. *Le Carrosse* is a distorted photogram: the image is shot through with a "vibration" that viewers discover as they get closer. I like it when the gaze is called into question after the initial moment of identification, and when the spectator's position is an element of the gaze. Looking means taking a position, in every sense of the expression. The fragmented image is recomposed by the spectator's brain. We are familiar with the fragmentation of our surroundings and it is up to us to put them back together to understand them. The work's appearance is conditioned by the spectator's gaze. This gaze opens up as visitors stroll through the exhibition, which, like Versailles and its grounds, unfolds like a landscape.

MICHEL GAUTHIER — The second work that the visitors see is *The Naked Woman*, in the Royal Courtyard. Doesn't the impact of this sculpture also lie in the tension between the naked body, unchanged for thousands of years, and a medium and modes of image production that reflect a given moment in history?

XAVIER VEILHAN — I'm interested in nudes, and in all forms that recur throughout art history—landscapes, portraits, still lifes, history painting, funerary, ritual, and commemorative art, propaganda art, and so on. Culture suffuses our bodies. I'm interested in the way we all present and stage our bodies, and the way the image of the body is recreated by artists and technology. The supposed permanence of the body highlights the impermanence of its surroundings. I think of a whole series of statues I produced as figurative McCrackens, such as *Laurent (Deutsche Grammophon)*, for example.

MICHEL GAUTHIER — You're thinking of John McCracken's monochromatic, rectangular-sectioned columns?

XAVIER VEILHAN — McCracken's objects are unanswerable examples, whether they are free-standing or leaning against a wall. Their minimalist rigor does not preclude a certain cool style that I also appreciate in John Armleder's work. Actually, the typology of McCracken's objects is close to statuary. In fact, I produced a self-portrait that is propped against the floor and the wall like his planks.

MICHEL GAUTHIER — Let's get back to *The Naked Woman* in the Royal Courtyard.

XAVIER VEILHAN — In actual fact, I always begin by thinking about the exhibition before the works. The Versailles exhibition had to extend along an east-west axis, at different scales, without being monotonous. The site for *The Naked Woman* was key: it is located at the point where the avenues leading out from the grounds into the city begin. The geometry of the site makes the strategic points so precise that they break free from space to become symbols. *The Naked Woman* is a small vertical sculpture planted in the Royal Courtyard like an acupuncturist's needle. It demands the visitor's attention, and the fragility of her nude body is counterbalanced by the hardness of the titanium. The nude as a genre features throughout art history and is present everywhere at Versailles. It is supposed to represent the permanence of humanity, yet it reveals the cultural aspect of the body itself, which evolves over time, and the diversity of the ways in which it is represented, associated with mythology, religion, and eroticism. The work is the product both of the image that the model wishes to project and of the artist's gaze, whatever the period.

For *The Naked Woman*, I also thought of Helmut Newton's *Big Nudes* and Julian Opie's marvelous swimmers from the series *Christine Swimming*.

MICHEL GAUTHIER —The tension between two contradictory principles is also present in *The Effigy* in the Marble Courtyard. The sculpture represents Yuri Gagarin, the world's first cosmonaut, who flew into outer space and orbited the Earth on April 12, 1961. He died six years later in a plane crash near Moscow. The first space cowboy was grounded for good. Speed and immobility, weightlessness and gravity.

XAVIER VEILHAN — I love the idea that Yuri Gagarin was the first man to see the entire Earth, as an object ... The contradictory tensions you mentioned are often present when you try to explain things. Art sometimes manages to reconcile them.

MICHEL GAUTHIER —A few months after Gagarin first orbited the Earth, Piero Manzoni produced his *Base of the World*. So the same year as Man saw the planet for the first time, an artist made it a readymade. Gagarin was the first person to see the work that stood on Manzoni's plinth.

XAVIER VEILHAN — He saw it, but of course he was unaware of that aspect. The first glimpse of the Earth transcends the political and technological aspects of the event as such. It was the first visual perception of the Earth as a whole, and at the same time as part of a wider ensemble—the universe. The cosmonaut in *The Effigy* consists of shapes inset in his body. I think he represents the way that the elements that constitute our bodies are only temporarily part of us before becoming, or after having been, parts of other elements.

MICHEL GAUTHIER —Let's go over to the gardens on the other side of the château. A great number of architects have been associated with the history of the Château de Versailles. Does the theory of the sculptures representing architects echo this?

XAVIER VEILHAN — Deciding to represent people means asking what it means to celebrate someone: after producing portraits of a group of close friends for whom I felt a kind of physical attachment, I needed to identify new heroes. I had already asked myself the question for my exhibition at the Louvre in 2004. Then I chose to line the biscuit-ware *Illustrious Men* up behind a small statue of Laïka, the space dog, Gagarin's precursor and the first living creature in space. In the end, I thought to myself that Versailles called for the only contemporary figure to be both heroic and scorned and often mistreated by economic and political contexts—the architect. That's why I lined famous architects along an east-west axis, leading to the point where the king would stand at the center of the Parterre d'Eau (starting from the Château), going from the youngest to the oldest, Oscar Niemeyer. They take their place in the history built by Le Nôtre and Le Vau.

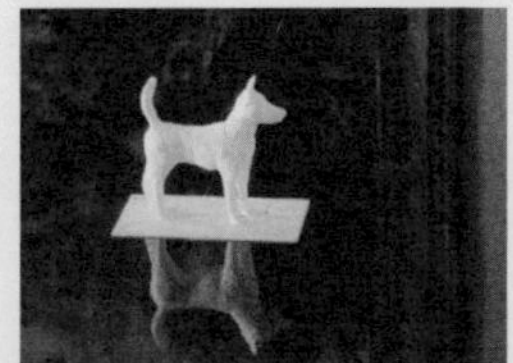

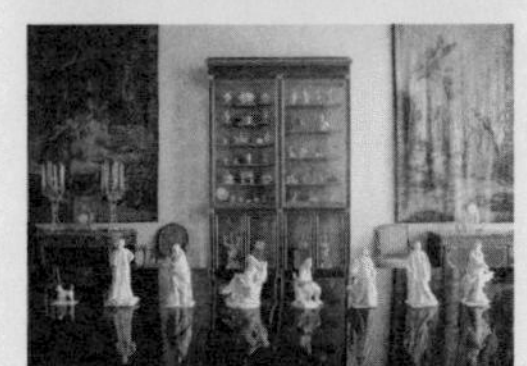

↗ *Laïka*, 2004

The age of Versailles means that those who participated in it are dead, but the technique I used—a three-dimensional scanner—implies that the subjects are alive.

MICHEL GAUTHIER — The layout of the château and grounds looks rather like a plane—a stealth aircraft. Did the large sculpture of the plane that you initially intended to display on the Tapis Vert lawn act as a mise en abyme of the site as a whole?

XAVIER VEILHAN — Of course, I place importance in symmetry as a construction that is artificial yet simple, maybe even natural. The geometry of the airplane is determined by the need for balance. That of the gardens and château evokes a body whose surface symmetry envelops asymmetrical organs, like the groves of trees and buildings in the grounds. This geometry is a program that dissolves as you move away from the château.

MICHEL GAUTHIER — Your exhibition at the Pompidou Center in 2004, *Vanishing Point*, explored questions of perspective. You return to these questions in Le Nôtre's gardens at Versailles.

XAVIER VEILHAN — Perspective is an illusion allowing the three dimensions of space to be represented in two dimensions, in a drawing or painting or on a computer screen. I admire Le Nôtre's ability to associate illusionism and reality—we are simultaneously in the realm of drawing and in real space.

MICHEL GAUTHIER — In the end, you decided to replace the aircraft with *The Moon*. A moon in the Sun King's gardens?

XAVIER VEILHAN — Since I was unable to produce the aircraft in the end, I decided to use the same principle of construction, putting together a motif from various discrete elements and calling on the spectacularly distorted perspective Le Nôtre created for the Tapis Vert. It's an anamorphosis materialized by spheres on the ends of rods. Their various sizes correct the effect of perspective to create an image of the moon, which is only fully visible from the king's standpoint in the center of the terrace.

MICHEL GAUTHIER — What with the recumbent statue of Gagarin and the moon, the exhibition is beginning to look like a Space Odyssey …

XAVIER VEILHAN — The exhibition's cosmic and mental dimension was not planned, but it is none the less powerful for that. I also included images of the moon in the rather dreamlike short film for the *Light Machine* series in the Queen's Staircase. Versailles is a cosmic place, both reified and imaginary.

MICHEL GAUTHIER — What memories did the project for this exhibition at Versailles bring to mind? For example, did you think about the sculpture park in Oslo, including works designed by Gustav Vigeland from 1924 to 1943?

XAVIER VEILHAN — The Vigeland Park is an oddity, a dead end in art history. But it is a humanist and hygienist celebration representing elderly people and babies according to a geometrical design that is as rigorous as any French-style garden. I love the way the set of statues populates the park and echoes the figures of the people strolling there.

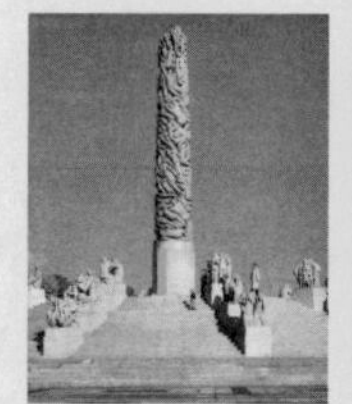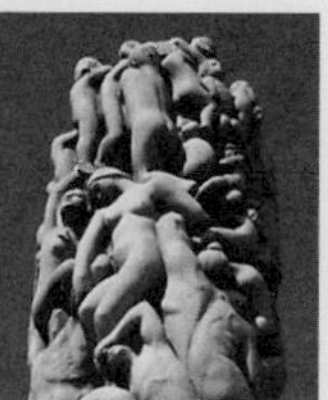

↗ Gustav Vigeland, *The Monolith*, Vigeland Sculpture Park, Oslo, Norway, 1924–1945

MICHEL GAUTHIER — You are one of the first artists after Modernism whose works draw on references and a realm of imagination that goes far beyond the

artistic field. You are just as interested in engineers and universal
exhibitions as you are in architects and masterpieces in museums.

XAVIER VEILHAN — I love it when making objects becomes an adventure. The objects may be
small or large, figurative or abstract; they may draw on craftsmanship,
folklore, architecture and landscapes, art, or design. When the creators of
old objects and paintings touch me, I hear them whispering in my ear, and I
find this capacity for communication across the ages immensely soothing.

MICHEL GAUTHIER — Versailles evokes a time when there was no ontological divide between engineers and
artists. There are illustrious figures like Carlo Vigarani, Keeper of the king's engines
and privy pleasures, whose name remains associated with the machinery he designed
for the *Pleasures of the Enchanted Isle* in 1664. You are also a man of performances,
and one might feel that you are closer to such creators than to the figure of the
artist as imposed by a certain kind of Modernism—the painter or the sculptor in
search of the essence of his art and scornfully overlooking science and technology.

XAVIER VEILHAN — Performances are in time, while exhibitions are an area and a landscape. The moment of the performance is shared by the actors
and audience, while a different exchange takes place in the visual
arts. I always wanted to combine the emotional power of music
with the formal mastery of the exhibition. I designed performances
and asked musicians like Air (*Aérolite* in 2007) and Sébastien Tellier
(*Ville Nouvelle* and *Val de Marne* in 2006) to provide music for them,
like an original soundtrack played for an audience. The result was
sometimes close to a concert, sometimes closer to a Constructivist
theater performance or a sporting event. I feel distanced from the
heroic solitude of the modern artist. The pleasure of art begins
with the discussion and potential for multiplication inherent in
teamwork. So I'm closer to a Renaissance artist, a film director,
or an architect. My work involves a chain of skills that shape the
artworks and enable them to exist. Working closely with other
people and companies often opens my eyes to new techniques.
I build rather than create. It's all already there, you just have to trim
away parts and make choices. Versailles as a whole is a place where
fiction and reality meet and where artifice encounters nature.
It's a place designed for festivities, politics, hunting, and love.

MICHEL GAUTHIER — What about *The Fountain*, the final exclamation mark?

XAVIER VEILHAN — I initially started thinking about works that would draw attention to the natural
elements, such as a huge flag indicating the presence of the wind, for example.
I've always loved the fountain on Lake Geneva as a visual event that is unsigned,
although it is obviously artificial. I like the idea that people will admire *The Fountain*
without asking themselves whether it's a work of art or not. The notion of the
author will sort of gradually blend into the gardenscape, as if dissolved in nature.
In fact I didn't plan this, but the monumental verticality of the fountain echoes
the magnificent horizontality of the water features designed by Le Nôtre. I'm also

moved by the impermanence of spurting water. Its demonstrative side doesn't mask its fragility: if you turn the tap off, it disappears and goes back to horizontality.

MICHEL GAUTHIER — The two works at the far ends of the layout are, then, *Le Carrosse*, pulled by horses, and *The Fountain*. So, at the far ends of the axis that structures the exhibition we have a horse-drawn vehicle and water, together re-enacting Tuby's sculpture *Le Char du Soleil* [The Sun Chariot], representing Apollo surging forth from the water as he drives his horse-drawn chariot toward the rising sun. Tuby's work must be of great interest to you as the artist behind *Le Zodiac* (2004) ...

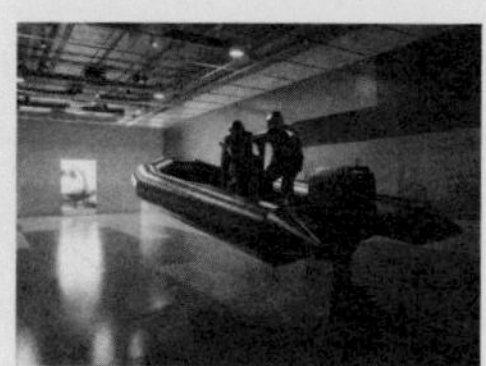

↗ *Le Zodiac, Vanishing Point,* exhibition view, 2003

XAVIER VEILHAN — I love the way that sculptural and architectural features are indivisibly linked with natural elements, be it *Le Char du Soleil* [The Sun Chariot], the Eiffel Tower, or works of Land art. Versailles is scattered with masterpieces of sculpture (Bernini's *Louis XIV*, Tuby's *Sun Chariot*, and Girardon's *Pyramid*, among others). You have to take these surroundings into account, but without inhibitions and without quoting them. The context and conditions of my invitation to exhibit at Versailles create a different setting to that of Louis XIV's artists: all I have to do is blend into the contemporary context while respecting the history of the site.

A JOURNEY THROUGH SPACE   MICHEL GAUTHIER

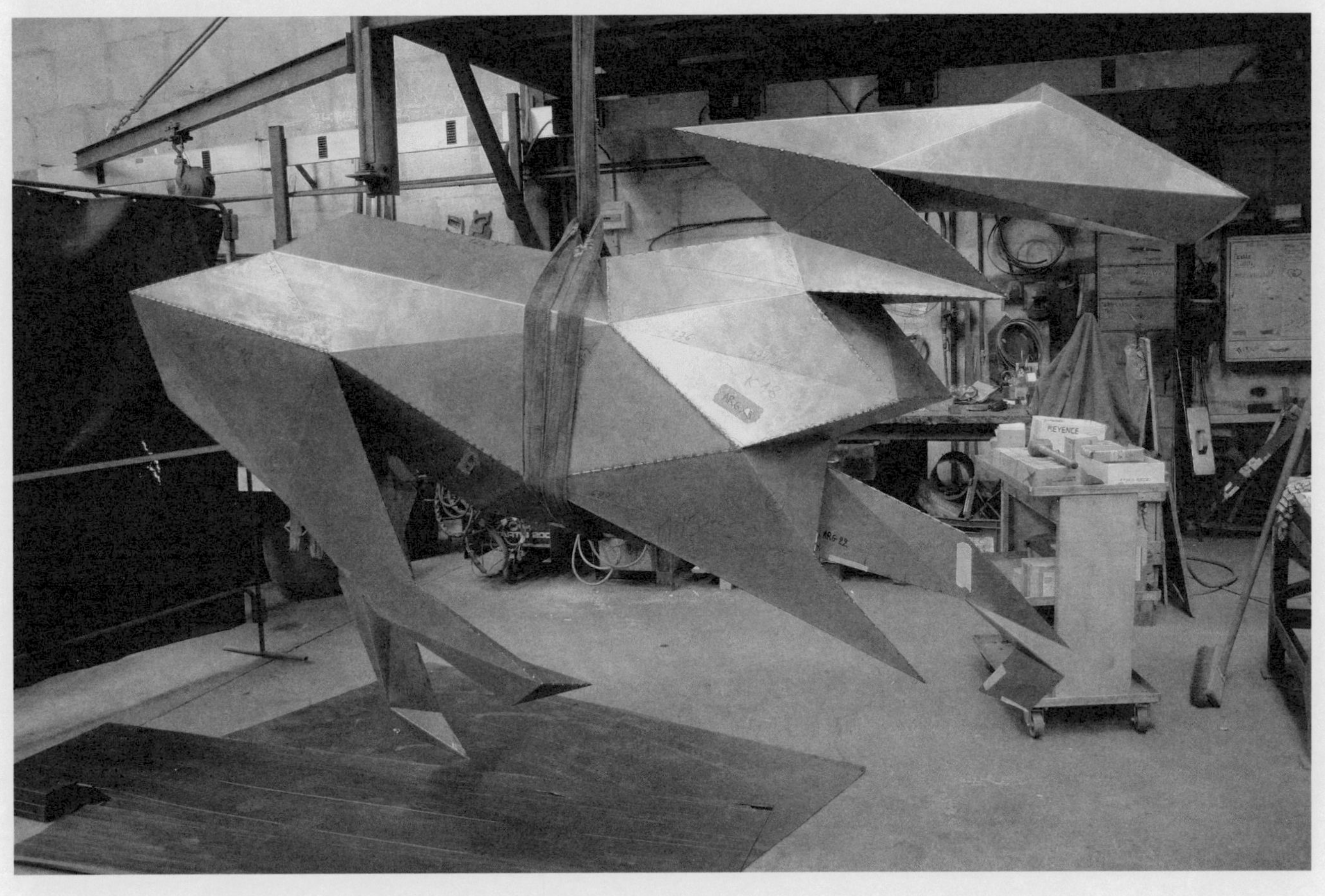

ONE OF THE HORSES FOR **LE CARROSSE**, ÉTUDES ET DIFFUSIONS, BONDOUFLE, 2009

Jean-Jacques Aillagon
— FORMER MINISTER OF CULTURE
— PRESIDENT OF THE PUBLIC ESTABLISHMENT
OF THE MUSEUM AND NATIONAL ESTATE
OF VERSAILLES

The Château de Versailles, often imitated by other European monarchs but never equaled, bears magnificent testimony to the glorious golden age of French art. Louis XIV, the Sun King, commissioned the greatest artists of the day—Le Vau, Le Nôtre, Hardouin-Mansart, Le Brun, Bernini—to design and decorate the château and grounds, while the master composer Lully and the playwright Molière were invited to provide courtly diversions. The château's unparalleled collections were later enriched by artists such as Lalande, Lemoyne, Nattier, Rigaud, Riesener, Mique, and Gabriel. In the 19th century Louis-Philippe invited some of the greatest masters of the age, including Delacroix and Horace Vernet, to update the château's rich 17th- and 18th-century architectural and artistic heritage. This period saw the completion of such masterpieces such as the Galerie des Batailles and the Salle des Croisades, as Louis-Philippe wished to turn the château into a museum of French history.

The Public Establishment of the Museum and National Estate of Versailles, the body responsible for conserving, restoring, and facilitating public access to this site of major historical significance, is proud to uphold a fine tradition by inviting contemporary artists to exhibit their work at Versailles. Following the huge success of *Koons Versailles* in 2008, I have chosen to honor one of France's finest contemporary artists, Xavier Veilhan, with a solo exhibition. Xavier Veilhan has made the bold choice to create and exhibit all new works at *Versailles Off 2009*, marvelously curated by Laurent Le Bon of the Pompidou Center. Each sculpture enters into dialogue with its setting, casting a fresh light on the splendors of centuries past. The works are arranged symbolically along the royal axis leading from the statue of Louis XIV, now on the Place d'Armes, to the far western reaches of the grounds, where the sun sets. From the Cour d'Honneur to the Grand Canal, Xavier Veilhan's playful handling of perspective masterfully captures the spirit of the place. The exhibition gives visitors a unique perspective on Versailles, enjoining them to explore the notions of time, history, and genius. I wish every visitor a very enjoyable visit and I hope Xavier Veilhan's art proves a memorable and thought-provoking contribution to the magnificence of Versailles.

JEAN-JACQUES AILLAGON

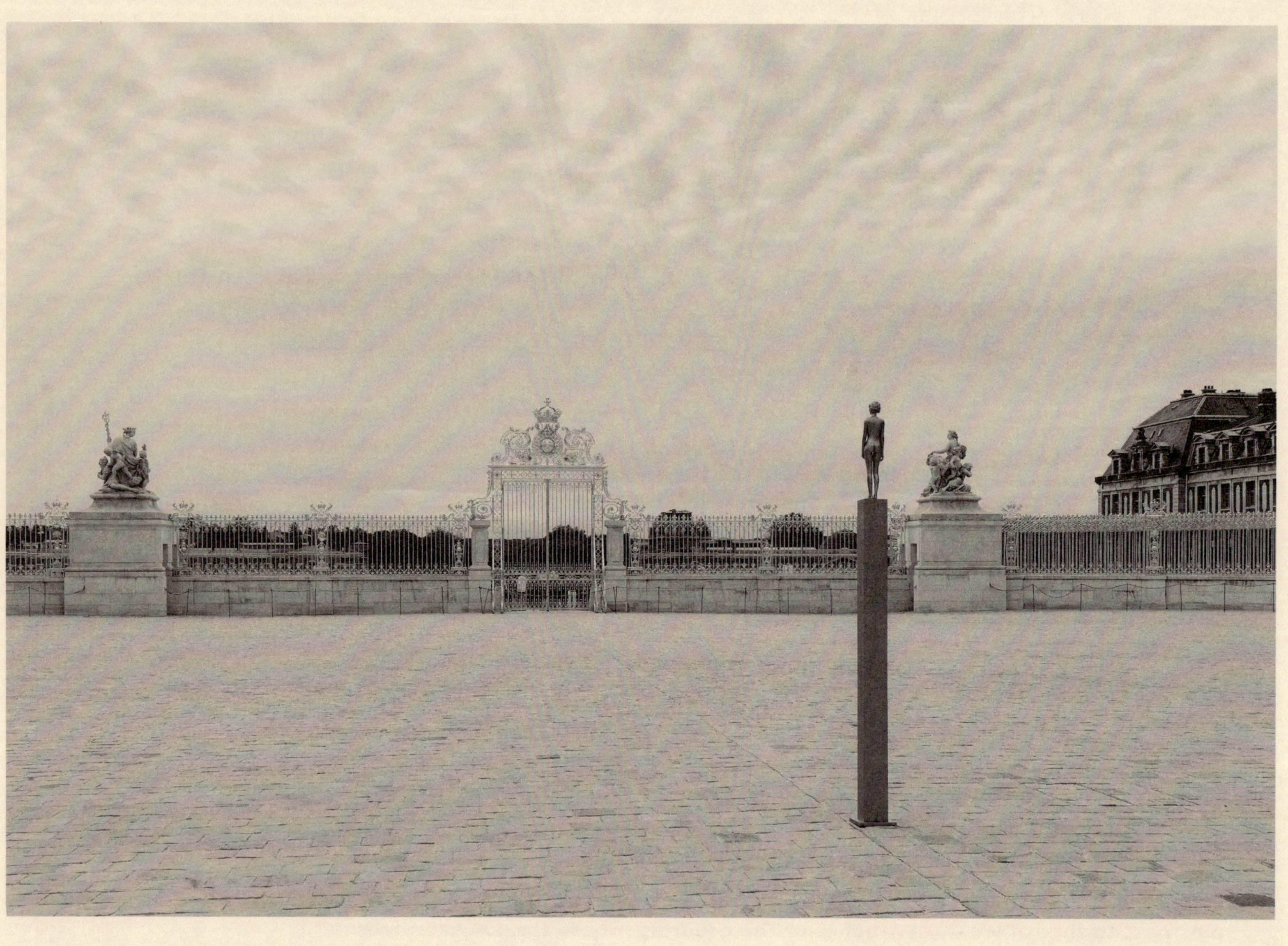

LA FEMME NUE (THE NAKED WOMAN), VERSAILLES, 2009

A FRESH VIEW ON VERSAILLES
XAVIER VEILHAN

Laurent Le Bon
— CURATOR OF THE EXHIBITION
VEILHAN VERSAILLES

Veilhan Versailles is an exceptional event which sets out to reconnect the Château de Versailles with the artists of its day, by means of an exhibition which (re)introduces visitors to a site that is familiar and yet unknown. If there is one place where the risk of creating a truly contemporary event rather than a facile pastiche pays off, it is Versailles. Contemporary art creates a new vision of this living monument and its ever-shifting reality. Far from being the inert model of a single, hard-to-pin-down period, Versailles (like every aspect of our heritage) is the fruit of a complex stratification of gazes and interactions down to the present day. The exhibition plays a part in demolishing the clichés associated with the site, which take the form of a practice of place, which is on occasion conventional and highly concentrated. The aim is to propose new viewpoints for a monument that everyone assumes they already know, thereby revealing its contemporary complexity, its substance, and the depth buried beneath layers of habit.

Veilhan Versailles is a walk, an itinerary, a journey through the landscape and territory of Versailles. It is not a retrospective of the artist's work. The works—all new commissions—are often masterpieces of technology that the elusive mass of visitors will be able to see and appreciate. The exhibition features seven new creations placed along an east-west axis across the entire site, from the forecourt to the Grand Canal. The location of each sculpture—the medium chosen for the exhibition—has been selected very carefully in relation to the decor, architecture, and role of this axis, the most prestigious and symbolic in France's cultural heritage. The allegories and myths enter into a dialogue with Xavier Veilhan's work, which, as has often been pointed out, regularly engages with the classical/baroque dialectic. Xavier Veilhan's Versailles vocabulary includes statuary, speed, vehicles, fiction, anthropomorphism, and contemporary heroes, creating a new way of showcasing the site and playing with visitors' perceptions. As he likes to point out, "I build more than I create."

The temporary installation of works by one of France's best-known contemporary artists in one of the world's most-visited monuments creates an intriguing mise en abyme, underpinned by the question of what it means to see works in situ. In recent years, many cultural institutions have set up dialogues between their historical heritage and contemporary works. Whether they take the form of echoes, dialectic, opposition, or counterpoint is not up to us to decide. The primary aim of this unique event is to encourage visitors to explore the notion of the contemporaneity of our monuments and the vital necessity of modern-day creation. Notre Dame, the Invalides, the Pantheon, the Louvre, and Versailles, to list some of the best known, reveal a series of architectural strata, each one an intervention that was contemporary in its day, alongside which *Veilhan Versailles* is modest indeed. Yet its objectives were always the same: not to destroy the uniqueness of each artistic act and not to turn the artist's distinct imaginative vision into mere "heritage." This unique three-month experiment was guided by a few basic principles: avoiding the trap of "integrating" contemporary art into the historic monument; (re)discovering the site; drawing on the knowledge and skills of the site staff, particularly the fountain engineers; enjoying working with a living artist and the emotions, setbacks, and surprises arising from such a collaboration; providing pleasure. The exhibition sets out to entrust one of the finest artists of our day with the creation of a new Versailles—a Versailles for the modern world and a living monument in terms of its use value. It aims to create pleasure for the senses as the visitor explores the new Versailles labyrinth whose sole purpose is to divert, in both meanings of the term, taking visitors beyond the usual clichés. It is a fleeting folly and a risk, as Versailles, once a multidisciplinary site and experimental architectural laboratory showcasing the boldest artistic creations, particularly during royal celebrations, is worthy of the contemporary artistic gaze.

Xavier Veilhan invites us to the largest exhibition space in the world. The visitors (or walk-on actors?) are on the same level and the same pedestal as the statues created for the occasion. The exhibition is highly fluid. Yet it is impossible to grasp the project in just a few minutes. Visitors must explore the monstrous dimensions of Versailles, which now features on the short international list of mythical places temporarily devoted to contemporary art. The sites are vast (the Tapis Vert is 330 meters, the Grand Canal over 1.6 km, and the facades overlooking the garden over 600 meters in length, while the grounds cover 800 hectares) and represent the antithesis of the white cube. Other such sites include the rotunda of the New York Guggenheim and the Turbine Hall at Tate Modern. Xavier Veilhan has put together a sort of negative imprint of Koons—an exhibition of commissioned works, mainly on display outside. The selected axis incorporates that used by Jeff Koons. Xavier Veilhan has decided to measure himself up to the site as a whole in order to create an ephemeral stratum and a new gaze to study the most familiar features of Versailles.

There is something of magic and alchemy in the work from the Veilhan studio, combining do-it-yourself craftsmanship and high-tech wizardry in the virtuoso metamorphosis of metal (soldered corrugated steel, smelted aluminum and bronze, and so on); the extensive digital manipulation of three-dimensional scans as a contemporary version of casting from life; the fascinating brio of *Light Machine*, with its electric lightbulbs arranged in an analogue grid, imitating a low-resolution video of a ghostly walk through the grounds; and the mysterious, powerful jet of a fountain. This new way of showing Versailles implies intimate knowledge of the site, which the artist has explored on numerous occasions. Veilhan loves garden history, from Louis XIV's follies to the Vigeland Sculpture Park in Oslo. *Le Carrosse* echoes Apollo's chariot. *The Architects* also take their place in the ongoing history of Versailles and Louis-Philippe's museum of history and its commemorative commissions. *The Naked Woman*, a talismanic needle at the nodal point of the axis, nonetheless exhibits its exacerbated contemporaneity, with her square bob and chimerical body. Like the terminal figures in the garden, she is integrated into her plinth, but unlike the architects' pedestals, it does not let the visitors' gaze past. She is there, outside the window of the king's bedchamber, forming a counterpoint to *The Effigy*, a new cosmic calamity after that of Gino De Dominicis, placed on a marble floor laid in the 20th century. The artist behind *Vanishing Point* and *Plein emploi*, accustomed to unusual exhibition formats, decided to incorporate this flooring into the artwork, using it as the platform for the moon landing—or rather crash back down to earth—of a hero as neglected as most of the glorious French heroes surrounding him. The echoes of the history of Versailles are on occasion more discreet, such as when the artist places his *Light Machine* on the Queen's Staircase, where the 19th-century landscapes have been removed. In the gardens, *The Architects* engage in dialogue, in both form and content, with the allegorical statues representing Architecture, Geometry, Art, Nature, Youth, Poetry, the 12 signs of the Zodiac, and so on, particularly those on the west facade of the central body of the building and the horizontal statuary representing rivers in the water parterre. Some of these echoes are doubtless far from inadvertent in the hands of the master of dialogue between the generic and the specific.

Unlike the kings of France, Xavier Veilhan has no programmatic intention. These are just snatches of screenplays, fragments of history, with varying gaps, breaks, and scales. While the project as a whole follows the main axis from east to west, the layout of the exhibition in fact follows a snaking line. Horresco referens in the kingdom of contrived symmetry! Although Xavier Veilhan has set up this winding visit, this allegory of a complex, fragmented monument— its history now a closed book to most visitors, who reduce it to a mere cliché of monarchy—he has not done so as a way of inviting us to a celebration on an enchanted isle. He invites us, in Louis XIV's terms, to "consider the situation." As he writes, "Art is an instrument that enables us to understand reality." We all have our own version of Versailles. The artist sets out to deconstruct the myth for us by taking us into the decor, the better to reveal its strange false-ness. Thanks to a foreshortening effect, the visitor passes through a ghostly landscape of hieratic statues in a palette of purples—the color of mourning. The reflections of the sculptures are anything but flashy. Like the carriage without a driver, going against the flow on the fringe of the crowds of visi-tors heading toward the château, Xavier Veilhan's works at Versailles are on the margins, omnipresent yet stealthy. The artist is not one of the glories of France: he is an anonymous figure. His project throws back in our faces the occasionally terrifying use of the monument that survives merely in a handful of postcards. His architects will be unable to intervene in a site that is now static. They take us to the point where the king stood and looked out over the grounds. The great fountains are no longer playing. A melancholy endgame. The only movement is a pitiful attempt to break a record, the ultimate anti-sculpture, isolated in the heart of a universe whose power no longer exists—the most powerful fountain jet in the world, destroying the mirror of the slack waters of the Grand Canal.

LA FEMME NUE (THE NAKED WOMAN), 2009
[→ P.130–131] LE CARROSSE, 2009

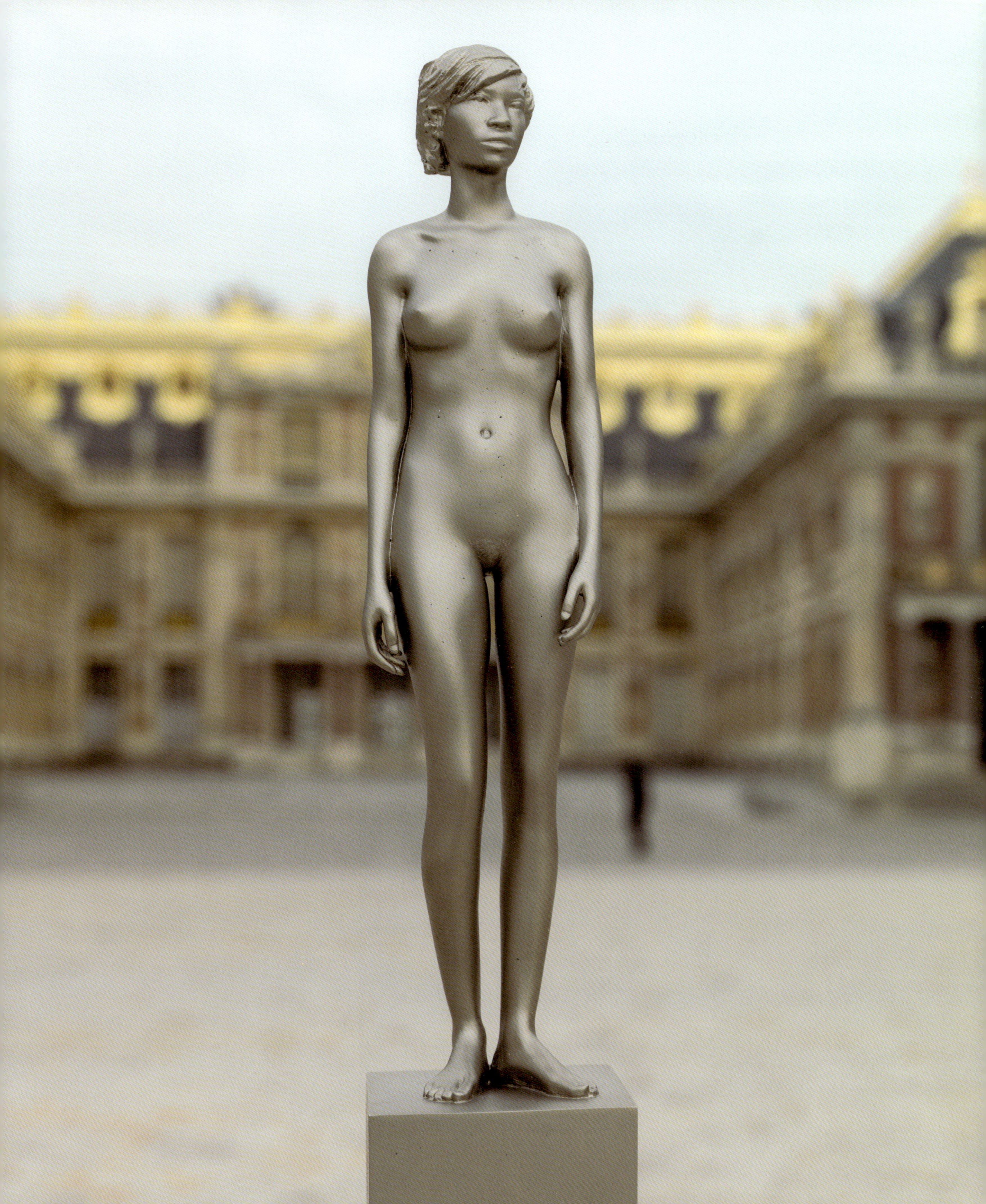

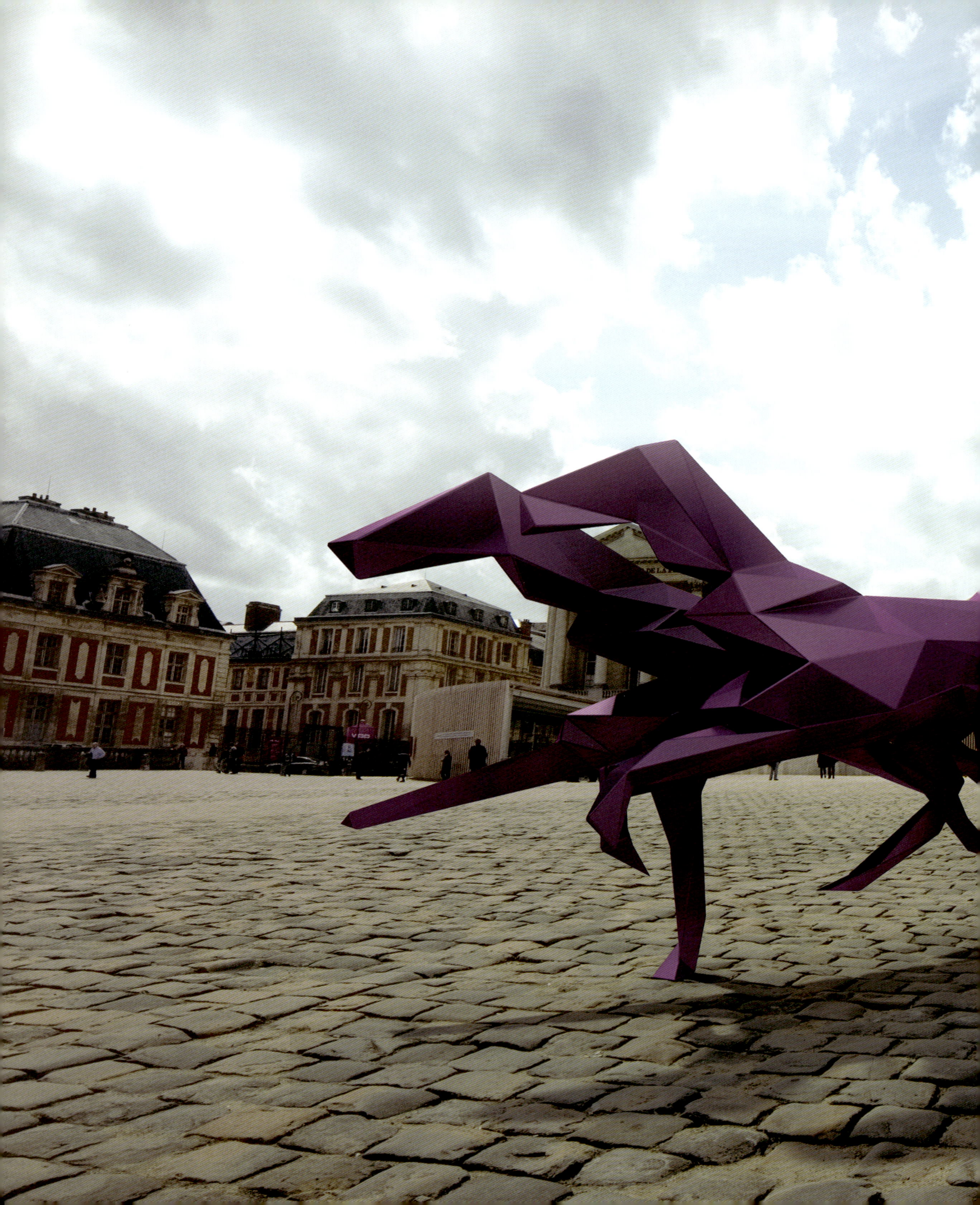

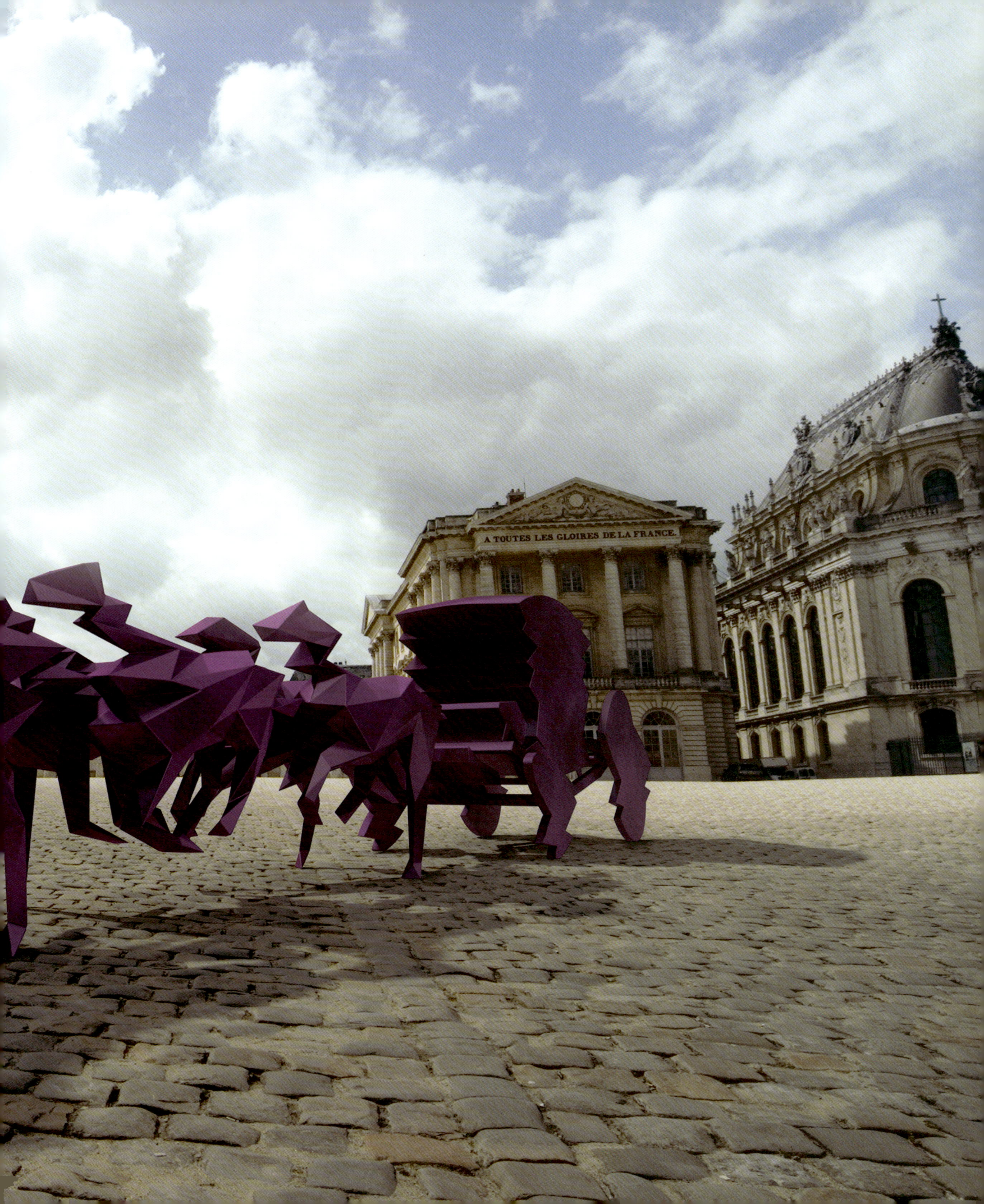
A TOUTES LES GLOIRES DE LA FRANCE.

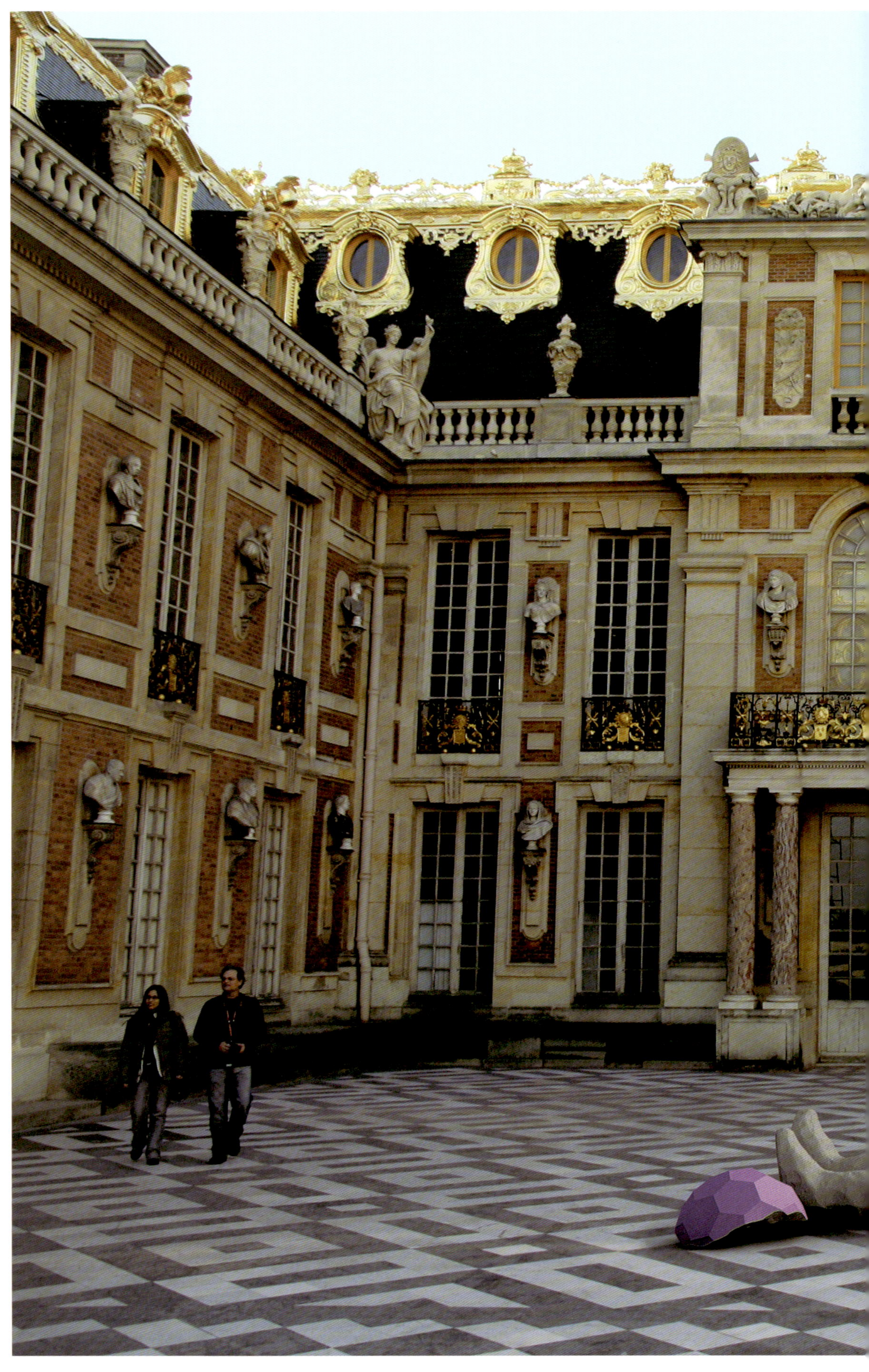

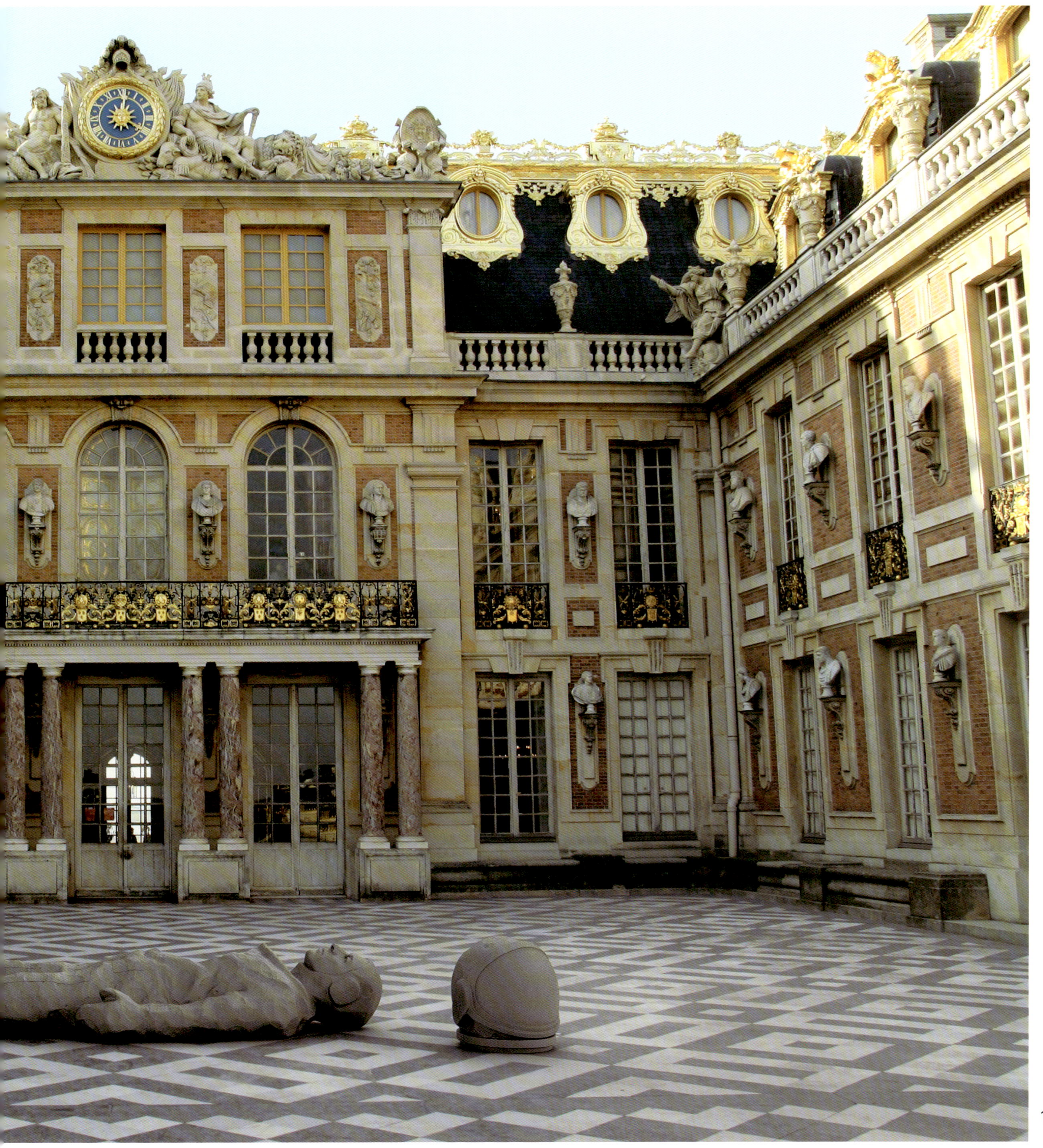

LE GISANT, YOURI GAGARINE (THE EFFIGY, YURI GAGARIN), 2009

MOBILE, 2009

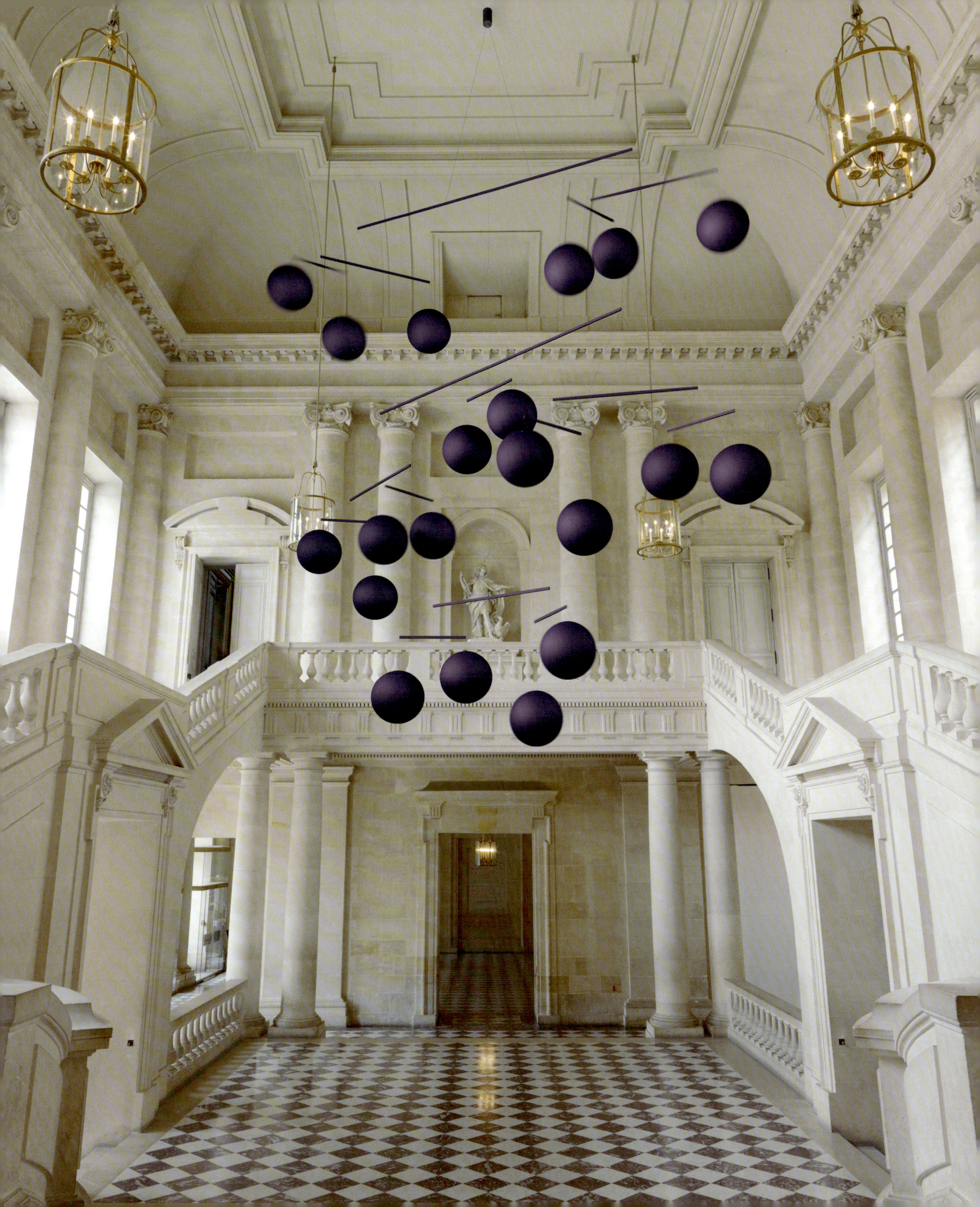

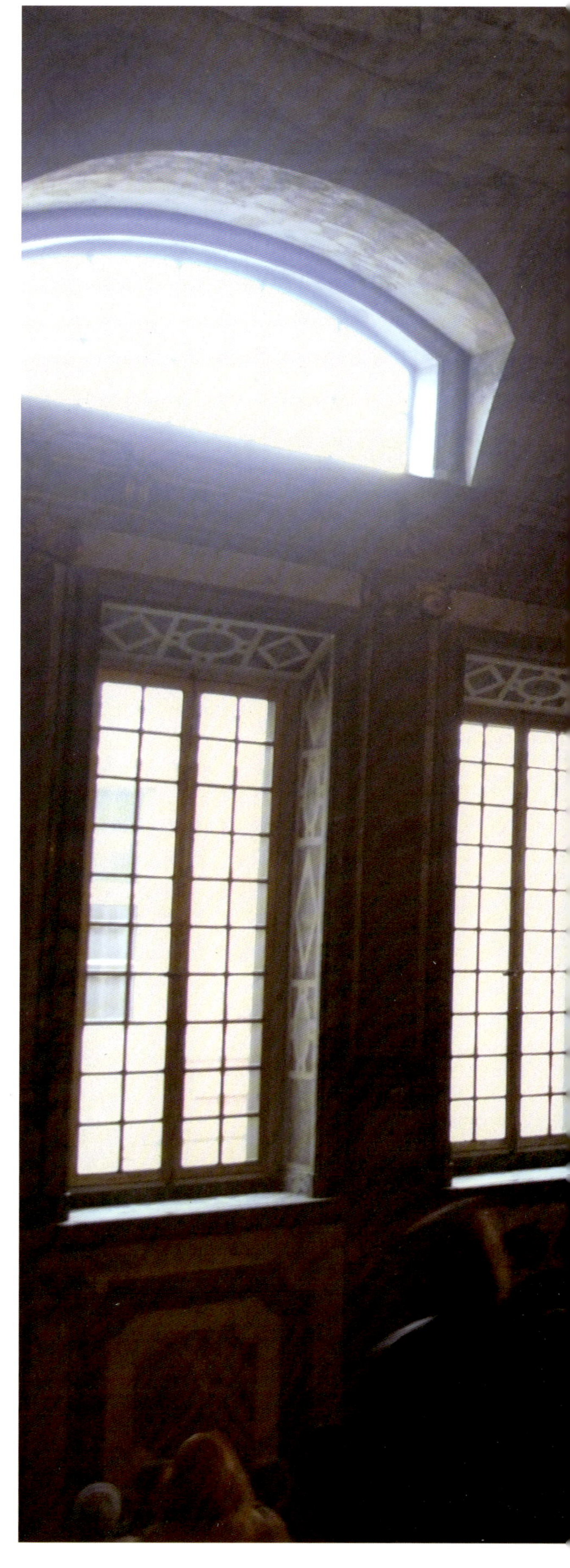

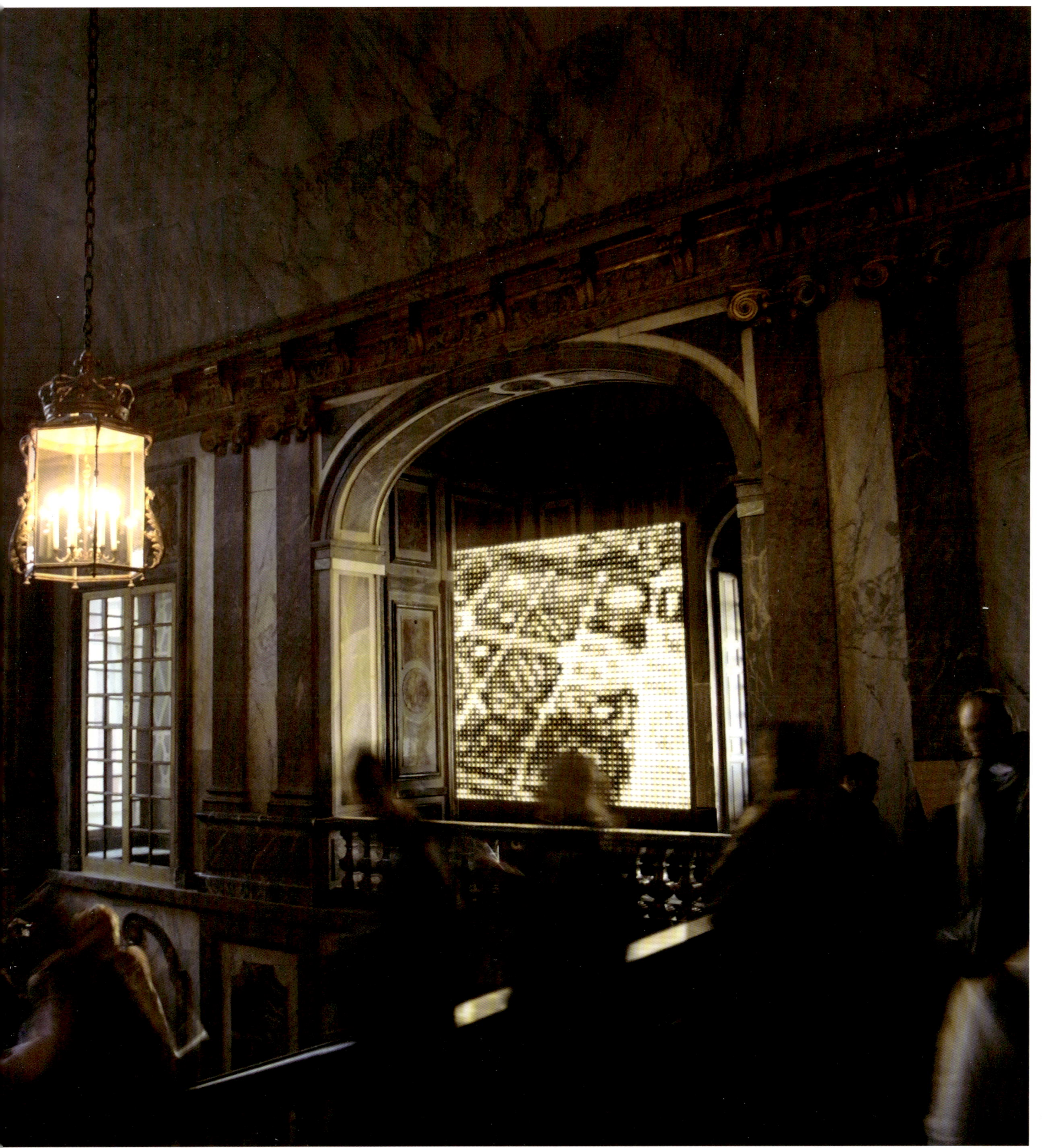

BIG LIGHT MACHINE (VERSAILLES), 2009

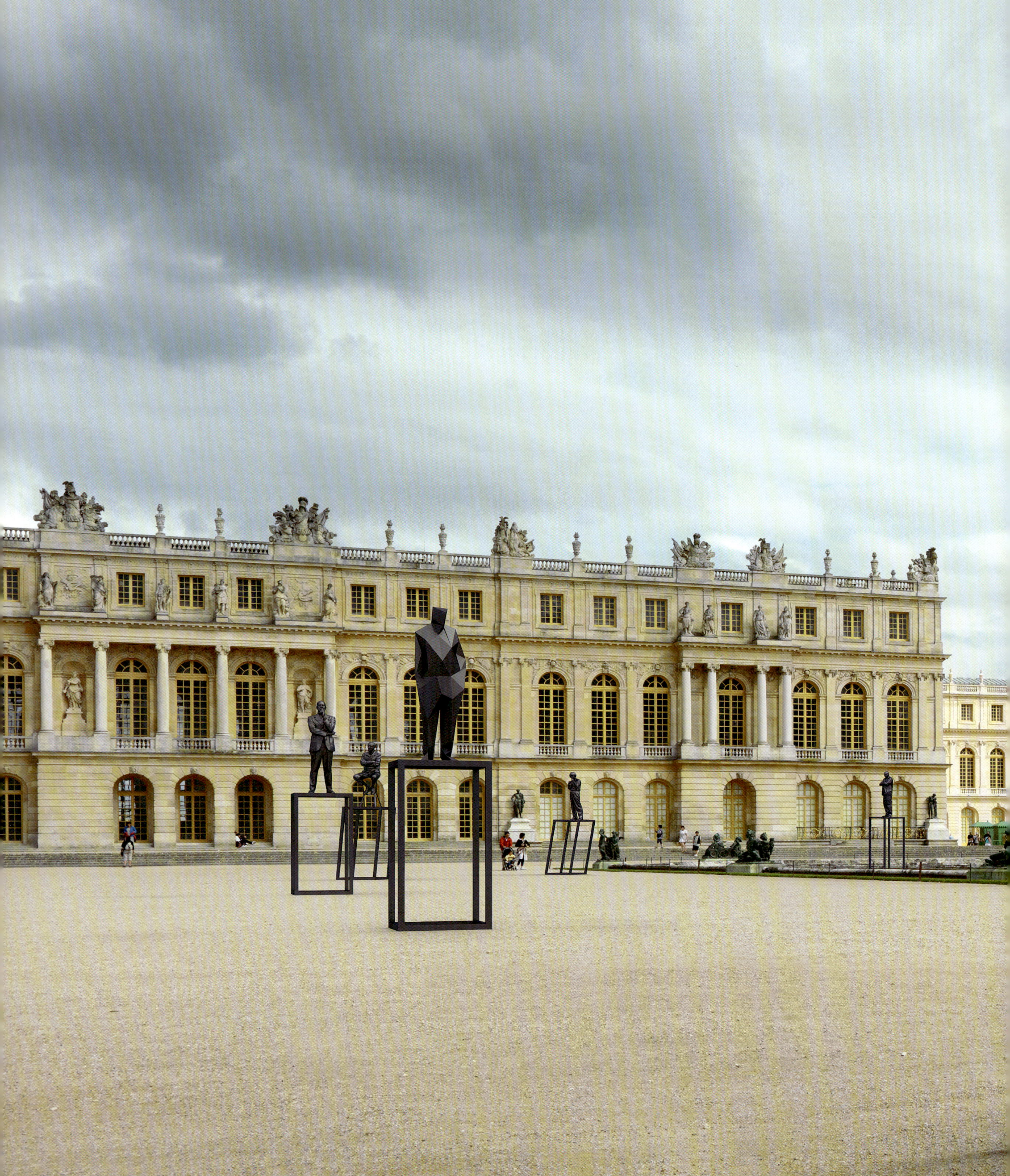

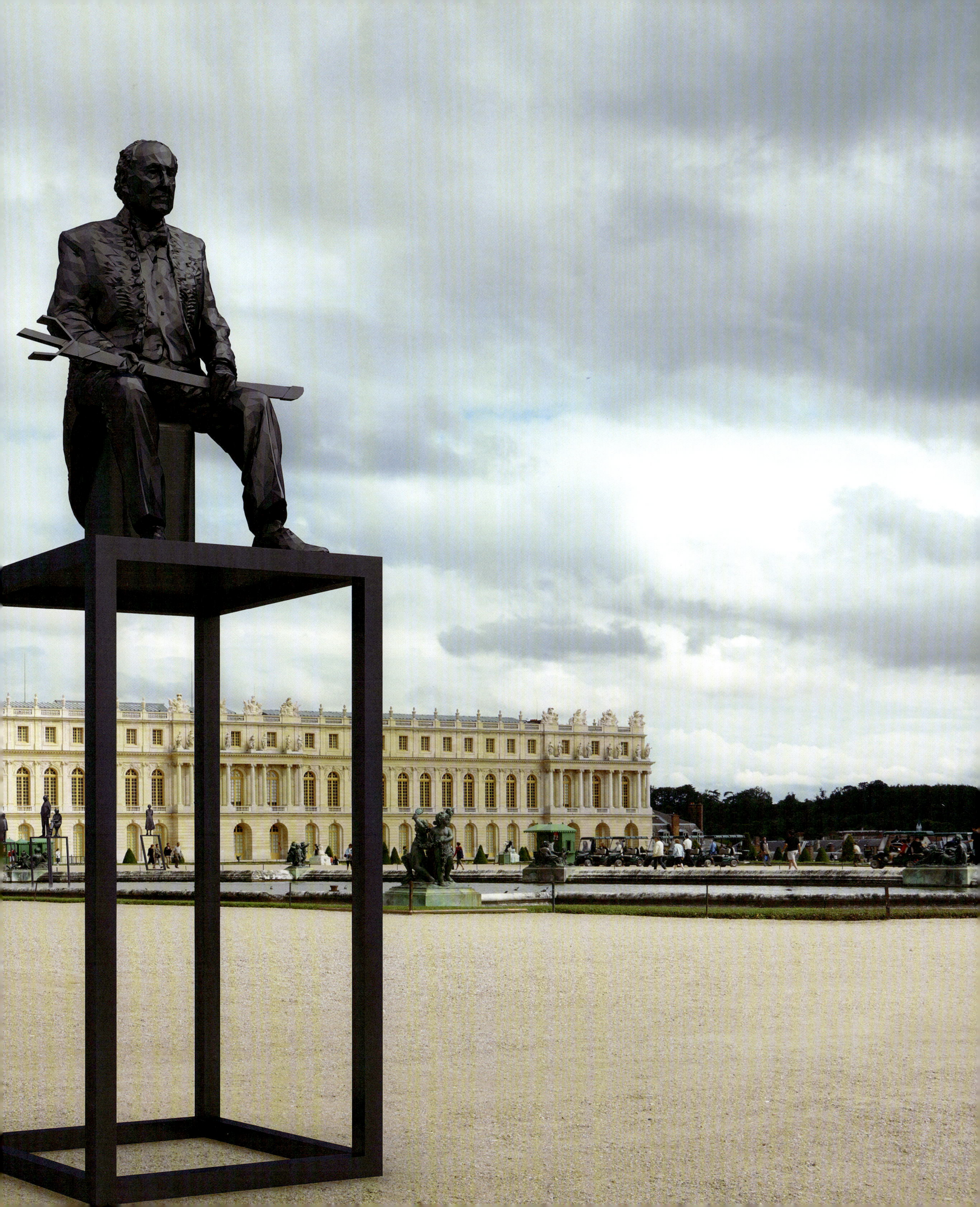

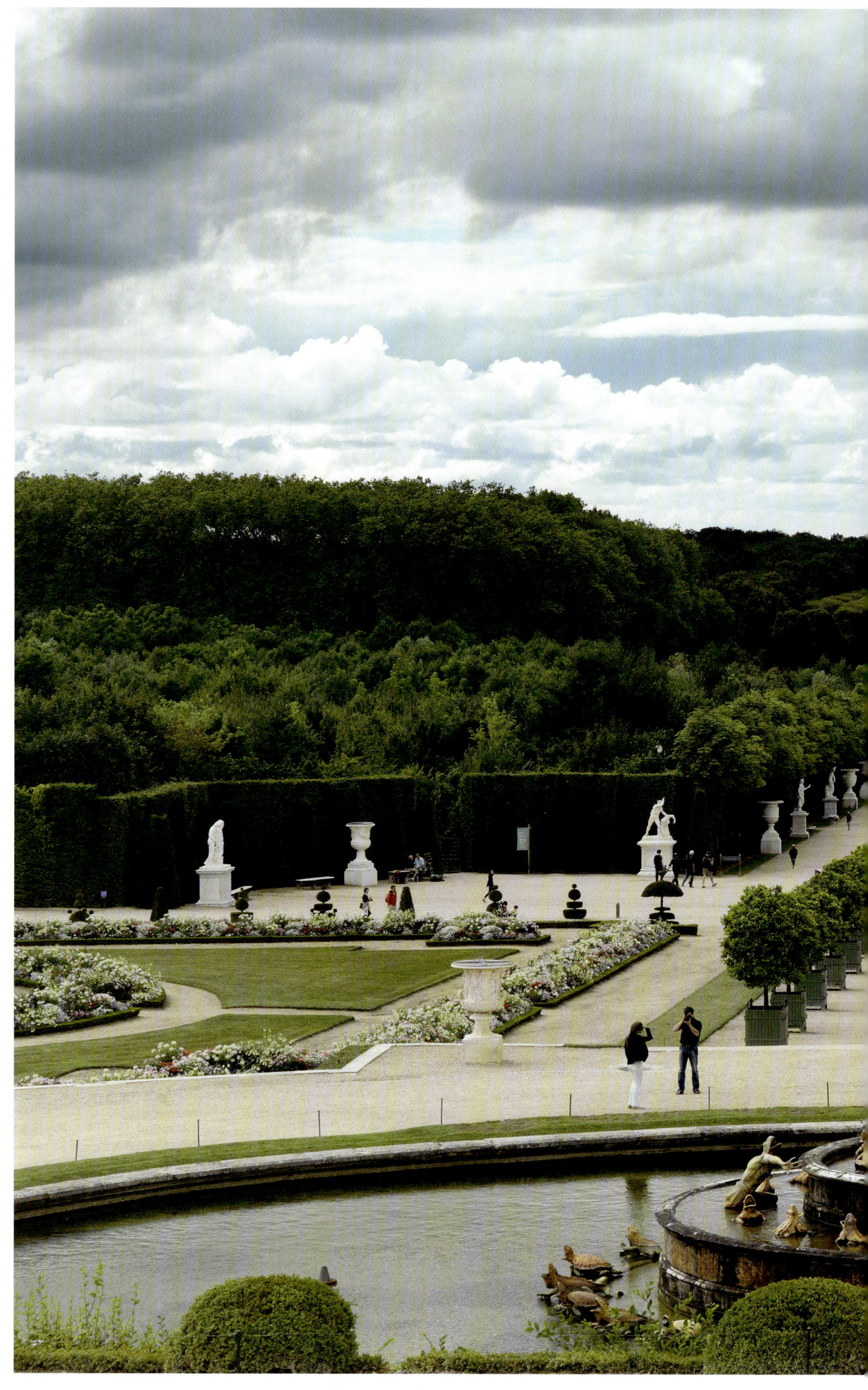

[← P. 138–139] **LES ARCHITECTES (THE ARCHITECTS)**, 2009

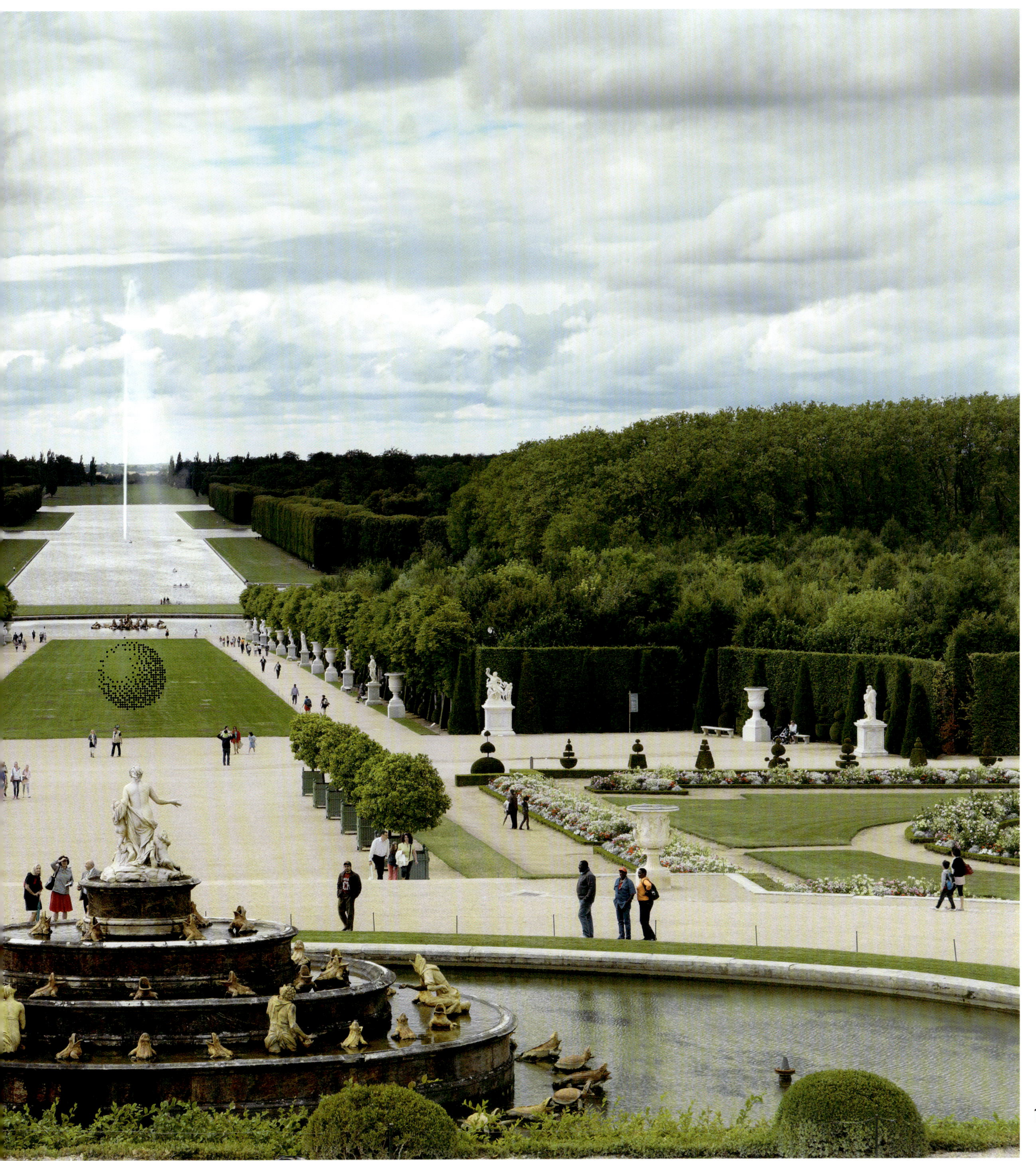

LA LUNE (THE MOON) AND LA FONTAINE (THE FOUNTAIN), 2009

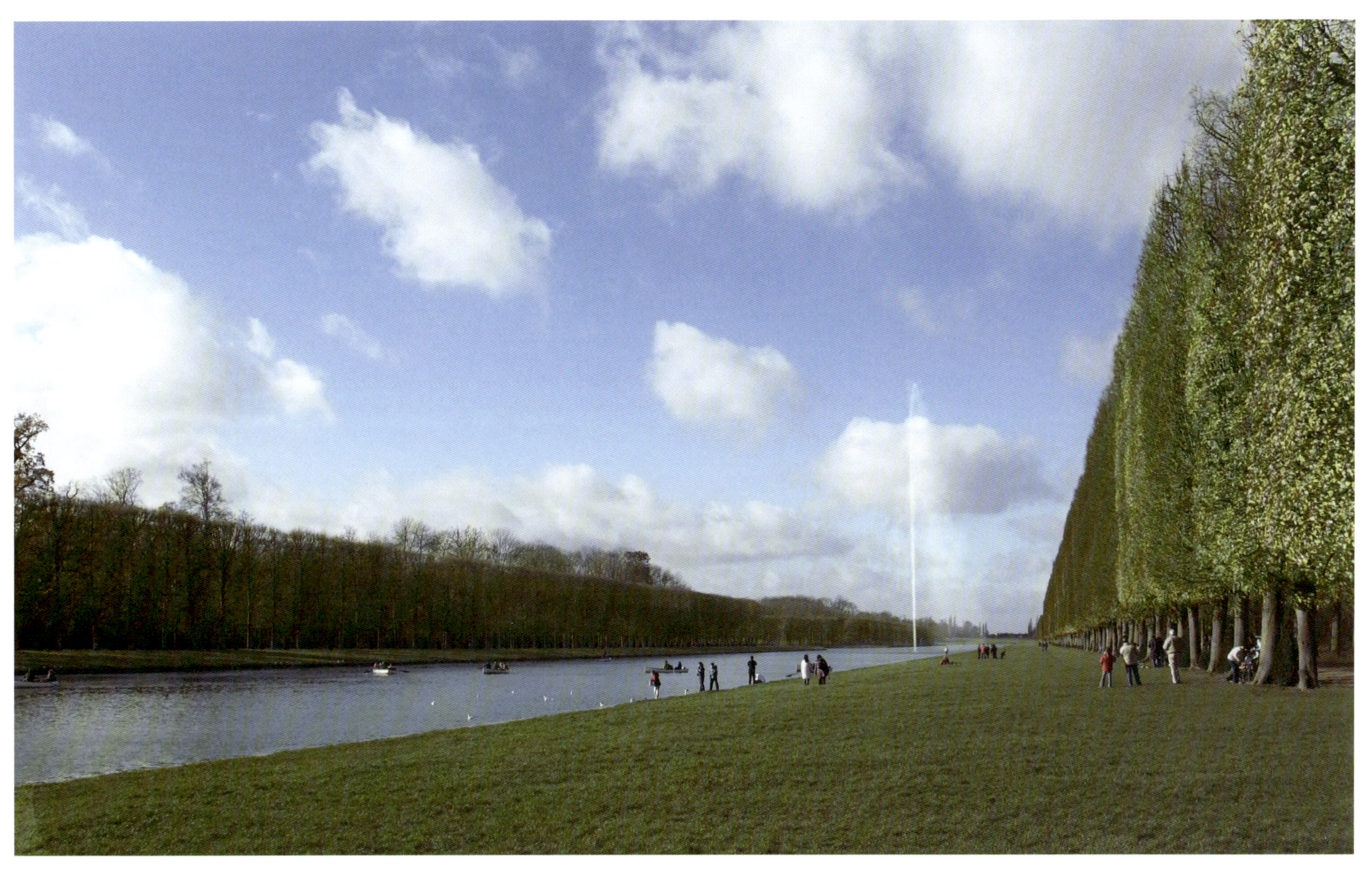

FOUNTAIN, 2009

GHOST LANDSCAPE N° 27 (SAINTE-MARINE), 2002

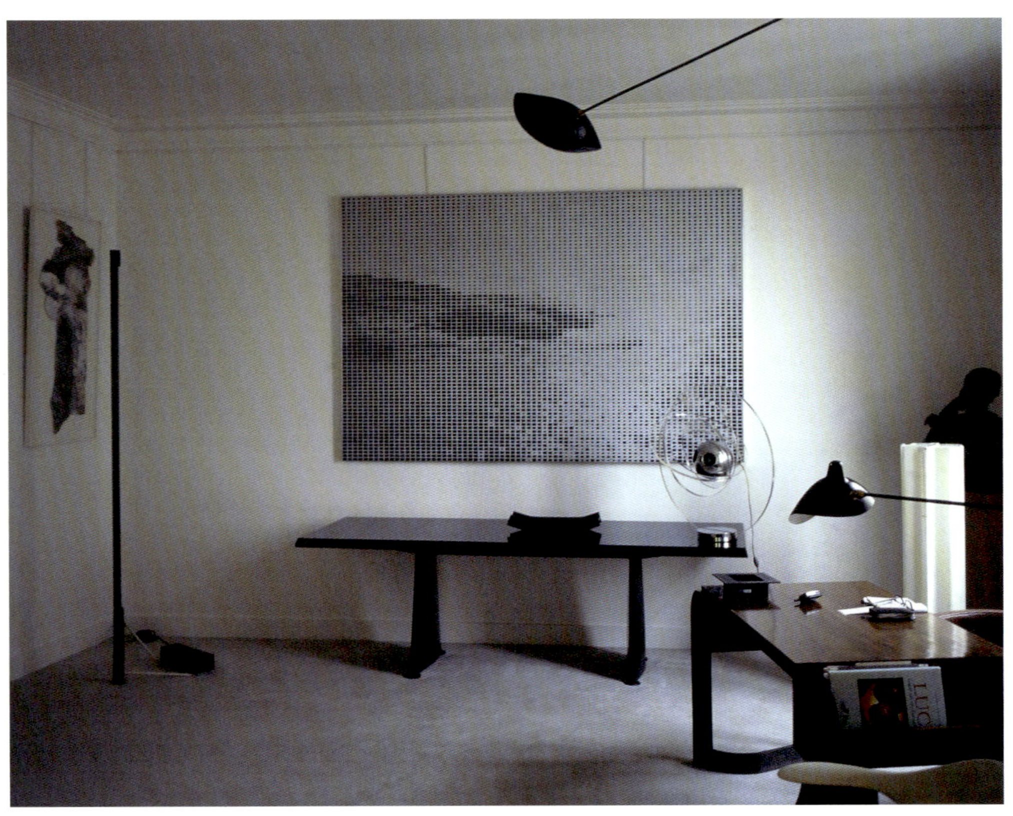

GHOST LANDSCAPE N° 4, 2002

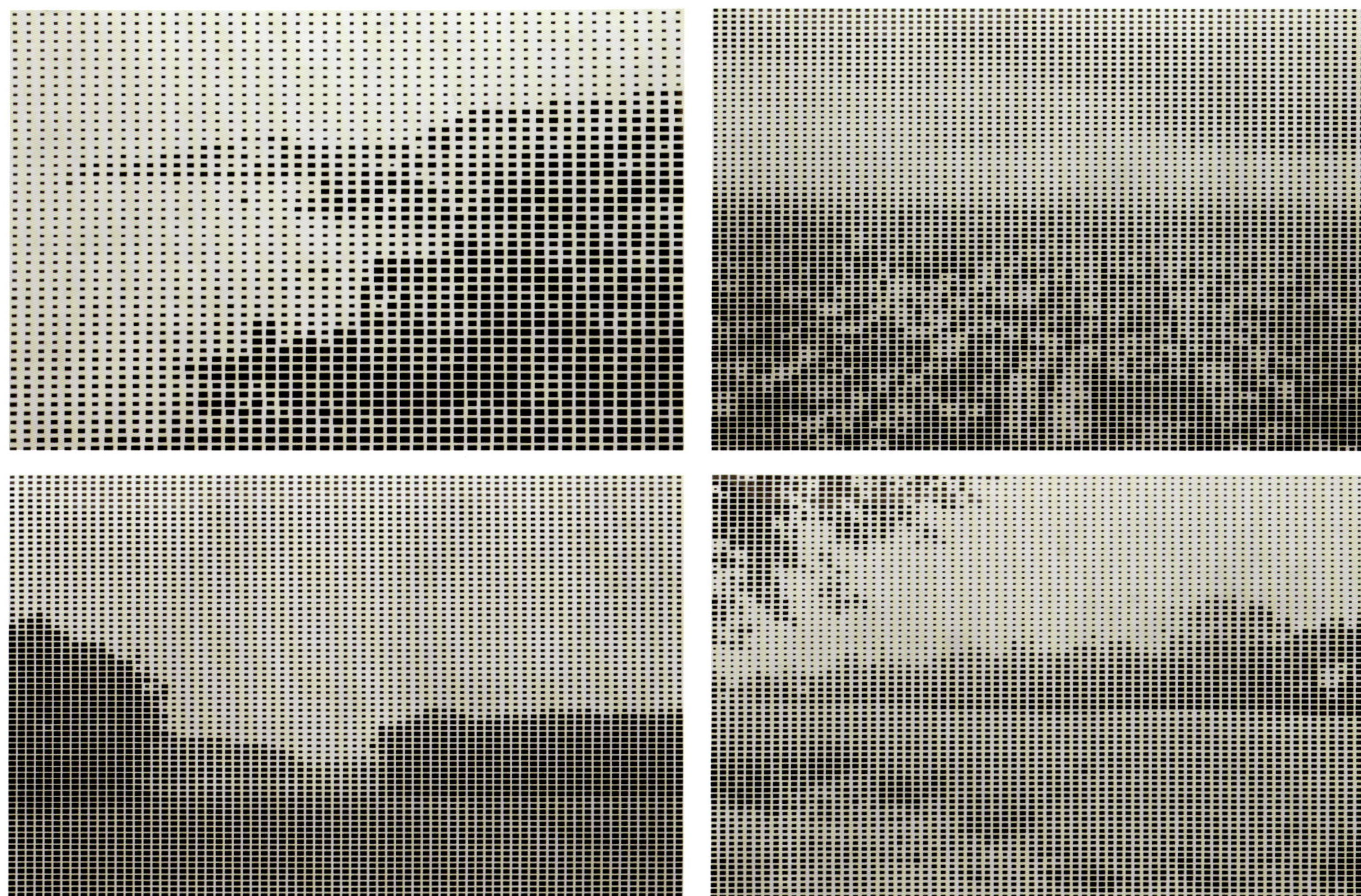

GHOST LANDSCAPE N° 23 (FINISTÈRE), N° 24 (BUENOS AIRES), N° 25 (ILE DE FRANCE) AND, N° 26 (ILE DE FRANCE), 2008

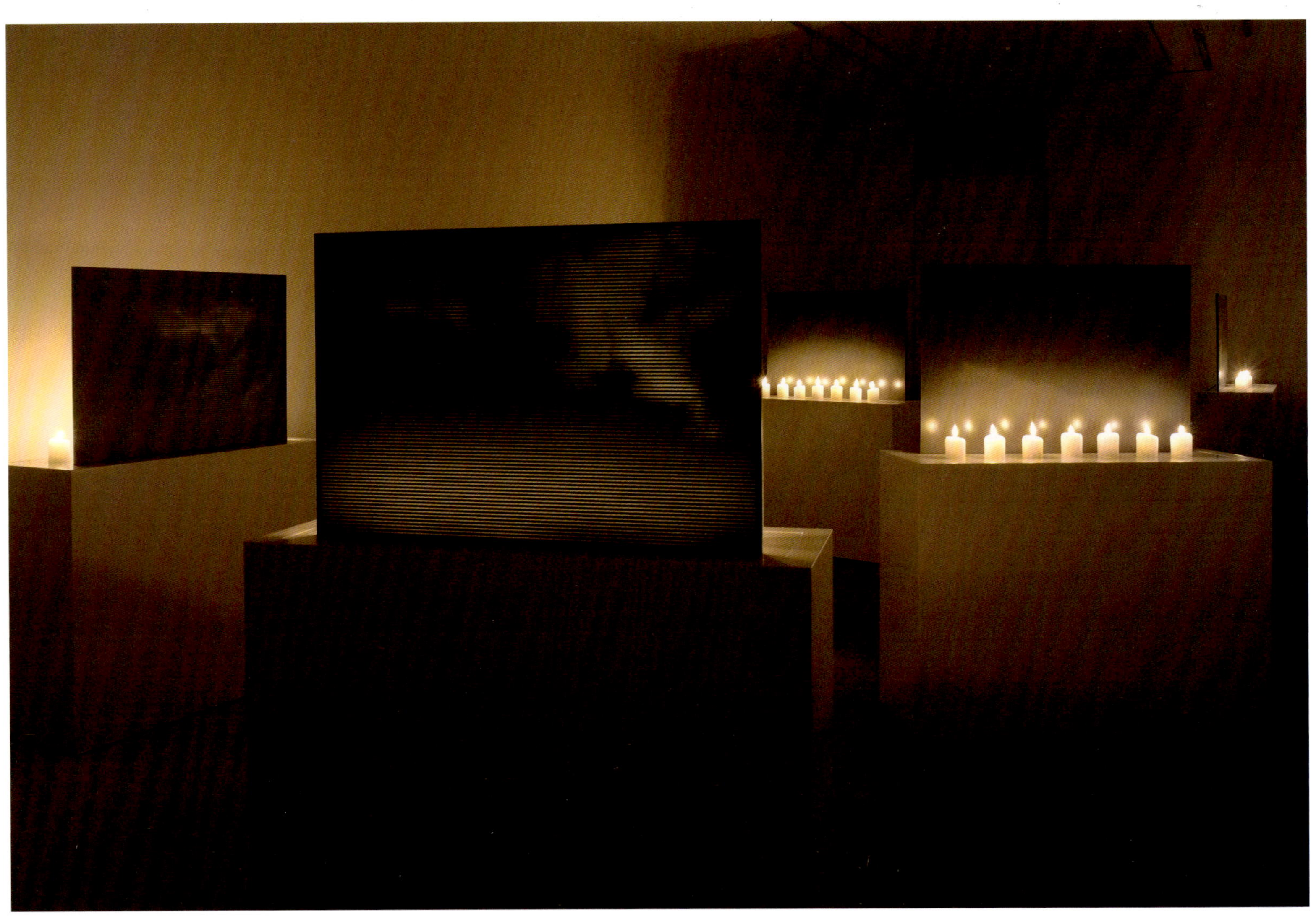

LITHOPHANIES N° 11–16 (NUAGES) (LITHOPHANIES NO 11–16 (CLOUDS)), 2008

LITHOPHANIE N° 12 (NUAGES) (LITHOPHANIE NO 12 (CLOUDS)), 2008

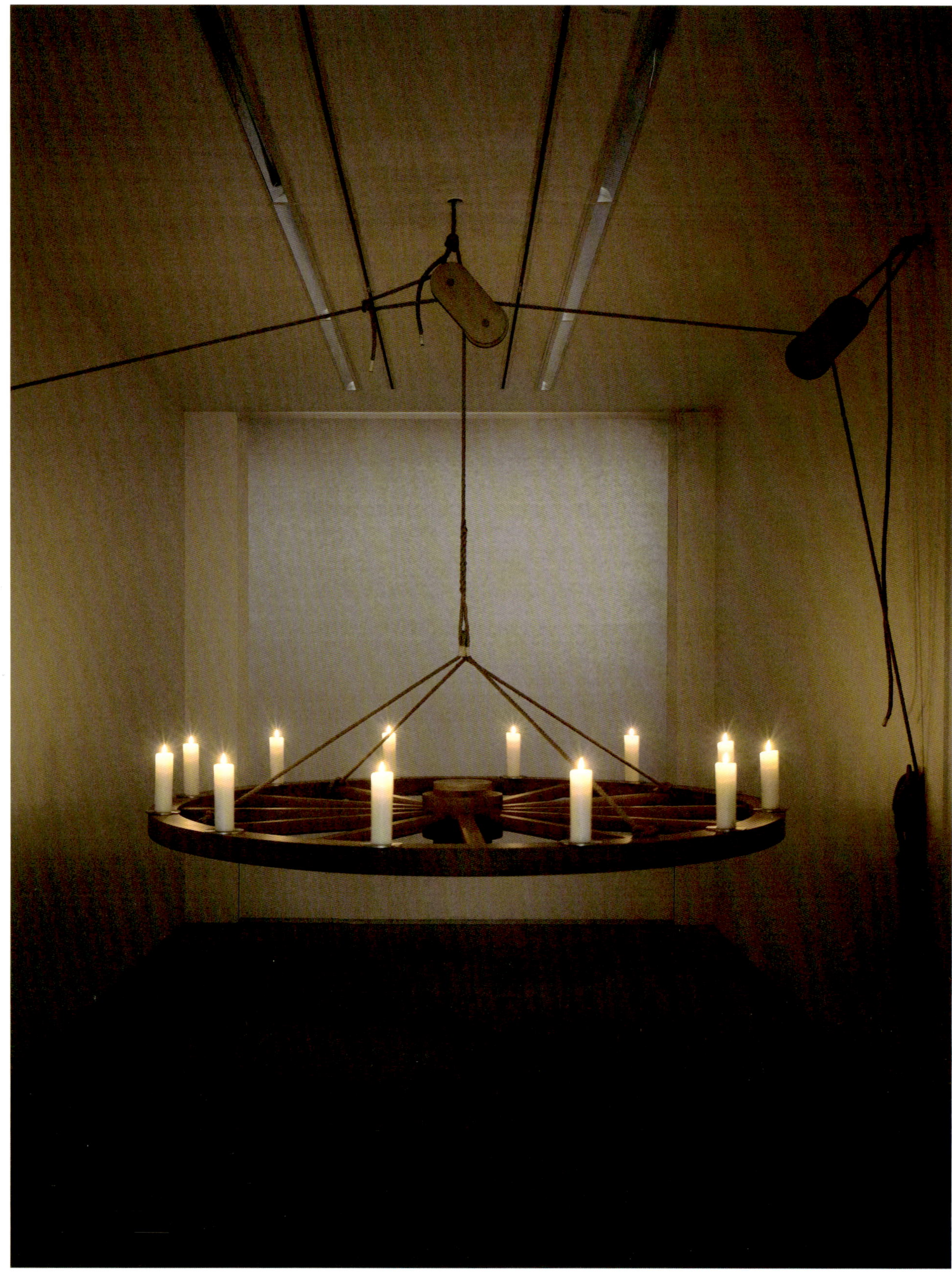

CHANDELIER, 2008

151

Xavier Veilhan is represented by the galleries Andréhn-Schiptjenko, Stockholm; Gering & López Gallery, New York; Galerie Emmanuel Perrotin, Miami / Paris, and Galeria Javier Lopez, Madrid.

AUTHORS' BIOGRAPHIES

Jean-Pierre Criqui, Editor in Chief of *Les Cahiers du Musée national d'art moderne* (Centre Pompidou), is notably the author of *Un trou dans la vie. Essais sur l'art depuis 1960* (Desclée de Brouwer, 2002).

Arnauld Pierre, professor of the history of contemporary art at the Université Paris IV-Sorbonne, is the author, among other books, of *Francis Picabia, la peinture sans aura* (Gallimard, 2002) and of *Calder. Mouvement et réalité* (Hazan, 2009). He is also co-director of the magazine *20/27*.

Writer **Pierre Senges** is the author of a dozen books, among them: *Veuves au maquillage* (Verticales, 2000; Points Seuil, 2002), *Essais fragiles d'aplomb* (Verticales, 2002), *La Réfutation majeure* (Verticales, 2004; Folio, 2007), *Fragments de Lichtenberg* (Verticales, 2008).

Michel Gauthier teaches the history of contemporary art at the Université Paris IV-Sorbonne and is a co-director of the magazine *20/27*. In 2009 he published *Gerwald Rockenschaub* (Ides & Calendes / Supervision) and *Les Promesses du zéro* (Mamco / Les Presses du Réel).

Jean-Jacques Aillagon, former minister of Culture, is President of the Public Establishment of the Museum and National Estate of Versailles.

Laurent Le Bon is Curator at the Musée national d'art moderne, Centre Pompidou, and Director of the Association of Prefiguration of Centre Pompidou-Metz.

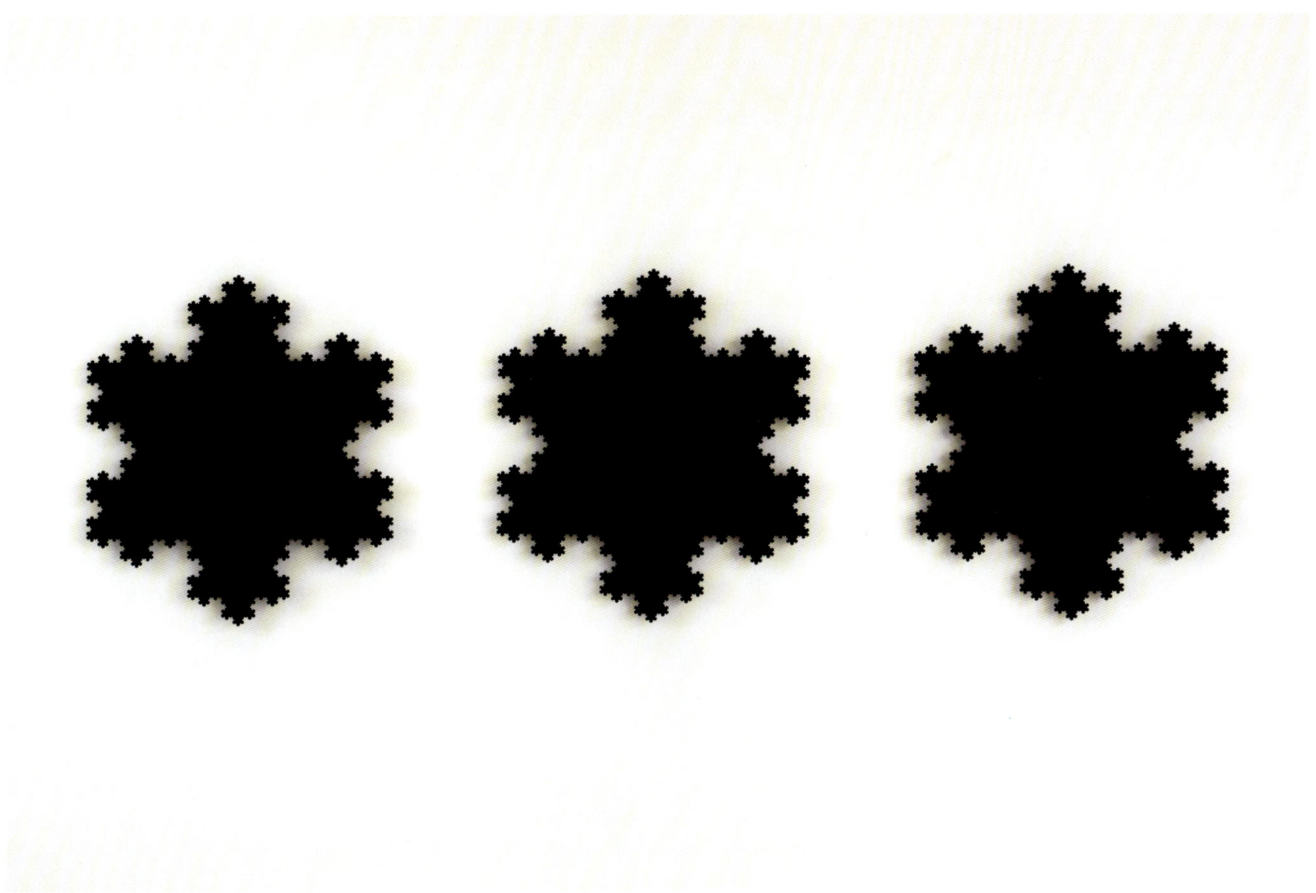

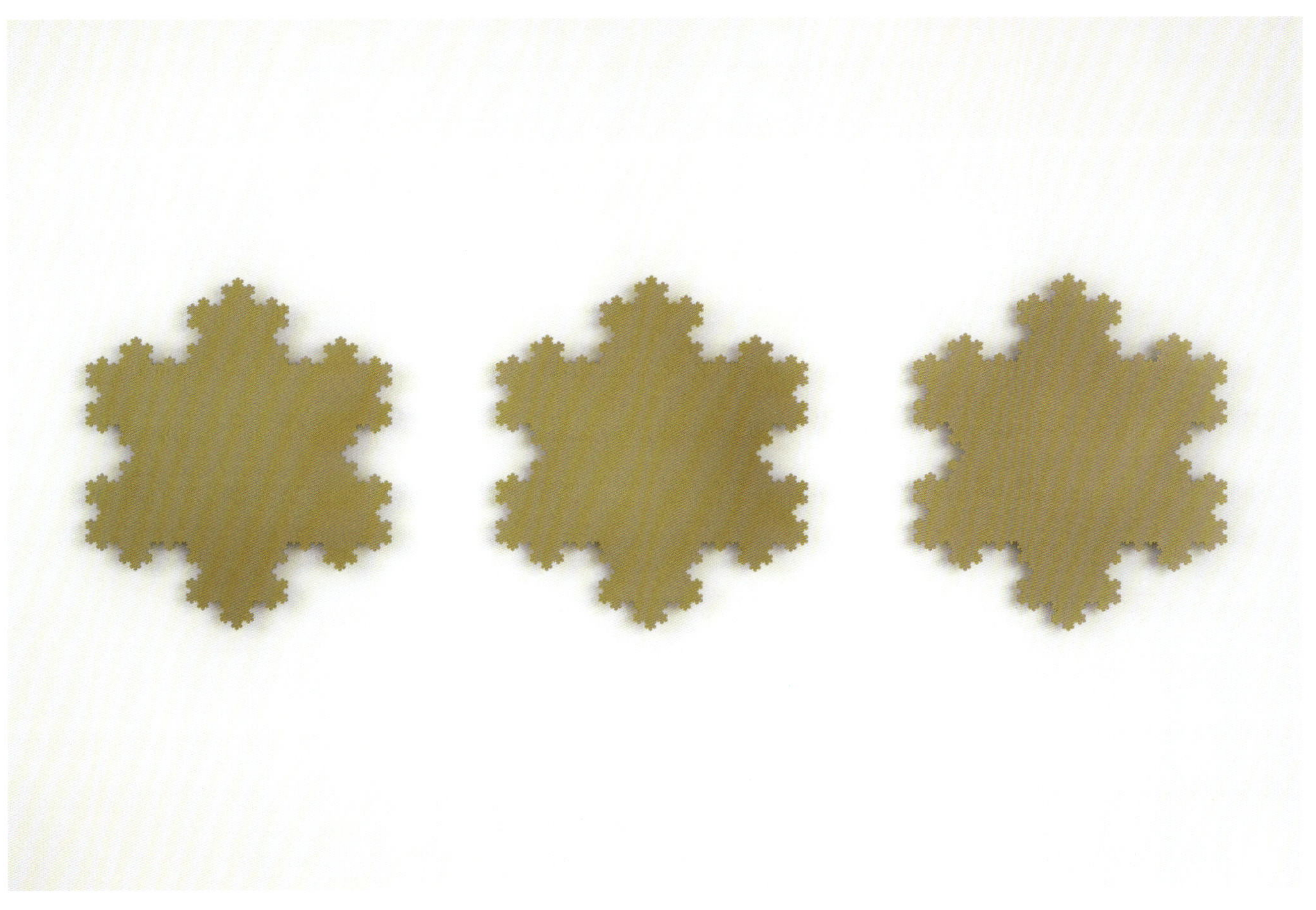

FRACTALS (**BLACK** AND **GOLD**), 2006

XAVIER VEILHAN

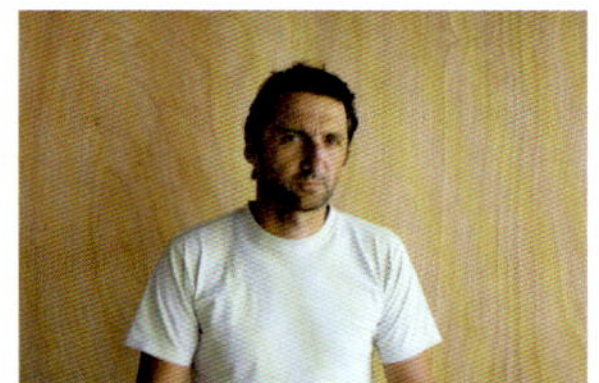

Born in 1963 in Lyon, France
Lives in Paris, France
www.veilhan.net

SOLO EXHIBITIONS / PUBLIC PROJECTS (SELECTED)

2009 — *Veilhan Versailles*, Château de Versailles, Versailles
2008 — *Furtivo*, Galerie Emmanuel Perrotin, Paris
  — *Furtivo*, Pinacoteca Giovanni e Marella Agnelli, Torino
2007 — *Metric*, Gering & López Gallery, New York
  — Andréhn-Schiptjenko Gallery, Stockholm
2006 — *Les Habitants*, Palais des Congrès de la Communauté Urbaine de
    Lyon, with Renzo Piano Building Workshop, Lyon (public project)
  — *Miami Snowflakes*, Galerie Emmanuel Perrotin, Miami
  — *Sculptures automatiques*, Galerie Emmanuel Perrotin, Paris
2005 — *Le Plein emploi*, musée d'Art moderne et contemporain, Strasbourg
  — *Le Projet Hyperréaliste*, Rose Art Museum, Brandeis
    University, Waltham; National Academy Museum, New York
  — *People As Volume*, Andréhn-Schiptjenko Gallery, Stockholm
  — *Fantôme*, Centro de Arte Caja de Burgos, Burgos
  — *Mobile*, Pinksummer Gallery, Genoa
  — *Éléments célestes*, artistic conception, Chanel Jewelry,
    Taiwan, Paris, New York, Hong Kong, Tokyo
  — *Le Lion*, Place Stalingrad, Bordeaux (public project)
2004 — *Vanishing Point*, Espace 315, Centre Pompidou, Paris
  — *Light Machines*, Fondation Vasarely, Aix-en-Provence; Écuries
    de Saint-Hugues, Cluny
  — *Keep the Brown*, Galeria Javier Lopez, Madrid
  — *Big Mobile*, Forum, Centre Pompidou, Paris
  — *Le Monstre*, Place du Marché, Tours (public project)
2003 — *Keep The Brown*, Sandra Gering Gallery, New York
2002 — Barbican Art Center, London
  — Galeria Javier Lopez, Madrid
  — Installation from the workshop, Center for Contemporary
    Art, Kitakyushu
  — Konsthallen, Göteborg
2001 — Sandra Gering Gallery, New York
  — Fundació Joan Miró, Centre d'Estudis d'arte contemporani,
    Barcelona
  — Pinksummer Gallery, Genoa
  — Andréhn-Schiptjenko Gallery, Stockholm
2000 — Le Magasin, Grenoble
  — *La Ford T*, 5th floor terrace, Centre Pompidou, Paris
  — Sandra Gering Gallery, New York
  — *The Rhinoceros*, Yves St. Laurent, New York
1999 — *La Forêt*, Le Consortium, Dijon
  — *La Ford T*, MAMCO, Geneva
  — Galerie der Stadt, Schwaz
  — Galerie Gio Marconi, Milan
1998 — Galeria Javier Lopez, Madrid
  — Galerie Jennifer Flay, Paris
  — Center for Contemporary Art, Kitakyushu
  — Centre d'art de Brétigny-sur-Orge
1997 — Sandra Gering Gallery, New York
1995 — Centre de Création Contemporaine, Tours
  — Sandra Gering Gallery, New York
1993 — ARC, musée d'Art moderne de la Ville de Paris, Paris
  — Andréhn-Schiptjenko Gallery, Stockholm
1991 — *Un centimètre égal un mètre*, Centre d'art contemporain,
    Parc de Pougues-les-Eaux, Nevers
  — Galerie Jennifer Flay, Paris
1990 — *Un peu de biologie*, Galleria Fac-Simile, Milan

GROUP EXHIBITIONS (SELECTED)

2009 — *N'importe Quoi*, musée d'Art Contemporain, Lyon
2008 — *Prospect 1 New Orleans*, Biennial of International
    Contemporary Art, New Orleans
  — *Modern Young People. Post Punk, Cold Wave & Novö Culture in
    France, 1978–1983*, galerie du jour agnès b., Paris
2007 — *The Incomplete*, Chelsea Art Museum, New York
  — *Airs de Paris*, Centre Pompidou, Paris (a project with Daniel
    Buren; *Aérolite*, a musical show with Air)
  — Galerie Rüdiger Schöttle, Munich
  — *De leur temps 2*, musée de Grenoble, Grenoble
  — *Rouge Baiser*, FRAC des Pays de la Loire, Estuaire 2007, Nantes
2006 — *La Force de l'Art*, Grand Palais, Paris
  — *Supernova: Experience Pommery #3*, Domaine Pommery, Reims
  — *Thank You for The Music*, Simon Lee Gallery, London
  — *Collection and New Acquisitions*, Viktor Pinchuk Foundation, Kiev
  — *Boucle*, place du Trocadéro; *Ville nouvelle*, Cour de l'Hôtel de
    Ville, Nuit Blanche, Paris
2005 — *Water (Without You I'm Not)—Thoughts of a Fish in a Deep
    Sea*, 3rd Biennial of Contemporary Art, Valencia
  — *Fundacion La Caixa Collection, 20 Years with Contemporary
    Art: New Acquisitions*, Caixa Forum, Barcelona
  — *De lo Real y lo Ficticio: Arte contemporaneo de Francia*, Museo
    de Arte Moderno de Mexico, Mexico; Bass Museum, Miami
  — *L'œil moteur, Art optique et cinétique 1950–1975*, musée d'Art
    moderne et contemporain, Strasbourg
2004 — *None of the Above*, Swiss Institute Contemporary Art, New York
  — *Genesis Sculpture: Experience Pommery #2*, Domaine
    Pommery, Reims
  — *L'Éblouissement*, Jeu de paume, Paris
  — *Contrepoint*, Musée du Louvre, Paris
2003 — *It Happened Tomorrow*, 7th Lyon Biennial of Contemporary Art,
    Lyon
  — *Coollustre*, Collection Lambert, Avignon
  — 25th edition of International Biennial of Graphic Arts,
    Ljubljana, Slovenia
  — *Glass Wall*, device conceived for *Faits et Gestes*, Atelier de
    mécanique, Parc des Ateliers SNCF, Arles
2002 — *Collections croisées*, CAPC-musée d'Art contemporain,
    Bordeaux
  — *La Part de l'autre*, Carré d'art, Nîmes
  — *Les Animaux sortent de leur réserve*, Centre Pompidou, Paris
  — *Light X Eight*, Jewish Museum, New York
  — *2002 Taipei Biennial: Great Theatre Of The World*, Taipei Fine
    Arts Museum, Taiwan
2000 — *Jour de fête*, Centre Pompidou, Paris
  — *Vivre sa vie*, Tramway, Glasgow
1999 — *Abracadabra*, Tate Gallery, London
  — *Côté Sud... Entschuldigong*, La Ferme du Buisson, Noisiel;
    Nouveau Musée-Institut d'art contemporain, Villeurbanne
  — *Bu!*, Palazzo delle Papesse, Siena
1998 — *Premises*, Guggenheim Museum, New York
  — *La Ville, Le Jardin, La Mémoire*, Villa Medici, Rome
1997 — *Selections from the Collection*, Fondation Cartier pour l'Art
    contemporain, Paris
  — *Need for Speed*, Kunsthalle, Graz
  — *Coïncidences*, Fondation Cartier pour l'Art contemporain, Paris
1996 — *Traffic*, CAPC-musée d'art contemporain, Bordeaux
1991 — *No Man's Time*, Villa Arson, Nice
1990 — *French Kiss. A Talk Show*, Halle Sud, Geneva

SELECTED BIBLIOGRAPHY
MONOGRAPHS AND SOLO EXHIBITIONS CATALOGUES
— *Xavier Veilhan. Un peu de biologie*, with an interview by
Nicolas Bourriaud (in Italian and in English), exhibition cata-
logue, Galleria Fac-Simile, Milan 1990
— *Un centimètre égal un mètre*, with texts by Eric Troncy, Liam
Gillick (in French and English), exhibition catalogue, A.P.A.C.,
Centre d'Art Contemporain, Nevers & Paris 1991
— *Xavier Veilhan*, artist book, Galerie Jennifer Flay, Paris 1992
— Xavier Veilhan, exhibition catalogue, musée d'Art moderne de
la Ville de Paris, 1993
— *Xavier Veilhan,* Centre de Création Contemporaine, Tours;
FRAC Languedoc Roussillon, Montpellier; Consortium, Centre
d'Art Contemporain, Dijon; JRP Editions, Geneva 1995
— *Tableaux*, 1997–1998, Center for Contemporary Art,
Kitakyushu 1999
— *Xavier Veilhan*, with texts by Dan Cameron, Liam Gillick,
Alison Gingeras, John Miller, Le Magasin, Grenoble 2000
— *Vanishing Point*, with texts by Alison Gingeras and Christine
Macel, Centre Pompidou, Paris 2004
— *Xavier Veilhan*, with text by David Perreau, Editions Hazan,
Paris 2004
— *Fantôme*, with text by Fernandeo Casto Florez, Centro de Arte
Caja de Burgos, Burgos 2005
— *Le Plein emploi*, with texts by Michel Gauthier, Patrick Javault,
Hakan Nilsson, and John Welchman (in French and English),
exhibition catalogue, musée d'Art moderne et contemporain,
Strasbourg 2005
— *Xavier Veilhan 256 jours*, Jordan Feldman, dvd, 90 min., bureau
des vidéos, Paris 2005
— *Light Machines*, Les Presses du Réel, Dijon 2007

EXHIBITION CATALOGUES
— *French Kiss. A Talk Show*, with texts by Nicolas Bourriaud, Eric
Troncy, Ijsbrand van Veelen (in French), Halle Sud, Geneva 1990
— *No Man's Time*, with texts by Christian Bernard, Nicolas
Bourriaud, Jean-Yves Jouannais, Eric Troncy, Dominique
Gonzales-Foerster, Pierre Ménard, Pierre Joseph, Aimee
Rankin & Ashley Bickerton, Johan Muyle, Philippe Parreno, Jim
Shaw, Lily van der Stokker, Xavier Veilhan & Liam Gillick, Sylvie
Fleury, Jean-Philippe Vienne (in French), Angela Bulloch,
Henry Bond & Liam Gillick (in English), Villa Arson, Nice 1991
— *Comme rien d'autre que des rencontres / Nothing but encoun-
ters as it were*, with texts by Florent Bex, Isabelle Vierget,
Edith Doove (in German, French, and English), MUHKA,
Antwerp 1993
— *Beyond the Borders*, with texts by Lee Yongwoo, Oh Kwang-su,
Kathy Halbreich & Rochelle Steiner, Sung Wan-kyung, Jean
de Loisy, Anda Rottenberg, Clive Adams, You Hong-june (in
English and Korean), Kwangju Biennale, 1995
— *Traffic*, with texts by Nicolas Bourriaud, Angela Bulloch
& Liam Gillick, Jes Brinch & Henrik Plenge Jakobsen, Maurizio
Cattelan & Philippe Parreno, Honoré d'O, Liam Gillick,
Christine Hill, Carsten Höller, Peter Land, Miltos Manetas,
Jason Rhoades, Christopher Sperandino & Simon Grennan,
Kenji Yanobe (in French and English), CAPC-musée d'Art
contemporain, Bordeaux 1996
— *Coïncidences*, with texts by André Magnin, Judith Bartolani &
Claude Caillol, Raphaëlle Jeune, Eric Duyckaerts, Franck Scurti,
Pierre Huyghe, Jean-Baptiste Bruant, Pierre Bismuth (in French),
Fondation Cartier pour l'art contemporain, Paris 1997

— *La Ville, Le Jardin, La Mémoire : 1. La Ville,* with a discussion
between Laurence Bossé, Carolyn Christov-Bakargiev &
Hans Ulrich-Obrist, and statements by the artists (in Italian,
French, and English), as well as autonomous publications
for each artist, Villa Médicis, Roma 1998
— *Coté Sud... Entschuldigung*, with texts by Karine Vonna,
Chantal Cusin-Berche, José Lebrero Stals, Jean-Louis
Maubant, Sergio Risaliti, Leonel Moura, Jean-Claude Conésa,
Miquel Molins, Francisco Jarauta, Marc Jimenez, and inter-
views by Karinne Vonna with Jordi Colomer, José Maldonado,
Eulàlia Valldosera, Pierre Huyghe, Pierre Joseph, Xavier
Veilhan, Liliana Moro, Alessandra Tesi, Grazia Toderi, Augusto
Alves Da Silva, Miguel Palma, João Tabarra (in French),
Nouveau Musée-Institut d'art contemporain / La Ferme du
Buisson, Villeurbanne & Noisiel 1998
— *Premises. Invested Spaces in Visual Arts, Architecture and
Design from France, 1958–1998*, with texts by Alison Gingeras,
Bernard Blistène, Alain Guiheux, Sylvère Lotringer, Denis Hollier,
D.W. Rodowich, Benjamin H.D. Buchloch, Dudley Andrew,
Philippe Abaïzar, Joseph Abram, Sophie Tasma-Anargyror
(in English), Guggenheim Museum Soho, New York 1998
— *Bú!*, with texts by Augusto Pieroni, Stefano Chiodi, Maria Perozino,
Chiara Bertola (in Italian), Palazzo delle Papesse, Siena 1999
— *Flashes. Tendências contemporâneas / Contemporary Trends.
Colecção / Collection Fondation Cartier pour l'art contemporain*,
with texts by Véronique Baton, Lionel Bovier, Hervé Chandès,
Hélène Kelmachter, Grazia Quaroni, Anne Bertrand, Margarida
Veiga (in Portuguese and English), Centro Cultural de Belém,
Lisboa Trouble Spot Painting, with texts by Cyril Jarbon (in French
and English), Hans Rudolph Reust (in German and English), Wim
Peteers (in Dutch and English), and an interview by Vincent
Geyskens with Narcisse Tordoir & Luc Tuymans (in Dutch and
English), NICC, MUHKA, Antwerp 1999
— *Abracadabra*, with texts by Nicholas Serota, Catherine Kinley,
Martijn van Niieuwenhuyzen, Catherine Grenier, Tanya Barson,
Jemima Montago (in English), Tate Gallery, London 1999
— *Jour de fête*, with a text by Sophie Duplaix & Catherine Grenier
(in French), Centre Pompidou, Paris 2000
— *Vivre sa vie*, curated by Tanya Leighton, Tramway, Glasgow 2000
— *Xn 00*, with texts by Lionel Bovier, Mai-Thu Perret, Oyvind
Fahlström, Michel Foucault, Robert Morris, Michel de Certeau,
Vito Acconci, Mary Mc Leod, Beatriz Colomina, Jean-Charles
Masséra (in French and English), Espace des Arts, Châlon-sur-
Saône 2000
— *Avant* and *Après*, with texts by Xavier Douroux, Franck
Gautherot, Robert Nickas, Anne Pontegnie, Eric Troncy,
Thierry Raspail, catalogues for the 7th Biennale d'art contem-
porain de Lyon, Lyon 2003 / 2004
— *Agua sin ti no soy / Water Without You I'm Not*, with texts by
Luigi Settembrini, Franck Gautherot, Seungduk Kim, Hongnam
Kim, Anna Maria Torres, Leonardo Santos, Maria Calabuig
(in Spanish and English), exhibition catalogue, 3rd Biennial of
Valencia Charta, Generalitat Valenciana, Valencia 2005
— *L'œil moteur, Art optique et cinétique 1950–1975*, Emmanuel
Guigon, Arnauld Pierre (in French), musée d'Art moderne et
contemporain, Strasbourg
— *Airs de Paris*, Christine Macel, Valérie Guillaume(in French
and English), Centre Pompidou, Paris 2007
— *Stream 01. Production, Création, Architecture*, Philippe
Chiambaretta (in French), Stream / PAC et Monografik
Editions, Paris 2008

EXHIBITION
This monograph is published on the occasion of the exhibition
Veilhan Versailles, September 13–December 13, 2009, at the
Château de Versailles, by the l'Établissement public du musée
and the domaine national de Versailles.
The publication has received support from the Château de
Versailles Spectacle.

PRESIDENT OF THE PUBLIC ESTABLISHMENT OF THE MUSEUM
AND NATIONAL ESTATE OF VERSAILLES
Jean-Jacques Aillagon

EXHIBITION CURATOR
Laurent Le Bon

STUDIO XAVIER VEILHAN
SCENOGRAPHY AND ARTISTIC COLLABORATION
Alexis Bertrand
STUDIO
Mahaut de Kerraoul, Violeta Kreimer, François-Thibaut Pencenat
DESIGN
Laurent Pinon
GRAPHIC IDENTITY *VEILHAN VERSAILLES*
Yorgo Tloupas
INFORMATION DESIGN AND 3D-RENDERINGS
Vincent Germond

AIA PRODUCTIONS
DIRECTOR
Renaud Sabari
PROJECT MANAGER
Tamara Charles
COORDINATION ASSISTANT
Lola Peiré
LOGISTICS
Céline Marchand

CHÂTEAU DE VERSAILLES SPECTACLES
MANAGER
Laurent Brunner
GENERAL SECRETARY
Philippe Chamaux
TECHNICAL DIRECTOR
Marc Blanc
PRODUCTION
Elodie Berthelot, Catherine Clément, Xénophane Canteaut
CORPORATE PATRONAGE AND PARTNERSHIPS
Amélie de Ronseray, Cloé le Roux
COMMUNICATION
Fanny Collard, Emilie Camjusan

ESTABLISHMENT OF THE MUSEUM AND NATIONAL ESTATE OF VERSAILLES
GENERAL MANAGER
Béatrix Saule
ADMINISTRATOR
Denis Berthomier
CULTURAL DEVELOPMENT MANAGER
Denis Verdier-Magneau
CHIEF OF EXHIBITIONS DEPARTMENT
Silvia Roman
PUBLIC AND SECURITY MANAGER
Thierry Webley
PUBLIC RELATIONS MANAGER
Olivier Josse
INFORMATION AND COMMUNICATION MANAGER
Ariane de Lestrange
ESTATE AND GARDENS MANAGER
Daniel Sancho
CHIEF OF GARDENS DEPARTMENT
Joël Cottin
ADMINISTRATIVE AND FINANCIAL DIRECTION
Nathalie Bastière

ACKNOWLEDGEMENTS
For their generous support to the *Veilhan Versailles* project, the artist,
the Etablissement public du musée et du domaine national de Versailles,
Château de Versailles Spectacles, and the exhibition curator would
like to thank the following private and public partners:
— Allard Palaces
— the Association pour la Diffusion internationale de l'art français
(ADIAF)
— the Centre national des arts plastiques (CNAP) and the Délégation
aux arts plastiques (DAP)
— Chanel
— the Conseil général des Yvelines
— Emmanuel Perrotin gallery, Paris/Miami
— Galeries Lafayette group

As well as Alexandre Allard, Sophie Calle, Natacha Carron, Catherine
Crozier, Amélie Darras, Jean-Olivier Desprès, Renaud Detalle, Frédéric
Devenoge, Christophe Durand-Ruel, Laurent Ghnassia, Guillaume
Houzé, Olivier Kaeppelin, Richard Lagrange, Anastassia Makridou,
Frédéric Migayrou, Hervé Mikaeloff, Sébastien Tellier, Guy Tortosa, Cathy
Vedovi, Timothée and Vassili Verrecchia; and the architects Tadao
Ando, Philippe Bona et Elisabeth Lemercier, Sir Norman Foster, Anne
Lacaton et Jean-Philippe Vassal, Claude Parent, Renzo Piano, Richard
Rogers, Jean Nouvel and Kazuyo Sejima.

PUBLICATION
EDITORIAL DIRECTOR
Jean-Pierre Criqui

PROJECT MANAGER
Clément Dirié

ENGLISH COPYEDITOR
Clare Manchester

TRANSLATIONS FROM THE FRENCH
Susan Pickford and Bernard Hoepffner (Pierre Senges)

DESIGN
no-do [Noémie Gygax & Yann Do]

TYPEFACE
AS Black by Aurèle Sack

PHOTOGRAPHIC CREDITS
Atelier Xavier Veilhan, Paris

SEPARATIONS, PRINTING AND BINDING
Musumeci S.p.A., Quart (Aosta)

THANKS
Xavier Veilhan would like to thank:
Mahaut de Kerraoul, Violeta Kreimer and François-Thibaut Pencenat, Alexis Bertrand, Pablo Cavero, Jordan Feldman, Virginie Marielle, Paulo Peirera, Laurent Pinon, Florian Sumi, Joséphine Théry, Yorgo Tloupas and François Valenza.

As well as Cilène Andréhn and Marina Schiptjenko, Sandra Gering and Javier Lopez, Philippe Joppin, Emmanuelle Orenga de Gaffory and Emmanuel Perrotin, Tamara Charles, Lola Peiré, Xavier Montagnon and Renaud Sabari.

Last but no least, Laurence Uguen, Jean, Alix and Antoine Veilhan.

For the *Veilhan Versailles* project: Yves Malka and Pierre de Poucques d'Enzyme Design, Valérie Roi Sans Sac and Eric Rollet of Créaform, Philippe Cléré and Vincent Germond.

The publication has received generous support from l'ADIAF-Association pour la Diffusion Internationale de l'Art Français and from the Groupe Galeries Lafayette, Paris, partners of the exhibition *Veilhan Versailles*.

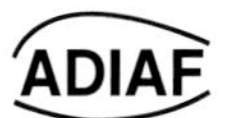

www.adiaf.com

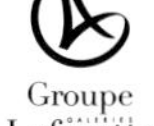

www.galerieslafayette.com

IMPRINT

PUBLISHED BY
JRP|Ringier
Letzigraben 134
CH–8047 Zurich
Tel. +41 (0) 43 311 27 50
Fax +41 (0) 43 311 27 51
www.jrp-ringier.com
info@jrp-ringier.com

ISBN 978-3-03764-077-7
(French edition available by Les Presses du réel, ISBN 978-2-84066-353-9)

JRP|Ringier books are available internationally at selected
bookstores and from the following distribution partners:

SWITZERLAND
Buch 2000
AVA Verlagsauslieferung AG
Centralweg 16
CH–8910 Affoltern a.A.
buch2000@ava.ch
www.ava.ch

FRANCE
Les Presses du réel
35 rue Colson
F–21000 Dijon
info@lespressesdureel.com
www.lespressesdureel.com

GERMANY AND AUSTRIA
Vice Versa Vertrieb
Immanuelkirchstrasse 12
D–10405 Berlin
info@vice-versa-vertrieb.de
www.vice-versa-vertrieb.de

UK AND OTHER EUROPEAN COUNTRIES
Cornerhouse Publications
70 Oxford Street
UK–Manchester M1 5NH
publications@cornerhouse.org
www.cornerhouse.org / books

USA, CANADA, ASIA, AND AUSTRALIA
D.A.P. / Distributed Art Publishers
155 Sixth Avenue, 2nd Floor
USA–New York, NY 10013
dap@dapinc.com, www.artbook.com

For a list of our partner bookshops or for any general questions,
please contact JRP|Ringier directly at *info@jrp-ringier.com*, or visit
our homepage *www.jrp-ringier.com* for further information about
our program.